The Nature of the Self
and the
Social Evolution of Humanity

Douglas H. Melloy

INNERCIRCLE PUBLISHING

The Nature of the Self
and the Social Evolution of Humanity
Copyright © 2007 Douglas H. Melloy

Edition

ISBN: 0-9728127-2-5

Cover Design by Douglas H. Melloy
Cover Creation by Chad Lilly
Interior Page Design by Chad Lilly
Edited By: Angela McKenzie
Cover Photo Credits:
http://antwrp.gsfc.nasa.gov/apod/archivepix.html

Are You Aware?
www.innercirclepublishing.com

Old tribes have fallen destitute by hands
Of golden iron marching drums to war,
To vanquish social lines by orders served,
To gather, hunt and fish to grow, mature–
Sustain the cultured traits conceived in time
Which draws the civilizing sons
To paganistic heathens felled by quest,
From righteous airs- their temper raged against
The flesh as aged on trails trod in dreams as dreamt.
This historic path reincarnates pasts–
The love of fear's false premise promising
The land bequeathed for Garden use to raise
The lives unlived above the tempered times.
From hardened hearts that hate- afraid, at odds
With the Imaged soul–the likeness few know,
But ghosts–a shadow self–a haunting call to arms,
To arms, laying waste claims as laid to rest
Attesting morals void of ethics lost,
Consuming vampiric'ly Spirit's blood
From Temple's skeletal fleshy frame formed
By thoughts as felt- willed to life, becoming…
Trampled under ego's false progressive guise,
Disguising true intents that mask–deceive
The mind and wishes–simple unconcern…
For ownership and acquisition's quest,
Enslaving liberty's lifestyle–amused,
Leaving homelands–deserted–destitute,
A wasteland reserved as promised land to give–
Vanquished refugees…a place, to waste, a w a y–
Enter extinction's blissed remembrance born,
Wombed to life through woman's nourishing drink–
An alcoholic bent on self destruction,
Enstaged, enraged, the rampage wound victors,
Unhealed and bleeding to death with war's cross-
A crux carried to crucify one's painful torment,
That to vi'lent hate–mirroring traits
Absorbed, sponge like, few know the hoop of fire
Tempering souls to purify the fallen sons
Having lost the battle of self displaced.

□——————⊢ Douglas H. Melloy, 1992

Table Of Contents

Dedication

This book is dedicated to my parents:

Elaine Barbara Lee Zum Brunnen Melloy
and
Robert Charles Melloy

Acknowledgements

I am always fascinated by the acknowledgements page when a lot of people are listed. I wish to express my sincerest gratitude to **Carol Bradshaw** for all the work she has contributed to this manuscript. Thank you for being the most authentic woman I know.

I would also like to thank **Phil Lawson** for all his input early on. I appreciate all the work **Chad Lilly** contributed to making this manuscript into a book, and all the editing **Angela McKenzie** suggested. Thank you all very, very much.

Foreword

My first association with Douglas H. Melloy began in 1998 with my reading some very profound truths he posted on a "spark list" for a group of thousands composing a Wayne Dyer study group. I replied to his writing by asking many questions. This began an ongoing correspondence between us that continues to this day. We are the best of friends.

There was something about his wisdom that stirred an inner knowing deep within me that prompted me to ponder, discern, ask, and know that this person was coming from a place of wisdom and truth.

We met and became close spiritual friends. I assisted him in editing his first two books, and have assisted him with his third book, The Nature of the Self and the Social Evolution of Humanity. This has been a great journey for me for the last eight years through our sharing as souls on a very similar path. Through my willingness to listen, address, and heal, my life has evolved immeasurably. I have witnessed some very profound changes in Douglas, observing that he truly "walks his talk" through persistent work with each experience. I witnessed him develop into full personal mastery in this lifetime. We can all do the same with personal intention.

These pages reveal a series of enlightened revelations, a personal knowing with each part growing more and more profound as the book progresses.

We each travel alone through the process of growth to the spiritual realms. It is up to each of us to do the required work, and to maintain a level of focused intention, to become our own master. The image of our creator becomes what we ultimately own. The responsibility rests upon each of us. We all in truth form one group body within the realness of God. This is the ultimate paradox. We are responsible for our own progress, yet we each are linked together in the oneness that is God. In this sense, we are indeed our brothers' and sisters' keepers, eternally linked in the evolving process of life.

It is with thanks and gratitude to have this opportunity to share a few words of possible affirmation in these pages. As we bring up our own vibrancy, our individual light and love will shine and assist humanity with its vibrancy. The personal experiences and individual revelations of each of us serve to add more luster and brilliance as we allow this transformational process to unfold.

It is both a privilege and honor that I welcome you as readers to The Nature of the Self and the Social Evolution of Humanity. This work is a living testimony of his life. A life in which becoming fully conscious is the truth of mastery lived.

Let each of us share the love and light one unto the other until our world is transformed for our highest and greatest good.

□———— Carol B. Bradshaw
April 2007

Preface

I remember years ago an interesting experience that lasted for 18 months. Every two to three days someone would approach me asking me to join his or her religious group. For 78 weeks this experience continued. I was surprised at how many different groups there were. What was interesting to me then was the conviction each person had about his or her particular version of what "faith" is, and what it entails. I found, in my search for meaning and truth, that given teachings or teachers failed to take enough into consideration about the nature of the self and what it encompasses. I discovered that most teachers and their teachings were mistaken and misguided because they were not taught what the nature of the self is. After dabbling in various religious disciplines over the years, I finally realized that going within is the only path one ever walks. I then began my personal search culminating with this book. This book attempts to answer some fundamental questions about the nature of the self and the social evolution of humanity. This book addresses what the nature of the self is, what one must choose, and how these evolve into what eventually ascends from the planet into the universe.

Part One of this book explains the nature of the self as will, love, light, and consciousness. These are the will of God as the mind, the love of the creator as the body, the light of the father as the spirit, and the consciousness of all that is, or universe, as the soul.

Part Two of this book explains that each of us must choose whom we will serve. Service polarity involves two paths that are either positive or negative (RA Material' Vols. 1-4 1984). The two paths are also called the right and left hands of God (RA Material 1984). They are sometimes referred to as self-service and serving others. Service polarity involves specific types of social behaviors. Self-service involves the philosophies of hierarchy, elitism, superiority, chosen-ness, and good versus evil, leading to the practices of conquering, enslaving, and destroying others through war, greed, and slavery. Serving others involves equality, balance, relationship, purpose, and harmony, leading to the practitioner living a life as a way-shower, deliverer, and healer.

How we recognize each path is what a person chooses to focus on. People who serve themselves aspire to the ideologies of the invader culture. Invader cultures live according to the practices of war, greed, and slavery. Self-serving individuals live according to false doctrine that conquers them, enslaves them, and destroys them through living denial, fear, and judgment. People who serve others live a simple life according to their design. We see this contrast as the historical conflict between invader cultures and indigenous peoples. The only struggle as conflict that exists is between individuality and collective consciousness. Individuality only involves 6% of the brain. From this perspective, the individual considers him or herself an entity unto itself giving him or her the notion he or she is an absolute, a type of false god. This leads to the need to empower the self through subjugating others. The emphasis is on self-glorification. Collective consciousness involves the other 94% of the brain. People who are collectively conscious know themselves as all that is unified into a state of oneness. People who serve others live their path as way-showers, deliverers, and healers, from a state of joy, peace, and freedom. People are faced with having to choose whether to live individually or collectively.

Part Three of this book introduces an idea that most people are unfamiliar with. That idea is collective ascension. Collective ascension is how humanity evolves from a planetary state of existence into an eternal ongoing-ness. Human evolution is the development of consciousness according to individuality, or collective consciousness. These evolve from a planetary state of existence into an eternal one through ascension. Ascension pertains to either individuality, or collective consciousness. The type of ascension accomplished determines how one evolves through the universe.

Individuality eventually ceases to exist. This is what death shows us. Death is only possible individually. Collective consciousness never ceases to exist and ascends en masse, and the highest levels of creation only involve collectives. The universe is one being—the being-ness of God. This is what collective consciousness realizes and lives personally, relationally, and socially. Collectives that ascend are conscious of their true nature individually and as all that is. Humanity is evolving into what collectively ascends, and this reality never ceases to exist. Humanity evolves beyond the planetary through collective ascension, and this evolves through the universe until it reintegrates back into the realness of God that surrounds it.

This book also contains 17 appendixes A-Q. Appendix A presents seven ideas about what the second coming pertains to. Appendix B addresses the attitude of business as "nothing personal" from the expectation and demand that greed and codependency remain unchanged, and the employee/management relationship exist as a form of socially accepted slavery. This appendix also addresses the social attitude of money as a form of economics creating class distinctions. Appendix C explains why God is an idea and ideal. Appendix D explains that two types of creation theories exist. One is human, and the other a type of biological robot, clone, or slave drone. The creation of the human being is positive, whereas creation of the clone or drone is not. Human beings have a soul, but the clone does not. Appendix E shares the idea that nothing in the universe is an absolute, not even God, and it explains why this is true. Appendix F is this author's version of the Mayan Calendars and what the end date 2012 pertains to, and what is involved with the numerology of 13 and 20. Appendix G defines enlightenment and shares several personal experiences. Appendix H addresses the problem of fixation upon seeking to attain an ideal state of awareness, like bliss, nirvana, or perfection. Appendix I states what God and universe are as a unified ideal demonstrated as a state of oneness. Appendix J explains the significance of Unidentified Flying Objects and the purpose they serve. Appendix K defines death as a form of fear, and that death of the body necessitates reincarnation of the soul. Appendix L is about meditation, how to meditate by focusing upon feelings, like joy or love and thoughts that prove to be true through experience. Meditation is the path of the seeker delving into the depths of being to discover what is real and true about the self that becomes the lifestyle one portrays. Meditation is the medium that expands depth of being and scope of knowing into an awareness that is both comprehensive and authentic rather than misguided, mistaken, or closed-minded. Meditation is embracing and owning inner states of realness, rather than pretending external appearances, worn as costumes, are it, making us who and what we are as human beings. Appendix M informs the reader that anything that exists is within. This appendix also presents the idea that the Big Bang is half of the origin of the universe. The very big also became the very small simultaneously. This appendix also states that change is an internal process mirrored back to us externally. Each of us is responsible for personifying those states we desire to exist as our reality. Each of us must be it in order for it to be real. By it, I mean such states as joy, peace, freedom, love, happiness, or compassion. Appendix N is my idea we are our own soul mate. Appendix O is there are two versions of oneness: oneness from a specific perspective, or oneness from a collective perspective. Appendix P states the Bible is a conflict between the Old Testament and the New Testament. Appendix Q explains the conflict between two differing cultures: invading cultures and indigenous people.

This book is a journey into self-discovery. It touches on what hinders personal growth and social evolution and assists humanity in the healing of dysfunction. It addresses development, both negative and positive, and gives the reader the means for becoming truly authentic. This book is a manual for being, living, and evolving. This book reveals the nature of the self and the social evolution of humanity. This is a manuscript written so one will become conscious of God and universe, and heal the fictions of disease, disparity, discomfort, and even death. The path is how this is accomplished.

Reality and truth are not easy to address and embody, due to so many people subscribing to false doctrines based upon denial, fear, and selfishness. This book strips away dogmas instilled leading to the personal fictions of pain and fear, becoming suffering and death, and the socially reprehensible activities of slavery, greed, and war. This book is about ending personally what soon becomes extinct—individuality as a self-serving elitism that thrives upon war and greed. This book is a personal journey of self-discovery from individuality to collective consciousness. It is written to assist the reader in resolving personal conflict and choosing to become fully conscious. This involves resolving the self-delusion of individuality existing as an entity unto itself. This requires becoming conscious of one's collective state of being and knowing. Evolution is how one fully activates his or her brain.

If the reader wishes to become empowered, healed, and authentic, it is advised to read this book with an open mind, and with the intention of becoming that state of being that is collectively conscious, rather than addicted and attached to his or her individualized identity. This book explains how to heal and ascend.

□———┤ Douglas H. Melloy

Introduction

The path of the seeker is a curious and interesting process, due to the fact that each of us is unique. No two people experience life in the same way. People think a given teaching or teacher's truth is greater than their own. Also, it is curious how people subscribe to the ideas that others state as their truth. I am always brought back to the question: "What is your truth?" Few people can answer this question honestly. Answering this question by reciting or literally interpreting the ideas of another does not count.

Seeking for meaning and purpose is part of what life entails. There is also enjoying life as an individual, while seeking to live a life that is honorable and authentic. Selfish individuals fool millions by claiming to know what is real and true, but is actually only false doctrine.

This book advises the reader to know the self, choose whom he or she will serve, and aspire to collectively ascend. My only advice is, feel something real, think something true, and share these in ways kind and conducive.

People do not do a very good job in addressing and assessing their humanity, so what is involved as a catalyst, like pain, fear, arrogance, or the like, remain denied and ignored. These catalysts are designed to assist us in being and knowing the nature of the self, so that it is easily grasped and lived. I ask this question: "What has greater relevance, your individuality, or someone, like Jesus, or Buddha, or Mother Teresa, or Billy Graham?" People frequently state that someone else is more important than they are. People fail to address self-denial that becomes projection. This leads to relying upon others and outside sources for what is true and real. The fact is, each of us personally portrays our own truth and realness.

I have found few people honestly seek for what is real and true. They rely upon the ideas of others and give their life away to those whom they feel are superior to them. This prevents many people from feeling and thinking for themselves.

People fail to address their own humanity. Individuals do not spend enough time resolving issues which act as a catalyst, like pain or fear, for personal growth and evolution. There is an unwritten rule: Deny yourself completely and only live what others want you to be and do for them. People fail to grasp what creativity is and how it works. They live to follow the dictates of others regardless of what is entailed and where it leads. There are no real visionaries now leading humanity into an illuminated spirituality and truer way of life.

Today, people remain indifferent and rarely speak up about injustices lemming our lives over cliffs into rude abysses of our own making. They do not do a very good job at recognizing what is really going on with the intentions others have. Those who follow ill-advised ideologies are usually mistaken and misguided through 'blind' faith. Avoiding these ill-advised ideologies is not easy. Walking away from everything and everyone is difficult. This is the only way one can come to be and know certain truths about the self without bias. Going it alone is very difficult for many people to do because they do not like being by themselves. There is an endless array of attention-getters keeping people distracted. Seeking outer-based sources that are dogmatically revered, like books and teachers, usually only reinforces what one already feels and thinks. People refuse to address issues, like fear or anger, afflicting their lives causing stress and discomfort. So-and-so says such-and-such: we blindly believe and follow whatever advice others feel is right for us. Rarely do we question authority: authority can lead us astray.

In this manner, humanity fails to heal. People insist upon embodying ideals that create disease, disparity, conflict, poverty, discontentment, violence, war, and even death. Where is the global vision in which all of humanity aspires to achieve? People aspire to die and go to heaven and that's about it. People assume life ends with death; however, choice is always involved. Dying is not living, and life is not death. Living the life of something eternal is one goal. Another is being happy and feeling good about living as flesh and blood. One can choose to feel good and enjoy his or her life as a human being.

This book focuses upon three aspects of humanity. The first

is the nature of the self. The second is choosing whom you will serve. The third is aspiring to collectively ascend.

A large percentage of the human race is unaware of who and what they are. Part One of this book defines the nature of the self as the will of God as mind, the love of the creator as body, the light of the father as spirit, and the consciousness of all that is as the soul. These are the basic or fundamental natures of the self that we individually portray as our biology and physiology. Part One also explains the roles pain, fear, darkness, and negativity play in assisting personal and social evolution. These four catalysts are the basis for how infinity, eternity, completeness, and what is total exist as individual states of expression. The entire creation is God stating, I am. I am-ness is God's individuality. This makes everything existent within the universe an aspect and quality of God. This is why the Bible tells us: "Unto the least of these ye do unto to me." Me pertains to God, not to Jesus.

Part One also explains what God is and where this exists. God is an all-encompassing state that is centered within the heart. As an observed state, it looks like a small dormant sun. When entered into consciously, this brings to life the realness of God, making anyone who does so a God-man, or Avatar. Coupled with this realness is embracing the soul. This is done by doing conscious out-of-body experiences, which frees the soul from its flesh cocoon. Meditation is how the aspirant enters into God and leaves the body. Before the seeker can do a conscious out-of-body experience, he or she needs to desire to return to his or her place and point of origin. God and universe as self are depth of being and scope of knowing. Coupled with this, are actualizing life and demonstrating what it is to be a human being.

Part One also addresses embracing and owning qualities, like joy, love, compassion, kindness, and peace. This is done through understanding what each quality is not. The path is how each of us heals those qualities that are negative keeping our life a struggle and full of strife. The first part of this book also points out the role the ego plays in our life. The ego is the choice maker. It makes all the decisions for our lives. The ego is fear felt as an individuality.

Part One also touches upon the unique nature of each of us. No two people are the same - this is the infinitude of God. Infinity is and means variable and variety of that which remains constant. God is the constant. The fundamental nature of the self is the will of God. God will's to be and know what individuality is like as an image and likeness. The universe is applied intention. We are also learning how to be effective co-creators. This involves applying God's will as what we each manifest as our experiences. This requires resolving the mindsets of either/or, opposites in conflict, lesser and greater, and perpetrator and victim.

Part One addresses the fictions of absolutes and dogmas. It also addresses the areas of denial, irresponsibility, rejection, and projection leading to the beliefs we are born, crucified, die, and then reincarnate. Coupled with this are their opposites - acceptance, responsibility, embracement, and ownership - qualities each of us desires to have and to know, sharing with others in ways kind and conducive. Part One also touches on the functions of mind, body, spirit, and soul. The mind is self-sustaining, the body self-regenerative, and the spirit self-perpetuating. The soul houses all our experiences. When one lives what mind, body, spirit, and soul truly are, suffering, struggle, and death cease as a personal fiction.

Part One also explains inverse reversal as the technique used to create binary vibrancy. Binary vibrancy is lived as our heartbeat, breathing, waking and sleeping, and finally incarnation and ascension. Our heartbeat is the pulse of God. It is the binary vibrancy between what God is and what God is not as each of us. Breathing is the pulse of life. It is the binary vibrancy between the inherent and the apparent specific to planet earth. Waking and sleeping are the pulse of the self or being. It is the binary vibrancy between our biology and our spirituality. Incarnation and ascension are the pulse of service. It is the binary vibrancy between how we serve others, and where this goes when one's purpose is served. The first part of this book explains that each of us exists as ten differing states unified into one ideal. They are, all encompassing-ness, presence, is-ness, realness, pattern, content, truth, I am-ness, all-ness, and God-hood, through what these are not: emptiness, absence, nothingness, illusion, chaos, void, erroneous-ness, I am-not-ness, specific-ness, and self-glorification. Each of us lives as a self-evolving individual reality. This evolves into service polarity and is the second part of this book.

(The RA Material is the only body of knowledge I have read that discusses what service polarity is as both positive and negative). The second part of this book focuses on the idea of choosing whom one will serve. Most draw a blank when asked this. They do not realize service involves both the positive and the negative as a form of self-polarization. These two paths are called the right and left hands of God. Each path focuses upon differing ideals. Self-service personifies an ideology that is based upon hierarchy, elitism, superiority, chosen-ness, and good versus evil, leading to the social behaviors of conquering, enslaving, and destroying others through adhering to the fictions of exclusion, negation, and aversion. These are the exclusion of God, the negation of life, and the aversion to all that is.

Serving others is the opposite of self-service. Those who aspire to the right hand of God understand this and personify equality, balance, relationship, purpose, and harmony, leading to the social behaviors of way-shower, deliverer, and healer, from knowing inclusion, affirmation, and involvement. These are the inclusion of God as our fundamental nature, affirmation of life as God's creation, and involvement with the universe consciously. The aspirations of the negative path are war, greed, and slavery. The importance of choosing whom one will serve is only those who have chosen service are harvested (RA Material 1984). These individuals compose the wheat of humanity, everyone else is chaff. The end of the world, as written about in the Bible, only involves people who are self-serving, and those who have not chosen whom they will serve.

The third part of this book explains what collective ascension is as an ideal (The RA is a collective of 6,000,000 souls that ascended as one state of being). Few have ever heard of this idea and even fewer aspire to attain this as a collective experience. Knowing the self and choosing to serve others culminates in collective ascension. This is positive evolution. The requirements for each aspirant are being and knowing the qualities of joy, love, light, kind-ness, and generosity en masse. Faith, desire, and intention assists personal and cultural experience based upon oneness, healing, and wholeness that collectively ascends. Collective ascension is integrating into the universe as an eternal process through connection (The wisest and most evolved material shared, through channeling and books are collective sources).

Accomplishing this requires healing all the social fictions selfish individuals establish as tradition, like war, class distinction, and what people become interested in, like politics, religion, science, economics, education, competition, or any other man-made ideology.

The final pages of this book contain seventeen appendixes. Each explains a theme. Appendix A details seven ideas of what the second coming actually pertains to and involves. My first idea is our returning to living our life as it is designed. My second idea is returning our understanding to the fact that male and female are actually equality and balance. My third idea focuses upon people choosing to live as one being as the body of Christ. The Christ is and means collective consciousness living as one ideal. My fourth idea touches upon the literal return of Jesus, which took place right after his resurrection and now is the channeled material 'The Course in Miracles.' My fifth idea posits the notion Jehovah of the Old Testament and Id the father of man return to battle one last time (Ramtha 1984). My sixth idea tells of earth returning to a garden state. This will require the elimination of anything and anyone that is not conducive to life as it's intended to be lived. My seventh idea touches upon two areas of interest: the return of those sources that have contributed to this planet, and those cultures people belong to from the universe.

Appendix B addresses the problem of business as nothing personal and the social implications of money as a means of exchange that is only a mask for enslaving people. This appendix deals with the fact that money only exists to create class distinction, and that bartering is more evolved as a form of exchange. Greed is the truth of money and creates, as a balance, poverty. No one seeks to end greed as a form of selfishness.

Appendix C touches upon the idea of God as an ideal to

assist people moving away from hierarchical and elitist ideas. The idea of one God is necessary for people to have reverence towards differing aspects of one reality. One God and oneness are useful in healing the fictions of opposites in conflict and greater and lesser, or what is established as class distinction, and the fiction that one aspect of creation is superior or greater and another lesser or inferior. Also useful is our learning to love and accept, rather than fear and judge. Everything is an aspect of God and any attitude we portray is how we feel, think, and act towards God.

Appendix D is titled: The Missing Link, and explains how two creations took place long ago. One creation was us as a human being, possessing a soul, and the other a type of clone or drone, a biological robot, used to do the bidding of what created it, and lacks a soul. These biological cellular constructs only function in conjunction with those who created them and only function for that purpose. Humans are a positive creation and the clone was a negative creation. The missing link is the difference in function and role of two types of ideals.

Appendix E states nothing in the universe is an absolute– not even God. This is due to infinity, which means variable and variety of that which remains constant. The universe is a state of differentiation. Nothing has greater or lessor value given each aspect of it contributes to its overall constitution. People make mistakes in trying to elevate given aspects of it into something absolute. The problem we all face with this is: what does everything else pertain to? Absolutes invalidate everything else and they prevent God, life, individuality, and the universe from becoming something personal and relational.

Appendix F is about the Mayan Calendars and their end date of 2012. I created them in a past life. It is a visual representation of Yahweh and Id, and the relationships between different star systems, and the roles they played in our creation and the contributions made by others. The calendars depict the development of two types of beings, one is human and the other is not. The end date of 2012 is the time frame when third density ends and fourth density begins (RA Material 1984). One of the keys depicted is the center, as this is where God rests waiting for people to give birth to God. Another key is people remembering where they have come from and whom they belong to.

Appendix G explains what enlightenment is. It is any experience that deepens one's depth of being and broadens one's scope of knowing. Enlightenment means 'in the light of this moment' from a place and state of being and knowing. What it accomplishes is acceptance and understanding, leading to even-minded-ness. Enlightenment is embracing and owning an awareness as a state of being that is real, true, and personal. I end this appendix by sharing several of my enlightening experiences.

Appendix H is my idea that our humanness are the unified states of God and universe. These combine into making us human beings. God is an all encompassing-ness and the universe is all that is that combined into a third state called human. As the personal, God is the mind and universe is the soul. When coupled with body and spirit, i.e., love and light, we are human beings. What we are as human beings is the infinite mind, the eternal body, the complete spirit, and total soul.

Appendix I addresses a serious problem for anyone on the path. People have this tendency to become fixated with ideals that are considered absolute. This is impossible given the nature and role of infinity and the magnitude and scope of the universe. Attainment of anything considered 'it' dooms the aspirant. Any state realized is only an aspect of a greater medium. Even when God is fully realized, it is only an aspect of the overall self. Absolutes lead to spiritual entropy and evolutionary death. Single states are the union of two differing states. Bliss or joy is the union of will and love. When addressing the relational, absolutes become irrelevant because they cannot be shared. Sharing is law and the natural way.

Appendix J addresses the phenomena of Unidentified Flying Objects from the perspective of observation, conjecture, and experience, and puts them into a context that has relevance and meaning for everyone. They have come and will return soon. It is very possible they come to retrieve people who are here that actually belong to that culture. They also come to let us know we are not alone in the universe, and that many other cultures exist throughout the cosmos.

Appendix K focuses upon the death experience as a form of fear. Living life is what ascends. Just as death pertains to the body, so does ascension. Death of the body is reincarnation of the soul. They are the same experience. Anyone who has passed will reincarnate again. The body is lived as love, or departed as fear. Love ascends as our taking our body with us when we evolve beyond planetary life, and fear dies leaving the body behind. We take with us our body as love. Fear is left behind and laid to rest.

Appendix L is important to grasp. It touches upon meditation. Meditation is going within to discover or become conscious of what is inherent. Meditation is how one becomes God conscious and universally knowing. Meditation is a form of relaxation. It is also a way to be and know what something is, and the purpose it serves. It is a way to understand experience, and is the mechanics behind effective creativity and manifesting. Meditation is discovering what one is in possession of that is then shared with others. Meditation is the path.

Appendix M states change is an inner process, and when each of us owns the state desired, like peace or harmony, conflict ceases to be a reality. This part of the book also posits the idea that the very small and the very big came into existence at the same time.

Appendix N addresses the concept of the soul mate. Love and light are its truest form. When my soul incarnated into my body, this gave my life a soul mate relationship, and is the only relationship I actually have. Woman is to love what man is to light. Woman is love/light and man is light/love, thus making our life the only soul mate we ever have.

Appendix O is my idea there are two ways to understand oneness. One idea is oneness according to individuality, or oneness according to a collective state. Oneness individually requires exclusion, negation, and aversion. Oneness collectively requires inclusion, affirmation, and involvement.

Appendix P shows how the Old Testament is the opposite of the New Testament. Teachings taught in the Old Testament are contradicted in the New Testament. I offer the argument that we as a society choose to live either according to the Old Testament or the New Testament.

Appendix Q explains how only two cultures actually

exist. One culture invades, while the other lives indigenously. Invading cultures thrive upon the activities of war, greed, and slavery. They exist upon the social attitudes of conquering, enslaving, and destroying others through placing faith in false doctrines taught as science, religion, and politics. Indigenous people live as designed as the image and likeness of God, thriving upon peace, bartering, and community.

People continually seek for outer-based sources to rely on, rather than going within to discover what is inherent. God, life, humanness, and anything else are within the self, and it is here one finds what is real, true, and sharable. Another problem facing the individual is, how does a given state of realization pertain to and involve the opposite sex?

This book advises the reader to know the self, choose whom you will serve, and aspire to collectively ascend. My only advice is to feel something real, think something true, and share that with others in ways kind and conducive.

□——— Douglas H. Melloy

The Nature of the Self
and the
Social Evolution of Humanity

The Nature of the Self

Where does one begin in his or her search for understanding and knowing what the nature of the self is? Our individual uniqueness is a journey of self-discovery. Some believe there is no self, and others believe an array of negative ideas, like sin, karma, guilt, pain, fear, the fall, or banishment is what afflicts us. Most of humanity never looks beyond or within their psychology, gender, race, issues acting as catalyst, like pain, fear, jealousy, and social biases. Adding to this confusion, are the many institutions offering an assortment of ideas about who and what we are. Then there are religious, scientific, political, cultural, and family traditions holding to very specific attitudes and ideals about the self. What these entail on a personal, relational, and social level determine how we evolve. Face value living is fine, but does not reveal to us our creator, or the purpose our ideal serves. If we take ourselves where we stand, what do we recognize about whom we are.

This book attempts to answer these ideas in a format that focuses on remembering God, actualizing life, and becoming conscious of all that is as the nature of the self. This unified realness is the self that exists within as being and outwardly as knowing. This evolves through choosing whom one will serve, and culminates in collective ascension. My purpose in life is to actualize and demonstrate what it is to be and know humanness as a state of being that knows, shares, and evolves the image and likeness of God.

One of the ironies life presents is, no two people come to know in the same way. Each of us is our own paradox that we alone resolve. It is left to each of us to discover for ourselves whom we are, what we are, and where we are going. Books are fine as teaching aids, as are techniques, teachings, teachers, and applied forms of discipline. Eventually, though, these must be set aside, so that all that remains is the self, unencumbered by ideas disseminated by external or foreign agencies, regardless of how evolved, enlightened, and loving they may be.

Truth is tailor-made; customized by each one of us. This makes it personal and unique. Part of the path is discovering what one's truth is, thereby knowing what one's purpose for being is. Individuality is how one comes to grasp what the nature of the self is. Solitary time spent alone is the path to being and knowing all-one-ness, and that all is one state of consciousness, or universe, or song of God. This does not mean one must remain alone and isolated for one's entire life. One should only do so for as long as it takes to heal one's 'dark night of the soul,' and only for as long as it takes to remember God's inherency within the context of one's purpose for being.

The realness of God individually is centered within the heart that each of us can bring to life through discipline, understanding, and the intention of doing so. This gives the seeker the basis for knowing personal realness, and moving from such catalysts as pain, fear, darkness, and negativity. These catalysts are the experiences assisting us in personal and social evolution. They do not exist independently, but only in conjunction with ideals that have an eternal value. Catalysts also assist us in choosing whom we will serve. They are the basis or foundation for what we feel, think, and contribute to this planet and the universe.

How does one accomplish this task? It is up to the seeker's faith, desire, and applied intention that determines what heals. Healing involves resolving to let go of a certain quality, like pain, fear, guilt, arrogance, and ignorance that hinders one's ability to be real and know truthfully any idea that has an eternal value to it.

Details tell us our entire history. They compose our entire story, showcasing what we believe in and aspire to become. Depending upon whose truth we subscribe to, determines what our life embraces. Faith is holding to the 'evidence of things unseen.' Desire develops our faith; applied intention fulfills what our faith and desire is placed on. Applied intention is the application of any principle creating a specific type of experience we embrace through God's will. The work we engage in is based upon how attached we are to the outer, and what is it that causes us to feel pain and fear. Denial, pain, and fear are the three basic catalysts that assist our life and what it touches upon day by day. This gives us the opportunity to grasp what these are, and what they do in assisting the entire creation; this is the basis for personal evolution. Healing denial is the path to acceptance. Healing pain is the path to joy. Healing fear is the path to love. Healing darkness is the path to light. Healing negativity is the path to living life positively.

It is useful to the seeker to understand what denial, pain, fear, darkness, and negativity do to assist us in healing. We deny and project them, which only prolong their active roles in our life, thus giving them identities that do not exist, yet we are convinced they are very real. Pain denied and projected becomes Satan the tormentor. Fear denied and projected becomes God the destroyer. The real culprits for all negative experiences are pain and fear, not Satan or God. In grasping what purpose catalysts serve, we need to examine them as what each does. Pain individualizes God into a specific ideal. Fear isolates this. Darkness distinguishes this from all else. Negativity repulses everything, so the ideal will stand alone. These give God the opportunity to exist independently, and experience a myriad of differing ideas. Experience is the sole purpose of creation. Experience gives God the ability to state I am this idea or ideal.

What purpose does a given experience serve in my life? Patience is necessary. Some answers do not come until enough experience fills our life. Case in point: In May of 1987, I traveled to Key West, Florida for four days. During my stay, I met a man who began speaking to me in a heavy foreign accent while I was walking. He was a small man with very brown skin - Cuban, I believe. He told me we would meet the next day. Sure enough, our paths crossed again and he spoke directly to me about my life and times. He even mentioned that I thought he was crazy. He told me some truths about my life. Upon leaving Key West, Florida, I realized, had I not been so arrogant and closed-minded, I could have listened to him, and learned something of value as he was a master. Fifteen years later, I realized what he was showing me... that from the perspective of others, they would think of me exactly how I thought of him that day -- as crazy. I do know my insanity is the norm where I come from. The problem people face is that they do not know when truth is lived and shared by one who has mastered his or her life into purpose and wholesomeness.

Experience fills our life with what is relevant, so we will understand truth as it is. In lacking such experience, our higher-self remains silent, as we must have a basis for grasping what the truth is, based upon our life from the point of places or experiences. I call this 'experiential realism.' Answers come when I am willing to involve myself with what the truth pertains to. When I am truly seeking to know the truth, understanding will come through revelation or direct experience. This is a type of knowing that comes when one desires to experience what is real and true. Revelation is a very interesting process that comes as a type of direct knowing. The revealing of a truth only comes through experience, and the willingness to be and know continuously. Being is what is real and knowing what is true. These are versions, or forms, of love and light.

Everything is designed to assist us in understanding and knowing a given truth. It is truth, coupled with love, through which we create our reality. How attentive we are to the details involving our life determines whether a given clue is recognized and successfully resolved as we journey through life. Knowing the self is key to why we are here and what we are doing. What we discover as our path and purpose is being and knowing whom we are, what we are, why we are here, where we are from, and where we are going.

Every idea we believe in pertains to how our life is. What we feel and think shapes our life into what we touch on personally. Observation shows us different versions of one reality. The one reality is God and universe unified into a single state. Any idea we think and any observation we make is within ourselves. Everything is a detail showing us whom we are. Every idea is an idea about whom we are as well. There is the personal aspect of an idea and the relational aspect of an idea. There is also the reciprocal nature of an idea, leading to the ability to create. This can be thought of as the potential giving rise to the actuality of a quality, like joy, love, or kindness, that stands as a representation as our experience. When ideas, like God, life, universe, or love, and their opposites are pondered and grasped according to how each pertains to the self, the work is done, the task is completed, and we move on.

We exist to be and know the self. This requires patience, discipline, study, and humility. Each of us decides what to get involved with until it is time to move on. For some, this takes years to do. Sometimes the distractions are so enticing we never move beyond them.

The path of understanding and knowing the nature of the self precedes any further development, for it is from here all else develops. Most people are involved with the most basic aspects of living: pain, fear, denial, projection, guilt, and death. Healing these is deemed unattainable by many. The path is healing these catalysts. For many, healing is deemed impossible. Many choose to involve themselves with ideals to know what it is like to be that humanly. Experience is created and designed to make us feel at home. There is never any judgment made about what we create. Judgment is a threat we feel as fear and pain, based upon arrogance and hatred. This is impossible for God to feel towards any aspect of itself.

A useful meditation is feeling oneness toward something or someone and seeing the perfection of that as-is, now. Applied intention through meditation is the realization and actualization of a given state as a personal realness. Breathe in oneness and exhale perfection. Do this until each idea is felt to be real for you; particularly useful in areas of great stress. Love is acceptance and is key in living life, as it is this love that operates before anything else. Wisdom is the ability to understand, before acting or applying itself to a given situation. It is not for us to understand the dramas of others. We must grasp why we react as we do to the creativity of others in all cases, regardless of how it looks to us as outsiders to what is actually going on. The only conclusion I make when making an observation is, "I am this also." It is curious to me that nothing is acceptable to us, yet everything is acceptable to God. If something were truly deemed otherwise, God would simply erase it. Do not think that God does not have the ability to do so with any aspect of life or in the universe. I am always reminded when I judge something or someone, that I am only recognizing myself as this is how I see myself according to the judgment I am making. The outer only mirrors the inner realness ever and always. The inner is my being-ness and the outer my knowing-ness.

I remember reading Chuang Tzu, a contemporary of Lao Tzu's, who was of the opinion: "I am not you, and you are not me." My immediate response upon reading this was: "I am you and you are me, and this is why we meet." Everyone is a mirror revealing what we feel and think about ourselves as what we observe. Actually, there is only one person here, and each of us is that one person. My humanity is humanity. I have found when I meet someone, I choose to love them, fear them, ignore them through indifference, or I choose to be neutral about them. Also, I choose to accept them, inspire them, and be kind to them in some way, or I choose to fear them, judge them, and persecute them in some way. This stems from what I feel and think about myself. I only recognize in and about others what I am guilty of myself. Knowing the self resolves differences of distinction until one understands clearly oneness and perfection. This is an inner oneness and outer perfection with everyone and everything. This is what love and wisdom does masterfully. Life affords us the chance to become loving and wise all the time.

Accomplishing this requires letting go of those issues we are born with through tradition and family values. This can be thought of as coming from, and then working through to where each issue leads. We are born into what is not and what we are not. This is the path we walk. It is what is not, that leads us into being conscious of what is, in ways that are personal to us. Each of us touches upon ideas felt and thought that personalizes for us what makes us unique.

Opposites tension the universe so it stands. The catalysts for action, leading to the creation of the universe, are the points and places where love and light are separated into specific states of being. Without opposites, a given reality as quality would not, could not, and does not exist universally or personally. It is always through what is not that we come to know what is personally as an aspect of the self. It is our beliefs, our interpretations, that define who and what we are as a personal reality. We are the determiners of what is real, true, and personal.

While it is true that truth is the premise or principle that defines a given reality, it is always a personal performing that determines just what our reality is, as it always conforms through correspondence to where we are in our personal ideals of feeling, thinking, and doing.

God, others, the environment, and the universe correspond to our interpretations. Applied intention remakes reality into our desires and interests. Just as God's imagination created the universe, ours creates every aspect of our life, and all we desire to become the consciousness of. Traditional approaches are misguided, backward, and often mistaken about what is real and true; few move beyond what tradition holds as sacred. All observations represent an ideal created from some source, feeling that reality defines the self in and according to that reality considered a state of being. Our body, the planet, everything on the planet, our solar system, every galaxy, even the entire universe are ideals manifested by creators feeling that their reality is now. Just as everything man made began as an idea, someone felt was the self. So it is with the entire universe, it is God's ideal of itself as that which is infinite, eternal, complete, and total, thereby making us similar in fashion. All our experiences are representations of inner states sourced from that which contains the originating idea. Personally this is our mind. The mind creates everything in our experience, even our body, through the will of God.

What creation seeks is uniformity as a constant. This is accomplished when we resolve paradox, and live evenness between opposing states of existence.

Gravity is the relationship between the inherent actuality and the apparent representation through the medium-ship that creates it, and observes it, from being it, as the self, through self, to an 'outer' state so we can 'see' by observing for our self what we are as an ideal now. How do we define the self or know it in a way that helps us get along with others and still pertains to what is common to us all?

In dividing you have the reality of the self. But who or what divides? To answer this, we must examine four aspects, which when combined, make us who and what we are. These four aspects are: God, creator, father, and universe, or will, love, light, and consciousness. As it is now God, creator, and father are treated as the same. However, each differs in scope and magnitude. The observed or seen reality of God is the universe. It is only a state of consciousness. It is God's soul. It is God's ideal of itself giving God I am-ness. God's original state, its is-ness or essence, surrounds the universe. Both God and universe are equal in magnitude as a state of balance, relationship, purpose, and harmony. God is uniform and constant while the universe is diversified and becoming.

Just as the universe is within God, so is the likeness or essence of God within all parts making the universe what it is. God is in partnership with everything. And everything we observe represents an ideal. How we interpret these observations determines how well we recognize what is represented. The interpretations we make are the conclusions we draw. How personal our interpretations are determines how a given observation pertains to the self and what we come to know about the self through these observations.

God is that which gives rise to all that is- the universe. The creator is that aspect of God who created us in their image. The father brought us to life by imparting itself into us making us and giving us the ability to live and act individually. The creator creates what the father brings to life. The name of the creator is Yahweh (Ramtha 1984) and the name of the father is Id (Before Yahweh and Id will return to this planet they must be asked to do so by humanity through prayer). The creator can also be thought of as divinity. The father can also be thought of as deity. Divinity and deity are love and light using God's will to be and know to create and manifest ideals that are self-conscious giving God its I am-ness. I am-ness is God existing as a state of consciousness that is aware of itself as an idea of some kind representing an ideal that evolves or becomes more of what it is through experience and expression.

This brings us to the basic question each of us needs to ask our self: What is the nature of the self, and what makes us whom we are?

The difficulty we are faced with in answering this question is, we treat everything as distinct from, other than, foreign to, and separate from our ideas about the self, thereby missing the point a given observation shows us about the self we are. People hold to an either/or mindset. People also believe opposites are in conflict, rather than working in harmony. What people fail to realize is that everything is an aspect and quality of the universe - nothing is superior to anything else. Another culprit that hinders our ability to answer this question is, we believe we are the victims of perpetrators who torment and destroy us as gods of some kind. This is the result of denial and fear, leading to superstition and projection.

Many years ago I experienced an interesting insight about the self and observation. The gist of my experience touched upon the fact that in order to observe something outside myself, it is inherent within me. Ideas like God, life, truth, and the universe are all within composing myself. The entire point of observation is, it shows me whom I am as what I perceive I am. Understanding this allows me to move my awareness beyond dogmas held by those people and teachings that are shortsighted and misguided about the self. If I think it, I am it, with all ideas about or concerning the self.

If we break our observations down to four states of universe, galaxy, solar system, and planet, these outer creations show us that we are greater levels of self-expression. This helps us move our awareness about the self beyond ideas that limit us. In fact, we can know what the self is as four inner states of being and four outer states of knowing that combine into what the self is. Human being-ness can also be thought of as the consciousness of life lived as a planetary embodiment. But a problem arises: How do we interpret, understanding ourselves what ideas about the self are that make them personal, useful, practical, and real?

Touching upon the self requires a willingness to look at the self without the veils that shroud our ability to actually see it as it is now. This is not easy, as so many individuals live a life of charades costumed by facades of psychology.

The real essence of knowing the self comes from accepting everything as an aspect of the self that are either loved, feared, or treated from a place of even-minded-ness or judgment.

What and where is the realness of the observed as a personal existence, and what gives rise to them as an actuality we observe? What the realness is, is God, and where this exists is within. What gives rise to all aspects of creation is God's will to be and know. How God and life are personal is through our mind as an embodied state giving each of us our entire sense of being human.

Perhaps the most misunderstood aspect of the self is the mind. Most people think of it as the ego. The mind is not the ego. It is the creative nature of the self, and is similar in form and function to the sun. The mind is the will of God. The mind creates using God's will through our intention. Specifically, the mind creates the body. The mind utilizes God's will to create all the experiences we embrace or touch upon physically. The mind creates using God's will to create love, light, fear, and darkness. These make our life what it is. The mind uses catalysts to assist us in choosing whom we will serve. The mind also creates experience, so we will understand through that what a given idea is, and how it works personally. The mind holds the entire blueprint of the self as body, and what touches the body as an experience of some kind. (Psychology was introduced, as all healing takes place in the mind; it is here all changes must be made).

True intunement to the mind means the basic structure of the body and the life we are living will be seen. Like a computer program, any aspect of life we do not wish to touch upon anymore can simply be deleted. I caution the reader in doing this. All aspects of our life have meaning and purpose. It is wise to grasp what the meaning and purpose is to all the experiences our life touches.

Mindful is what we are becoming. We are becoming mindful about the self on all levels of being. This begins with the mind, as the mind begins the self as an ideal that stands alone. The mind is the closest thing to God as God is. This can be thought of as the mind of God. I'll add that what quantum physics is actually looking for is God, or mind, as this is the 'smallest' particle that the embodied self originates from, and that astronomy is the impersonal observation and study of the soul. The scientist considers both other than who and what we are humanly. Quantum physics is the study of the mind, and astronomy is the observation of the soul. The mind personalizes creativity. This makes our lives tailor-made. The key is application and owning by taking responsibility for our creations, both positive and negative, by embracing them as our experiences.

As it stands now, we attribute positive events to God, and negative events to the devil. But God and the devil do not exist or work in this manner. We create using our minds, bringing forth both positive and negative experiences, so we will understand how each aspect is used to compose our existence, and experience how the creation works. Application of God's will to be and know is how life works for all the creation. God's will to be and know is cause creating our experience through our faith, desire, and intention. What our faith, desire, and intention are become the effects we see. Depending upon what we create, determines how we react to what touches our life. The truth is, we do create our own reality. No different than God creating its reality as the entire universe by its willingness to be and know the self as all that is. We are a smaller version of this doing for ourselves in exactly the same manner. (What people fail to realize is science, religion, education, and politics are designed as system theories to ensure no one comes to be and know his or her true identity as the image and likeness of God).

The mind creates the body according to how life is and exists (RA Material 1984, Edgar Cayce, 'A Search For God, Vol. 1). There is a relationship between the mind and body that correlates to the same physiology and biology of earth. This can be thought of as integrated synthesis, or to use a modern analogy, the mind is the software and the body is the hardware giving the self form and function.

The mind is to the cause what the body is to the effect of manifestation (According to Edgar Cayce, "The body is the creature of the mind"). The body is the result of the mind's intention. Healing the body requires accessing the mind. The program of what needs to be healed, as a personal reality, is held in the mind. Unless the cause is addressed healing remains ineffective and undone. This is why healers rarely heal. Healing requires knowing one's own mind. Lacking this insight, the body is treated as its own creator, which is impossible. The body is a tool of the mind. The mind creates the body, as it is the body that gives the mind the idea it is something; just as the universe gives God the idea it is I am-ness. Ideas exist, giving God the notion it is something specific, like a sun, planet, moon, or any life form existing on a planet. (This is God as something other than whom it is and what it is as a uniform and constant, all encompassing-ness).

Mindfulness is all encompassing-ness within something as specific as the mind. The mind fills the body with all it touches on in the life we live. The mind creates the body that is a state that feels both positive and negative emotions. The spirit brings the mind/body to life giving what feels the ability to think both positive and negative thoughts. The ego, as an aspect of the mind, then is given the role of choosing what it wishes to feel and think. This clues us to what the ego is.

The ego is the sense we are our biology alone. The ego is to the self what I am-ness is to God. The ego is the notion we are this embodiment living as a human being and our identity is all we are or have ever been. The ego believes the self is only flesh and blood, gender and psychology, race and tradition. The ego is the choice-maker of our intentions. The ego is focused on our becoming either one who sacrifices the self for a cause, like a suicide bomber, or one who dedicates his or her life to a purpose of some kind that is positive, like a healer.

The ego is fear as an identity focused solely on individuality. Fear, ego, and individuality are all the same term and mean the same thing. The body is the mind, manifested as a state of love expressed and represented as something specific. Fear is individuality. Love is collective. Love is a unified state consisting of thirteen qualities. Each quality corresponds to each of the entities composing our creator. Jesus and the twelve disciples were a human portrayal of this reality.

The body might be understood if our idea about it is changed. The body is the embodiment of the mind's intention. We are the embodiment of those qualities the mind deems useful to our personal and relational evolution. Plus, there is the truth that the mind creates according to one's desire to be and know life humanly in a given way, whatever way that is. Each person living has created his or her life exactly as what happens during his or her life. The body is love manifested as a state of being human. The mind creates the body as the realness of love, making love an embodied state of being that shares. The mind creates the body, whereas the soul manifests the spirit, making the soul something specific. When the mind/body pattern is unified with the spirit/soul, this completes us, making us human beings that know and evolve. Evolution is the process of growth that follows when people apply themselves to their own development. Within the context of humanity as a whole, this process culminates in collective ascension.

The difference between God and creator is that God gives rise to all that is, but the creator is an aspect of God, creating specific details according to the ideals the creator feels contribute to God. The creator is what made us the image and likeness of God, using God's will to create us, making us its offspring.

Working in conjunction with the creator is what brought us to life. I refer to this aspect of God as the father. The name of our creator is Yahweh, and the name of our father is Id. Yahweh is a collective consciousness composed of thirteen beings existing as one ideal (Ramtha 1984). Id is a collective consciousness of twenty beings existing as one ideal. The love of Yahweh and the light of Id, coupled with the will of God, created us and brought us to life. God, Yahweh, Id, and the universe exist as a unified state called human being (or us). These four states, (or us), exist as our mind, body, spirit, and soul.

The mind is the will of God; it is the pool from which experiences arise pertaining to a given desire, issue, or path of service. This differs from the higher-self, in that the higher-self is the universal consciousness we come from as a soul, giving us insight into the purpose experience provides us. Consciousness is energy that is self-aware.

This touches upon the notions of past, present, and future. God is considered the past, life the present, and the universe the future. These ideas arise from the fact the mind is forgotten –treated as if it does not exist. The body is regarded as the present, while the spirit and soul are considered ideals that only become real in the future and after death. The past and future are psychologies stemming from denial, projection, and a lack of individuals not becoming aware of their higher-selves and what they do. Actually, the idea of future lies in our refusal to address the self as a state that it becomes. There is only now, there is only here, and there is only what becomes conscious. What we become conscious of – God, life, the Christ, and the universe – are the natures of the self that evolve individually or collectively. Our interest in the evolution of life and our species centers upon the issues of individuality as a state of hierarchy, or collectivity as a state of oneness.

God is a state of oneness, and exists as a collective we observe to be the universe. God's collective state of existence begins with us, and by extending and expanding includes all else. We either love or fear this.

Individuality establishes hierarchical organizations. The entire focus is upon the self, glorified and treated as an entity exclusive to itself. God is feared, life is judged, others are persecuted, and the universe is treated as an observation. The work we do in understanding the nature of the self is in choosing to focus on individuality, or collective consciousness as who and what we are as human beings. The art of living requires choosing what we wish to be and know, and then share that with the rest of the creation.

Individuality is negative. Collective consciousness is positive. Individual states do not truly exist; by nature and design, they are collective. This is the evolutionary development of oneness versus oneness (Read Appendix O to understand what this is and means).

The body gives us the impression we are individuals, existing alone as a solitary state. (One must remember it is the pattern of the mind's ideal of the self to be something specific according to the creator's ideal). The body is a collective state created within the context of this planet; thereby making us whom we are as the biology we live.

The mind is self-sustaining by nature, the body self-regenerating, and the spirit self-perpetuating, making us eternal beings. The soul is self-evolving by nature and design. Also, the mind is instantaneous, the body spontaneous, and the spirit simultaneous. The soul is all that exists as a state of consciousness. In living, there are the harmonious relationships between mind/body, body/spirit, and spirit/soul.

These relationships encompass all that is as our embodiment and spirituality that we embrace as experience and expression.

All mindations are our ensouling spirituality we embody.

Experience builds our perception into a state of conscious awareness that the self intends. Also, it means we become the consciousness of something through experience, making it real and personal. What we create is our idea of ourselves, as our experience in any given moment. This gives us being and knowing through our experiences. Every experience adds to our idea of the self, and each experience becomes our personal ensoulment, as these are what make the reality of the self who and what we are in this exact place and time.

The life you are living is the embodiment of those qualities, making your life a physical ideal. We are the embodiment of those qualities, making our life what we experience. Context and format are useful in understanding the nature of the self as a planetary embodiment. The body holds the pattern of those ideals, making our life an experience. What each of us feels and thinks in turn gives our lives the experiences we express. The work we do in consciousness is resolving that which hinders us. This requires understanding what is involved with healing, and what it is we heal. Healing is letting go of the idea that we are an 'entity unto ourselves' living a life that is strictly individual, and only for self-interested gains, where everyone and everything is treated as a conquest of some kind. This leads to a life of continuously taking possession of people, places, and things. Healing is choosing to live what we are humanly in possession of, then humbly and kindly sharing it with others. The conflict people face most in their lives is between taking possession of something, or being in possession of something. Value and meaning are given to things that are either owned as possessions, or shared as inherent qualities. These two arenas of living are controlled manipulation or creative manifestation. They define paths of service. Individuality seeks to control, through denial and fear, what a collective state creates.

In the arena of creativity, we find what we feel and think becomes what we experience. The mind is the blueprint of what the body feels. When there is relational function between the mind and body, one's life will show health and vitality, rather than disease, negative feelings about the self, and dysfunction. Peace and harmony exist when there is relational function between the body and spirit; wholeness and ascension exist when there is relational function between the spirit and soul (Ascension is discussed in detail in Part Three of this book).

Crucial to resolving the mystery of this paradox in creating holographic structuring is understanding what inverse reversal is, and what it does. To create effectively, inverse reversal must be understood (Give yourself time with this as it took me twelve years to understand it well enough to define it, after getting it intuitively and visually). The actual experience presented itself to me on four levels simultaneously. The experience was, God's will to be and know extends and expands, inversely reversing into a focused becoming source centered within a given ideal existing within the universe.

The mind and body exist through the technique used in creation of inversely reversing one reality into a binary vibrancy. This makes a relational reality. The entire creation works this way. It exists as a relational involvement that we perceive as a binary vibrancy. This technique converts a single state into a binary vibrancy that is oppositional and lives as a state of peace; both aspects exist as an equality, balance, and harmony. This is one realness existing as two ideals, like male and female, or positive and negative. This is created energy manifested into an ideal.

Notice your breathing. It is not two breaths - it is one breath manifested in two differing ways. Notice that point when inhale becomes exhale, for it is here that inverse reversal takes place. Living is the art of opposites working together, rather than being in conflict. There are those who would have us believe there is good versus evil, but this is impossible given the realness and nature of God; impossible also, given the truth of oneness. When two opposing states unify into a single realness, conflict ceases to exist as a possibility. Peace makes opposites in conflict impossible because they exist as harmonious. Opposites in harmony, is peace. Inverse reversal exists as being peace and relationally as harmony.

Any given state has two components establishing it as a

binary vibrancy. These are never in conflict or in opposition with each other. There is always peace, harmony, tranquility, and serenity between them. Reality, as a binary relationship, never conflicts with itself. Conflict exists when an aspect of God decides it is 'it,' then seeks to control and manipulate everything else. There is only equality, balance, relationship, purpose, and harmony between what becomes inversely reversed, for each is in fact the other.

Inverse reversal can be thought of as an alternating current. Notice how both establish the reality as it is. Inverse reversal is that point or place, whereby during the vibration or pulse, it changes or becomes the opposite of what it was. Every idea composing the universe has an opposite, as this makes it what it is. From the perspective of a given quality or state, its opposite does not exist due to the veiling process. This is so we can touch a given quality, embrace it, and move from that to where it leads.

It is important to ask and answer what inverse reversal is and what it does, as this is key to the nature of the self and social evolution. The mind and body give us our sense of life, the body and spirit give us our sense of self here on earth, and the spirit and soul give our sense of universe of all that is as the self. Inverse reversal is binary vibrancy we experience as our heartbeat, breathing, waking and sleeping, and incarnation and ascension. The mind inversely reverses into the body, body into the spirit, and spirit into the soul.

Love inversely reverses into fear, establishing holographic structuring. It is God's will to know love and light, and fear and darkness, which is why we experience and express these things (There is a state that precedes this. It is a state of pure joy and pure pain. Lao Tzu called this state the Tao. This is a state that is both present and absent). Love and fear unify into is-ness and nothingness. This is God as idea, or God as infinite. The difficulty we have with infinity is that we are specific and human as a manifested creation. This presents a problem when trying to understand the beginnings of holographic structuring. Your mind creates the medium of the body, playing the role of giving identity to the mind. Your body gives function to your mind's ability to create. Your body is the 'self' creation of the mind into a specific ideal, representing your mind's ideal of humanness on this planet. The body is the medium your mind works within. Mind creates the body as its manifested realness. They are not two things; simply one reality expressed in two different ways.

Notice how we think of the mind negatively and the body positively, which is incorrect. The mind is positive, the body neutral, and the spirit negative. The confusion about mind and body show our lack of knowledge concerning them. Anyone tuning in to his or her own mind will create instantaneously, and reliance upon outside authority ceases. Few people engage in practices assisting the self in truly becoming mindful and creative. Most are enslaved to ideas and ideals that disempower the self and prevent one from creating effectively. The entire creation is designed for one purpose - the ongoing evolution of created ideals that encompass and enhance the entirety of all that is manifested, while existing as self-consciousness.

Becoming effective at creating a reality that works on all levels of existence is the purpose of creation. Each of us must take into consideration the nature of the self and what it becomes.

The mind creates the body into an ideal that identifies it giving the body all of the qualities we embrace as experience. The spirit brings to life what the mind and body are - a single state of being that knows. As self-expression, the spirit brings to life everything we experience; it is the spirit that allows us to move about independently. The spirit is that which perpetuates, the mind sustains, and the body regenerates. Spirit is also simultaneous, allowing for differing states to exist at the same time. The spirit gives us our entire notion of time and space. It is spirituality that allows for all ideas to exist independent of all other expressions. Movement is how the spirit is expressed. The beginning of time and space is that point in creation when love and light became independent of each other as singular states of being and knowing.

The body and spirit work in tandem; the body being the mind's ideal of itself as something. The spirit brings this to life as a self-represented ideal, believing it is different, distinct, and separated from all else.

When there is dysfunction between the body and spirit, it leads to conflict, stress, and anxiety, giving rise to the notion of good versus evil. The body is in a continual state of rest doing nothing by itself. Spirit is continual movement. Combining them gives us our sense of reality. When there is equality and balance between the body and spirit (rest and movement), there is peace and harmony, rather than conflict and violence. The purpose life serves is healing the dysfunctions between mind and body, body and spirit, and spirit and soul. The mind supplies the body with energy. Our spirituality is any movement we do through activities of personal interest and pursuits of happiness.

On a much deeper level, the mind is God, body is life, spirit is humanness, and soul is service.

The idea we are here to become more spiritual is pure fiction, because the spirit is complete in and of itself. The body and spirit are unified, making our life and times who and what we are. Just as we cannot make ourselves more physical, neither can we make ourselves more spiritual. Only our sense of unworthiness makes us feel incomplete and needing something more. It is our lack of joy and love that creates dysfunction between our mind and body. It is our lack of love and light that creates dysfunction between our body and spirit. Light is our spirituality, it identifies us. It is our lack of light and awareness that creates dysfunction between our spirit and soul. Each of us is responsible for healing these three dysfunctions. We are either healing or destroying our life through what we feel, think, and act on humanly. Death is the result of people choosing to die, rather than ascend. Dysfunctions encompass disease, conflict, and death as the relationships between mind and body, body and spirit, and spirit and soul. Dying is fearing life as humanness.

The typical life can be health, vitality, peace, and harmony; it is this kind of wholeness that ascends. It is odd to me so many choose to die, rather than live a life that ascends. People choose to create all sorts of attention-getting negative dramas. They do this just to feel alive and draw attention to themselves – it's a common situation. Many feel the need for acceptance, attention, and recognition from outside sources (There is nothing wrong or inappropriate about this). We are looking for approval and recognition outside the self, rather than within. This is why the hierarchical comes to us, giving us solutions and answers we feel we need. As long as we give it what it needs, it continues to control and manipulate our lives through slavery and forms of social coercion. This is needed for self-empowerment through our self-denial. It sustains its structure until it self-destructs. Anytime there is demise, it points to and shows us the underlying framework shared by a hierarchical source. Oneness never dies or destroys itself, because it is self-sustaining, self-regenerative, and self-perpetuating. Notice also, what happens when the 'source' we rely upon outside fades away. We either become self-reliant or extinct.

We all know by now that even the smallest aspect of the universe contains within it the blueprint of the entire cosmos. The entire blueprint of the body, as well as the entire construction of the universe, is contained within the mind. It is mind of God that created the universe. Looking at the universe, we are seeing what the mind of God created as an ideal of itself. What we haven't grasped is the awareness we have consciously. This is the ability to perceive and recognize the self as those differing states of being, in their original states and as us. We can draw the analogies that the sun is the mind personally, the planet the body personally, the moon the spirit personally, and the universe the soul personally. Mind, body, spirit, and soul are the inverse reversals of sun, earth, moon, and universe. Here is another analogy that might be easier to understand.

I am fond of the idea that the self begins with God and universe. When these become specific, God becomes divinity and universe becomes deity. When these become even more specific, divinity becomes mind and deity becomes soul. When the mind and the soul become us, the mind becomes our body and the soul becomes our spirit, giving us our sense of being and knowing the self as human. What do these pertain to as the realities they represent?

Who and what makes us human beings are God and universe, Yahweh the creator, and Id the father. We are the mind of God, the body of the creator, the spirit of the father, and the soul of the universe. God is our mind, the creator is our body, the father is our spirit, and the universe is our soul. The mind is God's will to be and know, the body the creator's love, the spirit the father's light, and the soul all we are conscious of. We are will, love, light, and consciousness that personally exist as mind, body, spirit, and soul.

How do we know love is real? We know love is real because it is physical. Our body is love manifested and personal. Heat is felt, and this is physical love. The physical is love as an embodied state of being. Everything physical is love as something specific. The spirit gives love the ability to be and know individually and independently from all else, as the spirit gives love the ability to move. The physical is love representing a specific ideal. Our spirituality is contrasted to this as light. Love is physical and light spiritual unified into singleness. The work we do consciously is increasing love's mass and light's magnitude through sharing. This establishes the relationship between differing ideals that are composed of the same energies. People working together peacefully and harmoniously increase love and light into greater levels of realness. What we see as the universe is a collective of love and light existing as greater levels of mass and magnitude. This is divergence evolving into communities.

We move our awareness from the personal into the relational, social, and global; some then move it into larger versions of itself, like a solar system, a galaxy, and the universe. Notice how each is composed of the same elements, and are larger versions of each other.

The mind radiates, the body absorbs, the spirit illuminates, and the soul encompasses. These exist as a state of purity that becomes distorted, then refined through personal work, culminating in an ideal that is the crystalization of those ideas, qualities, and ideals we aspire to become, like joy, love, light, and happiness. Crystalization also encompasses any state as an applied realness, like playing music, writing books, or having fun. In its truest form, crystalization is what ascends. As a state of consciousness or personal awareness, crystalization involves those states and qualities that are continuous in nature.

There comes a time when time and space as distance and

placement cease to exist. This is what ascension is, as the healing of these divergent states that work harmoniously together. As long as we hold to the notions that joy and pain, and love and fear are conflicted, we will continue to experience life as disease, conflict, dysfunction, and death.

The mind is pre-physical, the body physical, the spirit nonphysical, and the soul is metaphysical. Few grasp what each is, and the purpose each serves in making the self what it is. Addressing both aspects as the negative and the positive is the work we do in choosing whom we will serve and what we will heal. Healing occurs when there is equality and balance between opposites and different states of existence living as one ideal.

To address or 'meet' each aspect composing the self, one must tune in to it as it truly is. This requires meditation, having an idea about what a quality is, and the purpose it serves before one will become conscious of this personally. This is the role experience plays. Experience gives us first-hand knowledge about catalysts. Notice how pain, fear, joy, and love are ways we feel about ourselves. These are then shared with others. Eventually one chooses to be and know either what is positive or what is negative as one's path of service. Accomplishing this is difficult, as few truly know the self in its entirety. Before service is chosen the mind, body, spirit, and soul must either be accepted or denied.

One also sees how each works, and the role each is designed to perform. The fact that a given state exists means it serves a purpose of some kind. This is true of everything. We, in turn, give everything the only meaning it has. Nothing in and of itself has any meaning, it just is what it is. We decide the meanings of everything to suit our intentions and desires based on what we feel and think about it. How we apply what we feel and think determines our service polarity.

The way it is as dogma or fact is pure myth. We decide what is so about everything. According to Neale Donald Walsch, in 'Conversations with God,' "This is our make believe." And, "We are making this all up as we go."

Reality is self-defined. Reality is our "make believe" using those truths making our experience what it is. The fact we believe in dogmas as 'the' truth is what gets in the way of understanding and knowing.

Conviction blinds us to insisting what we believe is the only truth. This is impossible given the fact of infinity. Infinity is and means variable and variety of that which remains constant. God is the constant. The only equation that truly exists is I squared with the infinity sign. I only exist within a medium that is created – the universe. "I am" is the only statement the universe makes. The universe gives God identity. The I, in my equation, can mean infinity, idea, ideal, ideology, individuality, ideation, identity, inversion, and so on. We continually decide the reality of the self, moment by moment. I've learned that the positive path accepts everything and everyone, as is when I am even-minded. It only matters to me if it does. Then we need to examine why we feel and react as we do to impersonal events. The art of living is acceptance, responsibility, ownership, and even-mindedness (I am responsible for accepting personal involvement with my self as a human that evolves and ascends).

Stop for a moment and think about something that you feel passionate about. Notice it only matters to you because you've decided it has meaning for you and to you. Notice, now, all the things around you that mean nothing to you. Take a few minutes and think about what matters to you and what is meaningless to you. Ask yourself why a given person, place, or thing has meaning or no meaning to you. Meaning is what makes life, God, truth, and everything else personal or not. Take a moment to reflect on meaning and purpose. Purpose is due to existence, this gives it the purpose it serves. Meaning is what we decide about something that pertains to something or someone whom we feel and think about in all areas of life.

What is curious is the bias that comes with the territory of our personal uniqueness. Biases are issues acting as a catalyst we can heal or develop. Bias also include gender, race, family, and the environment. We enter into life with biasing that gives us the natural tendency to look outwardly and away from, rather than inwardly and into the matter making our life what it is. Biasing continues with heart and head, male and female, right and left hemispheres, the physical and spiritual, etc.

Biasing veils aspects of the self, so they do not get in the way of what this reality here on earth is designed to assist us in and with. Biasing is the perspectives we hold and includes some of the work we do. Remembering is another opportunity for expanding our awareness, becoming aware of what is real and true is another. Another is accepting our biology and loving this while living it. This is what the work affords us. It gives each of us the opportunity to remember, we are God, accepting our biological nature, becoming conscious of ourselves as all that is. One can think about the self in terms of acceptance, responsibility, embracement, and ownership. Each of us is here to accept the responsibility of embracing and owning our life. It is also those qualities we feel and think we are not, like God and universe. Each of us will come to know who or what is the basis for the entire creation. This gives us understanding about this particular reality we find ourselves amidst.

This is necessary before any other truths or realities can come into our conscious awareness. This is why knowing the self is so important, as this understanding precedes all other knowledge. We can ask ourselves: What is it that underlies the entire creation? The answer to this question is God's will and consciousness. These are the premises on which our personal reality is built and based on. This gives rise to those truths we embrace.

The universe we observe is God's will creating, as a manifestation, consciousness that evolves and creates. Our uniqueness and our individuality are what we observe as the outer. It is from this perspective we grapple with what God and universe are personally according to what their reality is as our own. The universe is an ideal that represents not only God's intention, but desire as well. The universe is God's feelings and thoughts about itself as specific states of being. The universe is how God conceives of itself as something manifested. Through God's will, the universe came into existence. All aspects of the universe seek to become self-conscious and work towards connection and integration, rather than disconnection and disintegration.

How does one come into knowing God in a way of equal magnitude to the vastness of the universe? We do this by knowing our own mind and soul. How does one do this seemingly impossible task? By entering into the mind, bringing God to life, and doing conscious out-of-body experiences.

The Bible tells us, "Seek ye first the kingdom of God." We are also told to be still and know the self as God. But again we are up against how to unlock this mystery of just who and what God is. There are many maps, directions, clues, and paths. The Sufis tell us: "There are as many paths to God as there are people on this planet." Each of us is 'the path' that wanders amidst the many distractions, amusements, comedies, tragedies, and interests.

For surely if the universe, or song of God, is God's idea of itself as an ideal that stands, then surely God exists somewhere, but where? "The kingdom of the father is within." (KJV Bible).

Within what you ask? God is the source centered within every aspect composing and comprising the entire universe. Everything existent within the universe is an aspect of God manifested as an ideal we observe as the universe. The universe is within God's all encompassing-ness that surrounds it. God is within us. We find God as God is in a state of rest centered within the heart. We bring God to life when we enter into this realness consciously. This will make our life the life of God. The path is journeying within until God is discovered. Within the quietude of silence rests the voice, or song of God, funding our life with energy. This sustains it, regenerates it, and perpetuates it as its humanness. We are the image and likeness of God. And yes, with the proper faith, patience, trust, diligence, determination, and gratitude we can all come to be and know God personally. Did I say be and know God? Yes. Everything is a symbol of God, from the smallest particle, to galaxy clusters, to the entire universe.

God is all that is manifested as the entire universe. God is what our identity becomes when we bring God to life. The now is being, here is knowing, and that continually becomes conscious of the self as all that is. God already knows it is everything. God is now. Life is here. Humanity is becoming. Currently, we think of God as the past, identity as the present, and heaven as the future. God then ceases to exist, and identity is just a dying fiction, coupled with distraction, so that the future never arrives. Our life fades before we become conscious of the self as God and universe existing as a life lived humanly as love and light. Death and reincarnation continue until we finally choose to become conscious of the self as God and universe.

How do we go within and know our self as the like-ness of God? We do this by meditating. Meditation is the path to God journeyed within and without. By without, I mean having conscious out-of-body experiences. Going within gives depth and going without gives scope. Eventually, the inner and outer vastness are identical in size so to speak. All encompassing-ness and infinity have equal value. God and universe are identical, as the inner and outer making the self the completeness it is.

Meditation and personal work, coupled with purpose, determine one's path. These are the essential basics framing the essence of one's faith, desire, and intention. The path is feeling what is real, intuiting what is true, and assisting others in healing and self-empowerment. It is as simple as breathing and as difficult as dying. But we love our MTV. We love our distractions. We love our illusions giving us our sense of identity. We love the insanity that keeps us forever busy. We are already the "image and likeness of God," so why do we work so hard at living an ideal that is less than what we are and that isn't real or true?

There is perfection to living life as we do with all its imperfections. But, the planet, solar system, galaxy, and universe are only outer perceptions we have of inner being, realness, harmony, and fullness. They are outer symbols of inner states of being.

What is the personality of a given idea and quality? It is anything we choose to feel, think, and share. Accepting responsibility for embracing and owning those qualities, making our life what it is, is the path.

God is the only reality that truly exists. We are an extension and expansion of God through love and light. What we feel and think makes God, as the self, something personal. We know we change reality just by observing it. We determine what is real and true about everything just by what we feel and think. Our observation changes the wave into particle. This is how we observe the self within the medium of the universe that is an ongoing continuum. We see our uniqueness within what is always and only a continuousness. What we become is more conscious, until we know with certainty that we are God and universe as individuality. Observation recreates the universe into the specific as this is the perspective we exist as personally. We define reality as we are defined. Reality and truth conform to those agreements we hold by believing in them. These become whatever we decide about them.

There is a deeper, larger reality we are involved with. What we are observing is a recreated field of observation, which is the self, defined so that it makes sense to us. We can then manipulate it into our personal ideals of intention. Reality changes into what is specific and particular to our way of living. God's all encompassing-ness becomes the particular or infinite. As us, this is all we perceive and recognize. We are all within the infinitude of God, so our perspective will always be from this point of view.

We decide what the meaning is about everything, be it God, life, truth, reality, or the self. This is our "make believe." Reality always is in agreement with the decisions we make. Why? This is due to the nature of infinity, and God's will to be and know. God is infinite, there is nothing God is not. God is all ideas. The will to be and know is that aspect of God, which by its very nature, creates into being a given idea. This is true of everything within the universe.

The self can be thought of as God's will to be and know, love and light consciously. In our pursuit to grasp the self beyond confusion or ignorance, ideas are useful until one becomes conscious of the self as each idea. The role meditation serves the seeker is it programs God's will so that one will experience the idea/s meditated upon. In the areas of love, light, and consciousness, the work we do is resolving our convictions that we are separated, isolated, distinguished, and distanced from God, life, others, and the universe. It is through pain, fear, darkness, and negativity that give us the perception our reality is as it is. Pain gives the perception we have separated from someone or something. Fear gives us the perception we are isolated from someone or something.

Darkness gives us the perception we are distinguished from someone or something. Negativity gives us the perception we are distanced from someone or something. These are the roles each plays as 'forces' in the universe. These four 'forces' give God's will, love, light, and consciousness the perception they are infinite and individualized.

Being and knowing are the conscious states existing within us as to what we feel and think. These are our ability to share. Sharing is performing. People perform their lives according to what is felt and thought as the positive or the negative, giving rise to one's current affairs. Sharing is applying God's will to be and know to a desired end or outcome. God's will is on automatic pilot. God's will creates everything that exists and that we experience. Self-mastery is sharing through service from a place of wholeness.

Being and knowing unify our ability to apply our intent; creating our reality as a personal truth, while we continuously become more conscious. Application is creating one's reality as a personal truth according to his or her intention. The nature of creativity is the application of God's will into ideals that are ongoing and infinite. God's will creates both positive and negative ideals as experience. The work we do in consciousness is effectively creating. Becoming conscious is understanding what is involved with creativity as our experiences. True mastery, in applying God's will, is how quickly our creations manifest. When they are instantaneous, true mastery is exemplified. Attaining self-mastery is the path we seek.

In our pursuit of attaining self-mastery, we begin by examining and observing our behaviors and reactive mindsets with everything and every situation. This explains why we feel, think, and act as we do in response to every circumstance, condition, or catalyst. The will is that aspect of God that creates establishing the relationship between one idea and another. This is the basis for all experiences giving each of us what it is to be and know a given idea, do something with it, and enlarge our horizons or viewpoint.

Being and knowing are always within the self. God's will is the 'motivator' for being love and knowing light that becomes conscious of the self as our intentions, and then applies these to others in the hopes that others will become as like-minded, thereby increasing the mass and magnitude of our intentions. These states of being are always within making the self who and what we are. They establish every relationship we have that involves us with what we hold onto as our ideas about God, life, others, and this planet. Bear in mind, the work we do is resolving those issues that keep us believing pain, fear, darkness, and negativity are real to us. Pain and fear, through denial and projection, become the superstitions of Satan, the devil, and evil spirits that torment us, but are merely the puppeteering of the ego. The ego is the choice maker. The one decision the ego makes is choosing path of service.

Knowing the self evolves into one's path of service. Path of service delineates between sacrifice and purpose. Sacrifice requires the ego choosing an outer-based ideology to follow blindly, like that of a suicide bomber. Purpose requires tuning into what is inherent, and then, dedicating one's life to living the inherent as path of service.

The process, or plan, we grasp is how to use God's will effectively by being love and knowing light consciously. It is God's will that creates the being-ness of love and knowing-ness of light. Consciousness is the awareness that understands what is involved, so that when it is effective, creativity ensues. When consciousness is aware of the self as an ideal, like us, creativity becomes possible. The fact is, God's will never ceases to create at every level of existence.

We can understand that within the self is the potential giving rise to all outer-based ideals we touch. This is the basis for all experience. The outer is creativity manifested according to our faith, desire, and intention, so we know personally what we feel and think, becoming all outer involvements. God, life, and others never create our reality for us. The less we know about this process, the more we believe we are 'victims' of our own creativity; then we complain about how we are affected by negativity.

Every experience we are involved with personally is created by God's will, drawing from the potential into a state of being, that then knows what this is through its relationship with the manifested representation of it. It is something specific that is uniquely personal. This is our personal reality willed into expression through intention by what we feel and think.

All experiences are our self-created expressions, built and based on what we feel and think by what we share. This process (or technique) works with all aspects of the universe. Above all else, God will's to be love and know light consciously. Everything composing the universe are states created. God's will, love, and light become a specific state of consciousness that is God's I am-ness. This is God being and knowing itself as various ideas. Each idea manifested is God stating "I am." The infinitude of God is all the various parts making the universe what it is. How we relate to a given quality of God is ultimately how we relate to God. We then choose to love, or fear, or show an interest in, or show indifference towards that. Leading naturally to how we interact with what surrounds us. This begins with our own heart and body. As we move away from impersonal beliefs about the self into the actual mechanics of the self, we discover that we are divinity and deity as our humanity, or human being-ness. These two states of existence combine, making us the image and likeness of God. What we become conscious of is what these are as us and how they work. This is becoming conscious of divinity and deity. Divinity and deity are our creator and father. As us, they exist as love and light. Understanding this requires letting go of the idea our biological parents created us (Our parents are versions of divinity and deity; these are love and light existing as something physical and spiritual. God's will creates everything. Our parents are versions of the creator and father, so that we know something precedes that created us and brought us to life).

In the first chapter of Genesis in the Bible we are told, "Let us make man in our image, after our likeness, male and female created he them." Why the plural? Both the creator and the father are involved. The creator of man is a collective consciousness composed of thirteen levels of consciousness unified into a single state of awareness (RA Material 1984). The father is another collective composed of twenty states of consciousness existing as a unified state of awareness. This is the oneness of differing ideals existing as a single state.

Oneness is the inclusion of differing states, not the exclusion of differing states. The problem is our insistence that oneness does not involve a number of different things composing it as a single reality. Oneness and infinity say and mean the same thing.

Take a moment right now and notice everything making you whom you are now. You have bones, blood, cells, tissue, muscles, organs, feelings, and thoughts; these are all unified into a single state of being. This is the oneness of you. So it is with the creator and the universe, each is a collective unified into a single state of being. Notice that it is our uniqueness, as an individuality, that gives us the viewpoint we observe from. God became the specific. The specific is anything that exists as what composes the universe. These, in turn, become conscious of all that is.

God becomes what is. This, in turn, becomes all that is, one experience at a time. Actually, God becomes ideal or infinite that becomes conscious of everything else through experience. God becomes the specific that, in turn, becomes God. The irony is, it is all and only God, ever. God is this, and I am God. God's all-ness diversified itself into an infinity, which is where we find our self currently. We are God looking at what God became and what we become; because God wanted to be and know difference, change, and diversity. God desired to be and know I am-ness, and it is this that became the universe. We can think of this as, is-ness wanted to experience is-not-ness to see what contrast is like, and as our humanity, it is all the opposites we experience.

What do we know about our us-ness? It depends upon whose opinion and whose propaganda we listen to.

Our self-discovery isn't finished becoming what it is. And just what are we becoming? We are becoming conscious of God and universe as the self. Self is the oneness, the union of God and universe as a single state of being that knows it is. These combine into each one of us. We evolve God through the universe from a perspective of self-awareness that is being God and knowing universe as a state of rest that moves. Rest and movement combine, or unify, or singularize into conscious awareness. This is the ability to observe one's being-ness that knows itself through what it does. God is the potential that gives rise to every state of being, while the universe is the matrix giving rise to all knowing.

In our specific instance, the creator manifested us as the image we see creating the humanness of God. Human being means: God manifested into a state of being us. We are God's humanity. What role did the father play? Bringing to life what the creator created. The creator created our embodiment that houses the realness of God in a state of rest within it. The father brought the creator's creation to life by infusing it with its own nature. The father imparted a piece of itself, and it is this that animates, by bringing to life, our creation. This is our spirituality. The spirit assumes the identity, while still remaining true to its original nature. How do we come to know what the original state, condition, essence, or is-ness of the spirit is? We come to know this by doing conscious out-of-body experiences. This is when we become our true spiritual identity within our ensoulment. We also understand what the self is as love and light. Love is physical as our embodiment, and light is spiritual as our identity. The physical is love and the spiritual is light that unify into creation as we live it. The spirit has a dual role in that it is what the father is, and what this becomes as us giving us the ability to do as we do; not to be confused with what we do for a living.

Why all the distinctions? If we wish to know the self as it is, we must have an idea about it before we will come to know it.

There is within the self a state that is identical to that state which precedes the universe. The universe is a symbol of God's ideal of itself as something other than all encompassing. In order for this binary vibrancy to work, tension is needed to be incorporated into the design. The basic tension underlying this design is love and fear. These are the two primary, or basic, elements the universe is built on. Love and fear are coupled with God's will to be and know. Will creates love, and will and love create light, and will, love, and light create consciousness. In order for individuality to exist as a single state of being or consciousness, pain, fear, darkness, and negativity must exist. It is these that make what is infinite, eternal, complete, and total into all forms of creation including us. From this all else arises and comes into being and knowing. Love and fear are the tension by which the entire universe stands. Love and fear also have their own developments as well through service polarity. Love and fear comes with the territory. Fear disperses energy; love unifies it. Will creates energy and consciousness evolves energy into greater ideals of self-creation. The entire universe exists, due to God's willingness to be and know I am-ness.

The path is touching qualities both positive and negative as our own state of being. Every opposite is the path to what it is not. Pain paths us to joy, fear paths us to love, etc. This is the only way we can recognize what a given quality is and does. Personally knowing what a given quality is and does, is why we exist. Life is a type of experience where we live as we do touching what we do making qualities personal. Eventually, we begin to discover what true creativity is. Creativity defines the self. The self is a form of expression or consciousness that experiences according to what is willed within a context that is infinite and eternal. Fear and darkness are finite and temporal.

Fear and darkness are veils needed, so that love and light can be differentiated into a myriad of ideas, making the universe infinite. What clouds our awareness of the self is the veil of forgetfulness that comes with this territory (The RA Material 1984). Each of us is responsible for piercing or lifting the veil by seeking to remember who and what we are. To do this, we must have an idea about what it is we are seeking to remember. We have forgotten we are God through the creator and the father, as the life we are living, as the self we feel and think is our humanity.

What imparts qualities creating us? God imparts the will, the creator imparts love, the father imparts light, and the universe imparts consciousness. These four states make us the human being we are.

The mind is that aspect of God that is personal. The body is that aspect of creator that is personal. The spirit is that aspect of father that is personal. The soul is that aspect of the universe that is personal. Combined is our humanness.

The soul is to the self what the universe is to God. The soul is the universality of the self. Every experience we embrace builds the soul that houses them. Each experience adds to what we are consciously aware of as the self as an ensoulment. Every experience involved with, since the universe began, is recorded in the soul, and it is this that makes us unique and individual. We are doing what God has done. We are creating our reality as we desire to be it and know it. This is identical to what God did in creating that reality that truly represents God's ideal of itself as something.

The differences between soul and spirit are that soul is a consciousness that is infinite, while spirit is light that is specific as that which is identified. The soul is all that is, while the spirit is what animates creation. The spirit is light as an ideal, coupled with darkness and the unknown. The spirit remains constant, as well as adapting to what it animates, or brings to life. It is the spirit that expresses what love experiences. Light expresses and love experiences God's will to be and know consciously desire that intends. Will becomes love, and these become light, and these become consciousness. As a single state, this creates and manifests what we observe as the lifestyles of everyone. Basic to our entire being is experience, as it is this that makes something real and true for us in a way that personalizes infinity, or all that is. It is love as my body and light as my spirit that gives me the sense or notion I am Douglas. The soul is my consciousness, and the mind is my will, so that what we are is mind/will/God/extension, body/love/creator/experience, spirit/light/father/expression, and soul/consciousness/universe/expansion.

The soul is all that is, while the spirit is what animates the mind as an embodiment, or what we think of as our body; these work together. We can also think of spirit as both light and dark as it pertains to our humanity. If the universe is fifteen billion years old, so is my soul. The spirit brings to life a given ideal.

Love is the physical part of our body that we experience as the embodiment of love, just as light is our spirituality, giving us an identity that articulates. God wills to be and know identity as a condition of self-awareness. The soul is our consciousness, our awareness of the self as something different than and distinct from everything else. This gives each of us the ability to create and manifest ideals of the self that are personal and relational.

God will's to be and know love and light as a state of consciousness. As us, they each retain their originality, as well as experiencing and expressing what they are not as our body and spirit. Love becomes the body and light becomes the spirit as identified states of existence. This is what meditation assists us in becoming conscious of.

The mistake many make with meditation is thinking doing so is leaving this awareness for another, and then treating that state as if it is our true nature and identity. Any awareness realized must be brought to our normal waking consciousness and shared. Our identity is what we share with others. Our identity is what was created and brought to life. Our mind comes from God, and our soul comes from the universe. The body comes from the mind and the spirit comes from the soul. It is our humanness that we live as an experience and expression that we share and evolve—not states of consciousness meditated into. Humanness is what we are evolving.

Spirituality is both light and what it animates giving it the sense it is what it brought to life by making it something specific, rather than something infinite and eternal. God's will is infinite, love is eternal, light complete, and consciousness total. These make the self what is real and true. Spirit is light and dark as me simultaneously. When viewed as the self, it is seen as half light and half dark. Just as love is both my body and what it is and is felt as both heat and fear. Herein is a clue to why we do not do a better job in grasping the self as it is designed. We deny and reject what makes the self an ideal.

The self is the inverse reversal of God, life, and humanness that serve. When light is observed, it is seen as half light and half dark; it is the dark unknown that becomes observable when it enters into a given creation and gives light its function and form, making it useful and creative. So too all other aspects of the self, as this gives each quality purpose, function, usefulness, and applicability. This is why we are a binary vibrancy existing on several levels. The problem people face is that each one of us is given the specific catalysts of denial, irresponsibility, rejection, and projection to work through. Coupled with these are pain, fear, darkness, and negativity. These eight catalysts allow us to exist as individuals who are unique. The path is how well we resolve these fictions.

The problem afflicting and facing humanity is, the notion of 'one' state being 'it.' People seek to be and know single states to the exclusion, negation, and aversion of all else. This stems from an absolutist mindset. Another mistake people make is, thinking attainment of a specific state is the point and purpose of being. The truth is, we are all here to understand how to create effectively, and unify ourselves into a single state that will collectively ascend.

Think of the moon in all four phases. This shows us what light as spirit is as an ideal, and what it becomes as a polarity. Each quarter phase shows us male and female that either becomes full or new depending upon service polarity. The full moon is positive polarity, the new moon negative polarity.

The light of the self, as our spirituality, becomes more light or dark according to whom we choose to serve resulting in complete light, or complete darkness. These then attract those who aspire to become like-minded.

The soul is our universality. The spirit is our light. The body is our love. God's will to be and know is our mind.

The mind is the potential from which all comes personally. The mind creates everything we embody. The mind creates the body, which the universe, or soul, brings to life through the spirit. The body is the mind's love as an ideal, just as the spirit is the soul's light as an ideal matched or mated with the mind's love, an embodiment that lives independent of all else, giving us the perception we are alone. The universe is a creation from God, and through God's mind that wills to be and know all that is. This makes God infinite, eternal, complete, and total as the universe we observe as our own soul. We literally see God as the self as all that is as our soul. The universe is God's soul. Our soul is composed of all the experiences embraced since the creation of the universe. In one context, God's soul and our soul are identical. The body is the actuality of that which potentiates us into our humanness.

This is the mind willing to be and know itself as an embodiment. The soul then brings this potential to life by imparting the spirit into it, making the body a living ideal that is a representation of God as a human being that knows and continually becomes through faith, desire, and intention. The physical is love manifested as a definite, through which light animates. These make us the union of love and light that is the oneness of the physical and spiritual we think of as human being. True soul mates are love and light. When the soul incarnates into the body, this becomes its soul mate. The soul becomes mated to the body after it incarnates into it. Each person living is his or her own soul mate, not someone he or she meets and gets involved with. People are not missing or lacking something in their life - outer-based ideals do not complete us. (According to the RA, Seth, Ramtha, and Edgar Cayce, people whom we meet as soul mates are individuals who have come to earth for the purpose of working together from the same universal community).

There are ten states of being to address. These are will/consciousness, joy/pain, love/fear, light/dark, positive/negative, awareness/understanding, principle/condition, divinity/deity, universality/specific-ness, and connection/integration. These encompass the entire self, making us the ideals we are. These are what we tune into when we meditate. What we become conscious of determines what we know about the self. Mind, body, spirit, and soul are all states of consciousness, as are God, father, creator, universe, life, will, love, light, and anything else we can feel and think. Our task, our responsibility, and our opportunity is, becoming conscious of who and what we are as God and universe, divinity and deity, and creativity and manifestation as our experience and expression. This can be thought of as God becoming life, which becomes human, which chooses service polarity, that then understands and knows oneness, then the oneness of love and light, that culminates in a state I call all-ness. These then reintegrate into all encompassing-ness as a state I call God-hood. This adds to God all the experiences embraced during the soul's journey over time, through space. This entire process is the incarnation and ascension of God as ideal (This can be thought of as, from God, through God, to God, as God).

The difficulty with this is, everyone has a different view

about the self, due to the fact that each of us is unique, thereby making what we see strictly personal and tailor made. Some choose to live contrary to what this design is. Further complicating this, everyone has personal biases that color the horizon giving differing nuances and hues to the landscape of our self-created experience. Each of us walks alone, and it is this that gives us the ability to be and know what our faith, desire, and intention deems worthy for us to embrace as the self. Aloneness is the path to becoming conscious of the self as all that is, or all one state of consciousness that is willing to be and know ideas as ideals that continually become. The now is my being-ness, here my knowing-ness that becomes continuously those ideas I feel and think I am living, giving me all the experiences I embrace inwardly and outwardly as a human being that knows.

I am becoming conscious of the self as God's will, love, light, and the universe. These are then shared with others in ways that are empowering. I am becoming a way-shower, deliverer, and healer through living equality, balance, relationship, purpose, and harmony. This is my path of service; unless I choose to focus upon what these are not, thereby making my path contrary to God, and God's I am-ness. There are those who seek to serve themselves. This requires being and knowing is-not-ness. These involve pain, fear, darkness, and negativity as an ongoing path.

Some choose to use God's will in creating and manifesting pain, fear, darkness, and negativity as their path. This is the left hand of God. People who use God's will in manifesting joy, love, light, and the positive are the right hand of God. Each path has its merits. Each has its usefulness, function, and purpose. It is important for those who walk holding God's right hand to honor and respect what the left hand is and does. Honor and acceptance are what love does regarding our creation. Fear does the opposite through judgment and persecution. A simple test for each of us is, are we accepting or judging people, places, and things?

Essential to grasp is, forgiving ourselves for all we create that assist the left hand in its role, as well as assisting us in our right hand path of service. Forgiveness is resolved and unnecessary when one accepts the self as it is. Acceptance becomes even-minded-ness. Acceptance and even-minded-ness are the attitudes God has regarding and concerning any aspect of the universe. Each of us is that aspect of God and universe that either accepts or judges the entire rest of the creation. It is we who have created 'hell' and a 'God' that judges us. Forgiveness heals hatred.

The self is God and universe, giving both uniqueness as ideal, that we live as our humanity. The creator and father are our divinity and deity. We further refine these as our image and likeness. This is further refined as mind and soul culminating in what we live as body and spirit. These experiences are what we in turn express. The body is an experience of love, while the spirit is an expression of light. We feel love and think light, utilizing God's will to be and know, while seeking to become more conscious of the self as God and universe. These are not a duality, they are an extension and expansion of our realness through experience and expression (Human evolution is our evolving love and light from something strictly personal into something eternal and complete, making them universal and ongoing. Collective ascension is that point in evolution where love and light transition from a planetary state of existence into a universal reality).

As it stands now, the body is treated as an entity unto itself; something distinct, separated, and isolated from all else. This is the illusion of time and space (Time is duration. Space is awareness. Time is representation. Space is placement. Time is structure and space content. Time and space are durated awareness. Time is existence. Space is where this stands. Time is organization. Space is where this exists. Time is ideal. Space is possibilities. Time is idea and space is where this will exist).

The body, treated in isolation from the mind, spirit, and soul, then denies, rejects, ignores, abandons, and fears everything else. This is the 'fall' of man. In that, we have fallen into believing we are other than and less than whom we really are, because we have rejected, denied, abandoned, feared, and ignored the mind, spirit, and soul. This creates a "make believe" reality for us, where we believe our identity is egoic as our outer identity that surrounds itself with assumptions designed to insure its survival. How does one disengage from the ego's insistence that it is alone and the only reality? It is done through meditation assisting the seeker in moving his or her awareness into other aspects of the self.

Before meditation becomes useful one must feel and think one is more than just his or her body. One can tune into each aspect composing the self through intention and discipline. Meditation is the inner path, a personal way of becoming conscious. This will differ for each of us. No two people are the same, so meditation will intune each of us to differing states of consciousness. Finding what works is an art form, given the fact that each of us is different, and each of us has different issues to address and heal. One must be willing to let go by disengaging from strictly outer-based ideals that keep our awareness forever looking away from what is within. The inner being of all is veiled; we only see it as an outer representation. This is due to the nature of that which precedes. Namely, God and universe coupled with divinity and deity that create life and our humanity. Specific to the self is the mind that precedes the body, it is this we seek through meditation. The mind contains the blueprint the body represents. The body is the mind's outer representation. Similar in nature to life that surrounds us, and the universe that surrounds this planet.

The difficulty we have here is in the interpretations we make involving and regarding these aspects of the self, being viewed as an outer representation. We only recognize outwardly what we feel and think about ourselves.

We have the awesome task of deciding who and what the self is, and then what this becomes. Everyone has a differing point of view about the self, so it is difficult for people to agree upon basic tenets or truths about the self. Complicating this is the racial biasing, as well as gender. I remember some time ago realizing that anything I observe is inherent within me, or I could not see it or think it. Any idea I have about something or someone is an idea I have about myself, always. Denial, irresponsibility, rejection, and projection remakes life into pain, fear, drama, and death.

These prevent me from truly addressing myself as it is.

Race and gender are 'veils' used, so we are convinced our body alone is our humanity. There are also the veils of confusion (RA Material 1984), darkness, forgetfulness, time and space, just to name a few. Veils are used to convince us a given state is real and true. We are convinced these states are independent of anything else. The inner and outer are terms for being and knowing. The outer is a way for us to know what is contrasted to being.

The state we exist in is our current reality, so we grasp the basic mechanics making life work. Creativity requires knowing what is used and how, so that we will effectively create and manifest what we will be and know personally and socially. We are the actuality of God and universe as an ideal. The difficulty we have with this is that God precedes the universe. Life is an extension and expansion of the universe that culminates in our creation. Our current belief systems misconstrue these as past, present, and future. We believe God is the past, our identity the present, and the universe the future. What we are actually doing is remembering God as it is now, actualizing life as it is designed, and becoming conscious of the universe as our own soul. Becoming aware of these as the self requires meditation; this is due to each differing from the other in form and function. The observable representations clue us in to innate actualities. The mind will look like the sun as a state of being; the body like the planet as a state of knowing; the spirit like the moon as a state of doing; and the soul like the universe as a state that is becoming.

What is the potential giving rise to this actuality that stands as a manifested representation? God is the potential giving rise to all that is. God gives rise to the universe as its manifested representation.

Rest and movement unify into what is neutral. Will and light unify into love making it neutral. Will at rest makes it positive. Light is continually moving making it negative. When there is equality and balance between rest and movement, or love and light, this becomes self-awareness as our ability to observe. On a deeper level, this means our perspective and awareness as a conscious observer (both aspects of God and universe) can be recognized and known as each is, and as each pertains to the self.

Movement is light as wave. Rest is will as particle. Light is negative and will is positive that balances as equality into self-awareness. Becoming conscious means we are moving our awareness to encompass more and more of "whom we really are." This is why we meditate. As it is meditation that moves us from one state of awareness into another until both God and universe are known as the self that create and manifest what is willed into a manifested ideal. When movement is observed from a state of rest, it conforms to and becomes the perspective observing it. It is our perspective mirrored back to us, showing us who and what we are as the observed. In order to observe the mind, one must understand that it is what precedes the body. The soul is observed after it leaves the body. The spirit is non-physical. The perspective we are coming from determines what is mirrored back to us as a manifested representation, giving rise to all that is as an actuality the observer embodies. One is realizing what is observed as an experience one expresses, i.e., creates and then manifests.

It is important to learn, teach, be, and know the self. It contains and pertains to any and all aspects that exist by extending and expanding, through inversely reversing into a focused becoming source centered within and surrounded by love, light, fear, and darkness (Love and light are never in conflict with fear and darkness. They are not opposites in conflict idealized as good versus evil. They work and exist as a state of peace within, and the harmony between outer-based ideals, when accepted, owned, and lived). This state of consciousness wills to be and know experience that expresses whatever is intentioned through desired faith. We find ourselves at that place or point where God and universe stand as a single uniqueness that continuously seeks to be and know. Our perspective is the particle and wave as an awareness convincing us we are humans on this planet. Every relationship we find our self involved with is our perspective observed. Actually, experience is embracing what we express as the self. If we do not like where we find ourselves, or what we find ourselves involved with, we can change what we feel, sense, think, and envision, giving rise to what we embrace as our personality and personal reality. Our personal reality is defined by those truths we hold to be self-evident making reality what it is for us, as us. Reality is self-defined truth we embody and share.

Reality and truth are the very existence of every ideal on each planet and within the universe. These are specific to what is being created. They correspond to what is being represented as an actuality demonstrating what was applied as an intention manifested. Creativity manifested is reality as a self-defined truth that evolves into whatever is desired. This is the creation and how it works.

This is not easy to understand as we act as if we had nothing to do with what comes our way. This is impossible, as we create our entire reality through God's will, and those properties that become what we embrace as our personal truth.

Those holding to the perpetrator/victim mindset are steeped in the mythic traditions of fear, guilt, arrogance, and denial, creating these as one's reality. It is what we hold about the self that becomes our experience. This means we create everything we experience; this is sobering to know and humbling to accept. (It is also interesting the role that gravity plays, for it is the force that draws and maintains our relationship to our self-imposed ideals. Gravity is the relationship between what is within, and its outer representation we touch as our experience).

One of our shortcomings is that we don't take enough into consideration when drawing conclusions about what we observe. If we truly seek to heal, we need to address what we feel and think, as these determine what we experience. What does our personal reality entail? It depends entirely on what we feel and think that we behaviorize. What we act on determines our reality. Reality is created through God's will to be and know through what we feel and think from a standpoint of choosing. Choice is what we act on through all of the experiences expressing whom we are.

All of our experiences involve choices and intentions. It is this nature and role that God's will plays. The will is God's willingness to become anything we desire to create good or bad. Fear converts God's will to be and know into law. Every law we live by is based or built on a fear we have about something or someone. This is due to what organizes the uncontrolled into meaning, value, and purpose. Law is the myth behind social order and conduct. Laws are the judgments we have made regarding fear's conviction that it is threatened by the choices others have made. Fear is necessary as it individualizes love into an organized system of realness. In our current state of existence, fear rules love into the physical we live. Fear as law is never in conflict with love's unconditionality. Fear is that which binds love's all encompassing-ness into a specific format. In our case, this is our humanness. Fear sets boundaries, so that love will experience and express itself as something individual and unique. Fear coupled with gravity maintains the integrity of this designed ideal. Without fear and darkness, all you have is love and light that is all encompassing, rather than specific, unique, and individual.

Pain convinces us we have separated from some source. Fear convinces us we are isolated from all else. Darkness convinces us we are distinguished from all else. Negativity convinces us we are distanced from all else. To remove these four 'forces,' the entire universe would return to and become a single state known as all encompassing-ness.

God's will to be and know is the foundation the entire universe came into being through. When all other aspects of creation are stripped away what remains is God's will. This is coupled with consciousness. Will and consciousness unify into and exist as a state I call all encompassing-ness that precedes the universe, and gives rise to the universe. The very first state that resulted from God willing itself into being and knowing was a state Lao Tzu grasped as the Tao; a state of presence/absence containing nothing else as a direct contrast to all encompassing-ness.

This first state of creation was an extension and expansion of God's all encompassing-ness, not a duality that is in conflict with God's realness. People fail to grasp what extension and expansion are through the experiences and expressions we observe as something specific. This can also be thought of as the inner and outer.

In understanding what it is to be and know the self, it is useful to have a working knowledge of God's early work. God willed itself into the universe that continually refines itself by redefining what it is to be and know. Everything is God's ideal of itself as something unique and creative; it is this we discover and understand about ourselves. We realize that we create our experiences, and then redefine who and what we are as an ideal that evolves into something infinite and eternal. God became what it willed, and seeks to know what it is being; all aspects existent do likewise. We seek to know what we are the beingness of, as well as creating for ourselves a sense of identity that represents what we will through applied intention.

This is evolution - evolution is the development of consciousness through experience. It is also the development of God's will as it becomes more aware and encompassing.

We continuously find ourselves face to face with what we are being, knowing, doing, and becoming. These are God, life, humanness, and service. Service is the application of the self in an ongoing and continuous manner that is either conducive to all that is, or a detriment to all that is. We are being God, knowing life, doing what is our humanity, and then becoming what shares this with others. A slightly different version of this is, we are being God's will, knowing life as love as the physical, applying light that gives us our sense of individuality and identity, and becoming conscious of all that is. What we are doing is understanding how God's will to be and know works through using love and light consciously. Effective creativity is using God's will to be and know coupled with love and light, giving the applicant the ability to create life itself. The adept will be able to manifest upon demand anything. In contrast to this, are those who choose to use God's will, coupled with fear and darkness, to create death and destruction through war and enslavement. The un-suspecting never realize which path they serve. Each path can be thought of as that which either creates or destroys.

Knowing the self requires moving one's idea about the self beyond identity, gender, race, family, and issues. We can change our ideas about the self by understanding what God, life, humanness, and the universe are personally. God personally is will, life is love, humanness is light, and universe is consciousness. Or we can say, the self is God as mind that wills, life as body that loves, humanness as spirit that is light, and service as soul that becomes conscious.

The problem each of us faces is what these are as something personal. Herein lies the work we do in consciousness. Doing the work is becoming conscious of the self as it is. This requires letting go of ideas that are misguided, shortsighted, and erroneous.

Meditating on the mind one discovers what God's will to be and know is on a personal level. This will be a state that is known to the seeker as all encompassing, and similar in nature and scope to the sun. The mind and sun function in a similar manner. The mind is centered within the heart. The body is the mind's creation of itself into an ideal that works within and upon this medium of planet and physical life. The body is the embodiment of love as a physical ideal, existing according to the mind's willed intention. The spirit is the individualization of light that gives each of us the notion we are a singleness. The spirit as light gives each of us the conviction we are identity. It is the spirit that convinces us we are the self we are living biologically. The soul is the universe summed up into a single state of consciousness. Everything within the universe is God's way of saying I am. I am-ness is the oneness of God as a specific realness. The oneness of God, creator, father, universe, will, love, light, consciousness, mind, body, spirit, soul, infinity, eternity, completeness, and totality is identity. Identity then seeks for meaning, function, value, and purpose as an ideal that is relative, relational, and collective.

The work we do is to grasp what the mind, body, spirit, and soul are and do, as states of being unified into an identified single ideal. All ideals works at resolving chaos into patterns that are at peace, harmonious, and conducive to larger more inclusive states of existence.

The mind/body, body/spirit, and spirit/soul work together combining God, life, self, and universe into a single state of being that knows, shares, and becomes. For those people who seek to attain bliss consciousness; it is the union of will and love into a single state that fills the heart when realized. Just as love and light unify into peace, and light and consciousness unify into freedom. Joy and peace unify into harmony, and peace and freedom unify into adventure. Freedom and adventure unify into creativity within the artistry of oneness. This gives the seeker the ability to enhance his or her quality of life. Truly evolved souls do this throughout the creation. The left hand of God seeks to control and enslave using war, greed, and slavery. Those who serve others do so as way-showers, deliverers, and healers. Those who have not chosen whom they will serve observe both paths at work.

Creation is and works according to ideals that become larger versions of complexity; no different than atoms becoming solar systems, and solar systems becoming galaxies, and galaxies becoming the universe. So it is with us. Only we understand the nature of the self through consciously seeking to be and know the self beyond self-imposed limitations. This can also be thought of as what surrounds us being a larger version of our self.

How does this process work? We become conscious of the self as something concrete and specific. As we comprehend what is involved, we discover there is more to our ideal, so we continually seek to be and know consciously what is involved. This moves us into other areas pertaining to the self in accordance to what we believe is true. The problem we are all faced with is bias, as this prevents us from delving into ideas about the self that differ or conflict with what we deem is so about the realness of personal reality. Complicating this process is the fact that the mind is pre-physical; the spirit is nonphysical; while the soul encompasses all that is. If we do not have a measure for what the mind is and does, we will never touch upon it as it is. This is true also about the spirit and soul. Few people have a working model of the mind, body, spirit, and soul as they are and exist pertaining to the self, making us who and what we are.

The self is the sum of all things as a unique ideal. In dividing, we have this life that realizes it is. From this point of reference, we can move our awareness into any other state that exists. The ability to do this only takes focus, intention, discipline, determination, and patience. The self contains eight chakras. Each chakra corresponds to each density composing the universe, and the realness of the self. This is why there are eight chakras, rather than seven. Preceding first density is a state of presence and absence, that when accessed, comes across as a void or state of emptiness, or zero point. This state is the original condition of the universe that is the inverse reversal of God's all encompassing-ness. This state of presence and absence compliments God's all encompassing-ness. This state can be thought of as God's nothingness. In that, nothing exists except presence and absence. What this state feels like is a hollowness coupled with deep sadness. There is a longing like desire one will also feel. This longing is God's will to be and know all encompassing-ness once again.

The universe came into existence through division. Once division became the universe as an infinitude, it began to add itself back up. God became an I am-ness that exists as anything represented upon a planet and within the universe. God then incarnated into that. What incarnated then seeks one ideal. God incarnates into expression through the sperm. (The sexual urge people feel is the desired intention of love and light experiencing union and oneness. This is accomplished through conception and orgasm. Sexuality is love and light differentiated experiencing and expressing union and oneness with varied individualization. Sexuality is the union and oneness of love and light existing as independent holographic states). The ideal sought is the oneness of all that is. Oneness is all encompassing (It is this longing that creates and manifests everything composing the universe trying to recreate its original state. Incarnation and ascension is the path or journey of God from all encompassing-ness, through the universe, then back into all encompassing-ness once again. This is accomplished through experience. After enough experience is embraced, it is added to all encompassing-ness through ascension).

The work we do in consciousness is becoming aware of the self as it is designed. This requires meditation, as much of the self is not physical. How do we get back to being and knowing this design as intended? By seeking to feel what is real, intuiting what is true, speaking what is relevant, and meeting the need in the moment. We seek to find, ask to receive, and knock to open to who and what we are. Not easy to do, as everyone has a differing idea about the self. Few people touch upon the self on all levels of existence. This is due primarily to few moving beyond gender, race, and tradition into what is real and true about the self.

People are proficient at following the dictates of others through rules of conduct, and the socialism involved with group participation. We seek agreement, conformity, and to be one of those accepted in the family as those who live life a certain way. Few venture outside the box the group has decided it's the way it is. People insist everyone stand on the same plane living life the same way. It is not easy to break away and go it alone to discover what the self is. People fear being alone, being different. They fear things that differ from them culturally and environmentally.

One of the basic problems we have humanly is we do not take hold of what infinity is and what it means. Infinity is and means variable and variety of that which remains constant. God is the constancy that forever remains unchanged. Infinity is and means everything is an aspect of God's creation. Infinity is another name for the universe. It exists due to God's willingness to become all that is as the universe. Actually, it is God's willfulness that creates the universe that is infinite. To understand infinity, think about all the different versions of trees. Or, think about how there are no two snow-flakes that are the same, and how billions and billions have fallen over the centuries. Think about how no two people are identical, even with all the billions who have come and gone. Or think about all the countless stars in the heavens. Think about all the grains of sand on earth and how no two are the same. Infinity ensures God does not do instant replay with anything.

Infinity is a contrast to all encompassing-ness. All encompassing-ness inversely reverses into infinity. This establishes binary vibrancy. This binary vibrancy is the ongoing relationship between God's all encompassing-ness and the universe's infinitude, God's being-ness and God's knowing-ness. God's all encompassing-ness is its being-ness, while God's universality or infinitude is its knowing-ness. The contrast that exists is due to time and space as the now and here. The now is what we are being, and here is what we are knowing. When now here is applied it becomes doing. When now here changes it is becoming-ness. Our life is one of being, knowing, doing, and becoming eternally as that which is complete and total. Will and love are our being-ness, while light and consciousness are our knowing-ness. Being and knowing are a binary vibrancy when unified into a single state of existence (Binary vibrancy is never in conflict with itself. Conflict is only possible when one aspect of what is decides 'it' is 'it', and that all else must conform to its way of being and knowing. This establishes war and slavery. Greed is the attitude one is superior to another, and money is the means used to establish class distinction).

To move beyond the psychologies of birth, crucifixion, death, and reincarnation, it is useful to realize and understand that from the relative everything is in relation to all else. Relativity is the notion an idea exists in and of itself, and that time and space distances it and separates it from all else. This is impossible. From the relative, arise the relational and reciprocal, and then the creative, that manifests as an ideal, all according to levels of binary vibrancy. There are four we deal with everyday. The heartbeat is one, breathing is another, waking and sleeping another, and incarnation and ascension another. Each of these is an extension and expansion of our basic or primary creation. God will's to be and know the relative, the relational, the reciprocal, and the creative. The relative gives all the creation the notion it is, and gives God the ability to state I am (I beg to differ with the Bible's statement that God claims to be, "I am that I am." I am-ness only exists within a medium that is infinite. I am-ness is the claim identity makes about itself when it is specific and evolving. God's realness is all encompassing. It is a state that is uniform and constant. This state lacks what infinity is and does. Infinity is all encompassing-ness diversified. Only something self-serving claims to be, "I am that I am." This clues us in to the service polarity of what the Old Testament glorifies. The relative is in relationship with everything else, and what closes this binary vibrancy is the reciprocal, for it maintains the integrity of the pattern, and how it works within a specific medium or density).

For some, we are here to learn our lessons. This is in fact untrue. We are not here to learn in so much as we are here to grasp we are creating and manifesting all aspects that touch our lives. We are becoming conscious of what we create and manifest. It is only denial and projection that convinces us we are at the mercy of God, or a victim of some evil perpetrator.

We are given the opportunity to feel our life as it is and that it is enough, and to feel content just being and knowing what it is to be and know humanness. Nothing else is required, expected, demanded, or stipulated, ever. It is enough that we are being and knowing the self as this life on this planet according to everything our lives touch. Never are there judgments or expectations placed upon us to be and know, other than what we choose to feel, think, and share. God only sees the perfection of our creations, and is at one with such, forever. (Everything is acceptable to God, but nothing is acceptable to us). God does not condemn an aspect of itself. God loves everything about itself, and accepts everything as is. It is only our pain and fear that condemns and judges. The entire notion of justice is the conviction something will get even for our pain and fear's perpetration. Justice and karma are the same terms; however, karma clues us to what becomes of those who perpetrate.

To understand karma and sin, reincarnation must be understood. Karma and sin are the application of the self negatively. Anything applied must be balanced. Any act of perpetration will be balanced at some point in one's evolution. Every perpetrator will reincarnate as a victim of someone doing the same act. If a person perpetrates, he or she will become a victim of that later in life, or in another incarnation. Time and space are the cause and effect of the perpetrator/victim psychology.

There are those who focus exclusively upon aspects of the self, convinced this alone is what they are. For some, it is God consciousness, others bliss consciousness, compassion, enlightenment, cosmic consciousness, love, light, husband, wife, professional, bum, artist, gender, race, condition, personality, and so on. Take a look at anyone, and what you see is what they are focusing on as the self. For some it is disease, others fame and fortune, or the work they do. Endless are the portrayals of the self we create and manifest, giving us the belief we are as we live. There is nothing wrong or inappropriate with how a given person creates, and what they create for themselves, giving them the notion they are what they've created. God did the same with the universe. People oddly, seek to become something other than and contrary to their true natures.

We do not do a very good job of honoring and respecting the self. In addition, we do not educate people into healing or releasing disease or hardship. This is due to some needing to enslave others, so they can live life as wealthy, famous, or powerful. Slavery is the dependency upon another due to denial, guilt, and fear that enslaves anyone holding onto these as his or her identity. These compose most of our 'civilized' cultures. Most people are enslaved to the dictates of those who serve themselves. Self-denial and projection create the entire gestalt of the perpetrator/victim mindset. What we fear, feel pained, and guilty about are the lives we are living as our humanity. Much of the qualities we honor are denigrating to the self.

The curious qualities about our parents is they give us our entire sense of identity. These give the reality of the self the mediums through which we create our desires. Self-denial and projection lead to two behaviors – co-dependency and irresponsibility, keeping us dysfunctional. These keep us looking for outer-based modalities, enslaving us by reinforcing what we feel and think due to our self-denial and projection. Denial keeps God and life non-existent, and projection forces us to look to negative sources that are outer-based. This is why the entire myth of a Satan or a devil exists. Denial and irresponsibility prevent us from creating ideals about the self that are truly magnificent and awesome. They also keep us steeped in traditions by reinforcing the fiction that we are helpless and that life is beyond our control, and must be controlled by something foreign to us.

To move beyond this, we are wise to realize and understand that the relative becomes the relational; this in turn becomes the reciprocal that creates. Pure relativity does not exist. It is impossible for an ideal to stand independent of all else. Infinity is and includes everything. Everything is in relationship with and to everything else. There is the specific, the truth that an idea is self-conscious of itself as something; evolving into a binary vibrancy, which is the relationship between ideals, that is reciprocal in nature giving an ideal its ability to create and manifest. Reciprocity maintains the integrity of the entire system or pattern.

I like to think in terms of being mindfully purposeful, and applying myself through intentional determination. So that my manifested creativity is always and only what I intend it to be through my faith. It is faith that establishes and determines what takes place as my experience. We live according to denial and projection, or creativity and manifestation; people miss this. Denial and projection give us the scenario that we die and go to heaven. Fear and denial as projection are the death experience. When we accept, embrace, and then own creativity as manifestation, this is and becomes ascension. Ascension is and means to rise above, take with, and integrate into. What we rise above are all the lower states of consciousness that keep us stuck in the strictly human way of being and knowing. What we take with us is the body, and what we integrate into is the universe.

What we are faced with, as either death or ascension, is denial and projection or creativity and manifestation. These are what we experience and express as either death or ascension. The work we do in consciousness is healing death, by letting go of denial and projection giving us direct being and knowing of God's will to be and know love and light as the consciousness of all that is. The idea we go somewhere after we die is projection given action. We die to the unrealities we live as, and then go to what our projection is. Healing is letting go of who and what we are not, so that we can consciously live as those realities making us the self-conscious human being here now. The seeming time and space differential between the self and our life ideal is what we heal. Until the self is lived as one state of being, one will die. Sharing the self with other aspects is serving others and what ascends. Ascension means making a contribution within a larger medium.

The purpose of being is understanding oneness. This requires choosing to be and know those qualities making us who and what we are. When the self is lived as God and a life that serves others, then it is time for one to ascend. Ascension is our graduation.

This brings up a curious fiction, a mythic notion, about everyone coming to the same conclusion about something. This is impossible, actually, and only happens through blind belief a given idea is 'it' for everyone. Change is the fact that nothing is the same moment to moment. Nuance is the name of the game. This gives each aspect of God's infinitude a differing slant or view on what is. This is the entire point or reason God created the universe, to give contrast to what God always is, a uniform constancy that never changes. All encompassing-ness inversely reversed into infinity; an endless array of ideas all expressing God as something specific. Infinity is variable and variety within a state of constancy. The universe is God as an ensoulment giving God the awareness of itself as a diversified infinitude. Eternity is the ongoing-ness of God showing us creativity, as consciousness never ends and never ceases to create ideals of intention. The notion of 'it' as an absolute is folly, and only works from arrogance convinced 'it' is 'the' only absolute. The only states that exist that are convinced of being absolute are those souls who serve themselves. They state "I am that I am."

So just what is it we are creating as a personal embodiment? Look at yourself in the mirror, and you'll see your self-created ideal as the person you are living now. Plus, anything you embrace as an experience is your creativity at work.

To truly know the self, two other areas remain to be recognized and grasped - completeness and totality of the self. These make each of us infinite and eternal. We only lack what we feel and think we do. Those who seek for a soul mate to make them feel complete and fill their sense of loneliness and emptiness will find that no matter what comes along the longing to 'fill the void,' that sense of emptiness and longing, will remain unchanged. Half of me is not missing as woman. My femininity is the internal relationship I have with myself that when lived gives me fulfillment that I then share with others relationally (My feminine side is love just as a woman's masculine side is light).

Truly living humanly is when love and light are expressed as a unified state. When I feel content with myself by feeling the joy and love within, I feel at peace and happy with whom I am, and it is this I draw unto me as woman who mirrors as the mated state I exist as. It is this that endears her to me and me to her. I do not seek for a soul mate. It is my soul's mating within my body that makes my life the only relationship I have. This determines the type of relationships I have with women, the whole of humanity, the planet, and the entire universe. God as life, as me, as truth, as infinity, meets me where I stand. There is no out there to go or states of consciousness to realize. Because who and what I am is right here, right now as my humanity. As I continue to know myself as God, life, me, and infinity, they reveal themselves according to what I feel, sense, think, and envision.

The evolution of these develops into service polarity. This requires choosing whom you will serve. There are only two types of service polarity, self-service or serving others.

Who Do You Serve?

Part 2

Who Do You Serve?

Knowing the self evolves into service polarity. Conflict resolution is the path, and evolves into either serving others or serving ourselves. Some choose to serve the self. Some choose to serve others. Most fail to resolve enough to evolve into the conscious awareness needed to choose whom they will serve. This culminates the entire point of one's purpose for existing as a created and manifested ideal.

Culminated evolutionary development pinnacles with service. Service evolves and develops between self-service and serving others. In the Bible, this was demonstrated by Jesus when he was 'tempted' in the desert, his personal wilderness. Aloneness serves one essential purpose, it is the state, place, and condition from which and for which choice of service is made. Those who know their Bible can recall Jesus being tempted to rule the world through his abilities. This is what the negative path seeks to do, using pain, fear, guilt, denial, and ignorance to empower the self by enslaving others. Jesus responded to this offering by the 'dark side' by stating, "Get thee behind me, Satan!" But we humans, in our ignorance and arrogance, have erroneously made this notion of Satan into a 'deified' absoluteness in conflict and opposition to God. We have made Satan the antithesis of God. So we have those who serve God, and those who serve Satan as good versus evil.

What is missed is, Jesus wasn't addressing something foreign to himself. He was not tempted by an 'outside' agency. Satan was the term or name Jesus gave to his own pain and fear. His statement, "Get thee behind me..." was his finally letting go of his pain, fear, and attitude as a predominating psychology. Each of us is responsible for healing the division within the self that the belief of good versus evil is true. If good hates evil and evil hates good, what difference is there then, given the conflict is hatred, and it is hatred that makes good versus evil a possibility. Hatred is the attitude fear has denied about itself that is then projected onto others. Hatred is an anti-human attitude. The war-lord God Jehovah hates Yahweh's and Id's creation of our humanness, and seeking above all else to destroy it. Hatred is fear seeking one ideal—self-destruction, and the destruction of all else. Hatred expressed is disease, violence, and death. Forgiveness heals these fictions of the mind.

While it is true service polarity has two compliments of endeavor, neither is in conflict with the other, due to conflict defeating itself into nothing as death or destruction. Every experience is preceded by willed intention. What we each feel and think corresponds to our faith, desire, and intention. Each of us then interacts with ideas representing what we feel and think about who and what we are here and now. Always something precedes and follows from this moment. We think of this in terms of past, present, and future; however, the past does not exist here and now. Neither does the future exist here and now. This leaves us with only what is here and now. And it is this that defines and determines what our reality is here and now. The way we hold onto past, present, and future is odd, in that we think of this in the context of how we observe movement. It is also how we interpret linear time. But notice what happens when we put this into an applied realness. Try walking away from your past now and notice how it follows you wherever you go. We take with us everything we feel, think, and experience. All of our past, present, and future is right here, right now, forever. The actuality is the instantaneous, spontaneous, and simultaneous. It is only our growth that gives us the perception of a past, present, and future.

The past, present, and future format is useful in that it shows us something becomes from something over and over and over again. In our case, our parents, their parents, and their parents give us what we define as our genealogy. Technically, we can trace our roots all the way back to 'Adam and Eve.' However, 'Adam and Eve' are mythical fictions used to instill guilt by 'that which deceives' leading to what is then practiced as conquering, enslaving, and destroying others, leading to the entire psychology of the 'holy war.' (Jesus' purpose in life was his attempt at healing, war, greed and slavery, by people understanding these are the great lies perpetrated by selfish, misguided souls).

Most of us dying today do so due to our lack or unwillingness to live life, as it is as an ongoing realness that becomes truer and more real. When positive and negative are psychologically conflicted, each aspect that composes matter as biology, cancels and negates the other, producing and leading to the perspectives of nothingness, illusion, chaos, and void regarding God, life, humanity, and what these become as a purposeful ideal. When the self is super-imposed over these, this becomes or translates into serving the self to the exclusion, negation, and aversion to God, life, and others. Notice how the exclusion of God, negation of life, and aversion to others plays out as our 'civilized' humanity. This leaves us with pain, fear, guilt, arrogance, denial, ignorance, indifference, and intolerance as the primary motivations we idolize. These in turn lead to disease, disparity, competition, conflict, violence, war, and death. This is what conquering, enslaving, and destroying accomplishes as an ongoing state of existence that self-service needs to empower itself by disempowering others.

The ideas of absence, nothingness, illusion, chaos, and void serves negative polarity well in that it 'theoretically' eliminates presence, is-ness, realness, pattern, and content that is ongoing. However, in order for something to exist, there is something that foundates it (Foundates is and means the premise and principle used to create an ongoing state of existence).

God precedes the universe, and predates it by eternity. This can be thought of as all encompassing-ness diversifying itself into an infinitude. Everything is an aspect of God's realness. The past then is the original state, condition, essence, constancy, and is-ness of God surrounding the universe and inherent within anything existing as an ideal representing God as something specific. Everything within the universe is actually within the reality of God as an indwelling ideal that makes an ideal infinite, eternal, complete, and total. What contribution are we making for and towards this as our personal and social ideal?

We are serving others, serving ourselves, or not serving anything. We serve God, serve ourselves, or serve nothing.

Bear in mind that, it is only service polarity that is harvested from this planet in the time of the harvesting of souls (RA Material 1984).

Choosing whom we will serve is ultimately the only choice we ever make, as it is the only choice that is truly ongoing.

Both paths are available for us to choose. Self-service is based and built upon denial, fear, darkness, and unconsciousness. Serving others is based and built upon will, love, light, and consciousness.

The ideological stance of self-service is good versus evil, dividing the self into a fearing mindset that suicide's life into death. The ideological stance of serving others is oneness that unifies and heals the self into a loving mindset that assists others in living life as designed. Love and fear work together as a harmonious binary vibrancy. Love inversely reverses into fear, and it is this gestalt that creates holographic structure. Love is a collective state of existence working in conjunction with fear, individualizing love into a single ideal. Jesus and the twelve disciples were a human portrayal of the creator as a collective of thirteen beings existing as a unified and connected state (RA Material 1984).

Love and fear are what each path is built and based upon. We choose what is about the self as either love or fear, then share this with others as hierarchy or oneness. Love is all encompassing, while fear isolates what is. Love is God that fear individualizes into infinity. Fear seeks to control and manipulate infinity, while love seeks to embrace and heal it. Fear is the basis for love's individuality. Fear is singular, while love is a collective of thirteen states. Holding to our sense of individuality ensures fear remains the predominance in our life, eventually killing us. Fear is death. Love is life.

Those who serve themselves seek to divide, while those who serve others seek to be and know, educating others into what oneness is as that that exists. Division leads to conquering, enslaving, and destroying others. Oneness leads to healing, wholeness, and ascension. There are those who aspire towards what hierarchy is and does as an ideology. There are those who aspire to what oneness is and does as an ongoing realness. People will find themselves involved with teachers and teachings fostering the seeker to aspire to become either self-serving or serving others. Each of us chooses that ideology that corresponds to what we feel, sense, think, and envision is the way it is as our reality and truth. Most of humanity has not evolved into a working conscious awareness of what service polarity is. Many people refuse to choose whom they will serve, so their lives are stuck in a neutrality that does instant replay over and over and over again in what we call reincarnation. It is only service polarity that continues on from third density (RA Material 1984). Our refusal to choose or even consider whom we will serve leads to living a life of indifference, where one will ignore life, others, and creative inspiration.

Now, there is nothing wrong or inappropriate with someone who decides he or she is not ready to take responsibility for whom he or she will serve. There is a perfection to any life lived as it is. People are given freewill to decide for themselves what is so about anything and everything. It is wise for each of us to actively seek to become conscious enough and contented enough to choose whom we will serve. Getting in our way is the fact that we are ignorant about service polarity, and clueless to what each path entails as a methodology. What does service polarity use to empower itself? What does service polarity organize into as a social ideal? What is the emphasis used as an ideology that humanity subscribes to, not knowing exactly what is actually going on?

The negative path is those who serve themselves. They maintain control through manipulation; accomplished through fear and guilt that enslaves people. This is accomplished by instilling a sense of doom through a threat of some kind, or from the conviction one has violated some 'sacred' rule or law of conduct. The actual mechanics of self-service begin with either an erroneous doctrine of creation, or an erroneous theory about how 'reality' began. Both religion and science have accomplished this effectively. Following this, the enslaving self-server implements laws of obedience as a divisionary dogma disseminated as the 'faith' worshipped as 'truth' or fact by those who become the 'chosen ones.' Division leads to conquering, enslaving, and destroying others, due to the 'chosen' feeling they have the right to annihilate everyone who disagrees with their right to rule through dogma. The pattern is hierarchy, designated as an elite deemed superior to other chosen ones who believe good versus evil exists and is true, leading to the social activity of conquering, enslaving, and destroying others. All war and violence stems from this gestalt. Hatred is needed to make self-service ongoing.

Our current worldwide history is this as an applied fact. Going to war is the great false doctrine many people subscribe to. Many nations hold to the erroneous notion that God sanctions and deems the 'holy war' appropriate. No greater fiction exists than this (I am of the opinion Jesus taught what he did in the hope of eliminating the entire philosophy and psychology of military and war from this planet). God does not take sides in any conflict. The idea the 'winner' of any war was favored by God is sheer nonsense, and pure folly. This is due specifically that life exists through God's will, love, and light.

Self-service places total emphasis on individuality as an entity unto itself, and values outer-based items, like gold, jewels, land, and people. Self-serving individuals are like black holes. People who serve others are like suns, radiating love and light for others to feel and see.

What this tells us is that Jehovah, as depicted in the Old Testament, is actually a 'war-lord god.' Jehovah then disseminated the propaganda needed to begin the process of self-service on this planet. Jehovah uses the mythic fiction of Adam and Eve to make us feel guilty about being human. Jehovah hates what Yahweh and Id created and brought to life. This entity establishes the Jews as the 'chosen people,' and the notion that good versus evil is 'the way it is.' Hatred is a form of selfishness and arrogance. Chosen-ness is a form of social coercion. Jehovah demands strict obedience to laws implemented that are punishable by death to ensure 'his chosen' never stray, and never intermix with the greater whole of humanity. Many a social order is convinced it is 'God's' chosen people. There is nothing more ridiculous than this notion, given God is all that is. It is impossible for something all encompassing and infinite to have an attitude that anything within itself is greater than, lesser than, other than, or foreign to itself. It is only the arrogance and ignorance of man that believes God has a favorite race or group of people that are right or correct and everyone else wrong and condemned forever. There is nothing more foolish than the idea that that which created us would also create a place of punishment and turmoil lasting for an eternity. Nothing and no one is this inhumane except those who serve themselves.

Notice what the ideas do involving sin and law. They keep the faithful fearfully stuck within the tradition positing such nonsense. Fear and guilt are the two main ingredients ensuring the adherent remains enslaved to the ideology. The focus is always 'out there' and the goal is the continuous taking possession of what one places the most value upon, rather than understanding what has true value within that is then shared with others.

Fear, law, and war are the covenanted ideals of Jehovah. Fear and guilt maintain the psychology, law retains the ideology, and war attains the 'promise' through adherence and application of those ideas leading to and insuring elitism, superiority, and chosen-ness remain unchanged. The doctrine of good versus evil ensures people will conquer, enslave, and destroy others. Through the promise, one is entitled to take the life and land of those who are not 'God's' chosen people. One must understand God is centered within the heart, and does not exist out there somewhere.

Jesus taught love, forgiveness, and doing unto others as a resolution to fear, hatred, and selfishness becoming the social mores of conquering, enslaving, and destroying others through war, greed, and oppression. While Jesus was teaching his truth to others, John was given his vision of the Revelation. This was a warning to us all. If we insist upon perpetuating fear, hatred, and selfishness, this would be the collective experience of everyone perpetuating social discords (The serpent mentioned in John's revelation is Jehovah). Anyone who holds to such nonsense will always be afraid, feel guilty, and use violence as a means to an end. Many a lost soul believes that God destroys and Satan torments us endlessly if we do not use some form of protection against our own self-created ideals. Namely, fear denied and projected becomes God the destroyer, while pain denied and projected becomes Satan the tormentor. This leads to everyone to feeling guilty for being alive, and that we are guilty for being human. The reason for this is Jehovah condemned what Yahweh created, constituting our ideal as a sin. According to Jehovah, what Yahweh created is a sin against God, and by its very existence, continues to sin against God. So what we have are lots of ideologies denouncing humanness as an ideal leading to all sorts of strange practices that miss the point entirely of what humanity is, and who humanity is, and why humanness exists as it does. The Bible tells us we are, "The image and likeness of God" and that we are, "the word made flesh." This makes us like God and as God. Our failure is that we hold onto fictions that make us less than this through what we believe. People believe their humanness is other than and not God's offspring. This is impossible, given everything is an aspect and quality of God. People do not discern what they consider our creator to be. The 'God' of the Jews is a case in point.

Jehovah arrived around 9,000 BC. The Jews were selected as his chosen people. Judaism is the ideology of faith maintaining the relationship between Jehovah and those who were chosen as its people. According to Seth, "Retention of the Star of David and recreation of the state of Israel necessitates the return of Jehovah for his people." The return of Jehovah means everything and everyone who participates with invader culture ideologies will be destroyed by him, as this is what conquering and enslaving promises and insures.

According to Ramtha, "Jehovah was defeated by Id, and the last great battle fought over this planet will be in the heavens between these two entities. Id will defeat Jehovah again. This battle between them will last seven days." Everything and everyone supporting and involved with the invader culture mindset will be destroyed during this time.

However, as long as we live fear as opposed to love, law as opposed to forgiveness, and violence and war as opposed to doing unto others, we maintain and live Jehovah's ideology, rather than the ideology of what works according to life's intended design. Each of us is responsible for choosing whom we serve through what we feel, think, and act on. Those who hold to negative modalities will be removed from this planet, as what comes are peace, love, kindness, and that which is life itself. Each of us is responsible for choosing love, forgiveness, and doing unto others, or what is antithetical to these. Essentially, if we hope to be 'left behind' as the harvested, we must be and know the reality that comes as fourth density upon this planet. Fourth density is the 'new age' dawning. Everyone who holds to fear, guilt, arrogance, and denial will find their ideology ceasing to exist as a planetary realness. It is wise for all of us to ask, who disseminated the ideas we hold as our social ways of living? Important in this regard, in that asking honestly and openly will lead us into knowing what is so about all ideals we aspire to and what is the underlying basis for such as our social ideology.

Humanity is wise to start implementing programs to heal the psychological intentions creating discord and disharmony. Humanity is also wise to discern what exactly is involved with negative service polarity and stop contributing to that psychologically. History only repeats itself when ideologies are retained as a disseminated ideal that humanity continually reenacts generation after generation. This is why it is so important to end our personal and social involvement with untenables that soon become extinct. 2012 is the timeline for what ends and what begins.

Everything that is not socially conducive ends as a personal portrayal due to being an untenable that is not real or true. The means by which a given state thrives will cease to exist as an ongoing reality if it is based upon self-service. This will be no different than mammals replacing dinosaurs causing their extinction as they no longer worked according to what creation deemed the next evolution in consciousness development. Plus, everything that is unloving, unforgiving, and undoing unto others will cease to exist as an ongoing becoming-ness. This planet is a positively created ideal that assists humanity in continuing the development of will, love, light, and consciousness as these evolve into an ongoing ideal that remains eternal. The only ideal that remains ongoing is what collectively ascends. Negative service polarity is removed from the planet and taken elsewhere to continue its development as this is what the harvesting of souls does with self-serving individuals (RA Material 1984).

The 'second-coming' involves the return of Jehovah for

his people, the return of the father in defense of his offspring, and a return to living life as it is designed. Living this design means learning, teaching, being, knowing, doing, becoming, actualizing, and demonstrating what humanness is as a single state. Christ consciousness is humanly portrayed when everyone living understands that we are each other. I am you and you are me, and this is why we are all here at this time. This is why living love, forgiveness, and doing unto others is so important now. Only what is conducive to life remains as life and continues the evolution of our species. Anything contrary or detrimental to life biologically and humanly will cease to exist as a catalyst, due to these aspects no longer applying to the new reality that comes. What comes is joy, peace, and freedom for everyone 'left behind.'

Service polarity is the application of love or fear as these pertain to the self. We are either loving or fearing, as the content of our character as an applied state of being that knows through experience. Evolution is the development of service polarity over time, through space until the time of the harvesting of souls. The harvesting of souls takes place at the end of third density and beginning of fourth density. In our specific case, this will be in the year 2012.

The historical facts about us as a creation involves Yahweh, who created us, Id, who brought us to life, and Jehovah, who taught us what it is to be and know negative service polarity. Negative service polarity is based upon the notions of hierarchy, elitism, superiority, chosen-ness, and good versus evil, leading to the social behaviors of competition, conflict, control, manipulation, greed, and dependency upon an outer-based entity or ideal. Those ideas that instill us into feeling fearful and guilty about ourselves, coupled with denial and projection leading to death and reincarnation, are how the negative path works. The alternative involves living life as it is designed according to the creator's love and the father's, light making us the humanity we are being and knowing. We are being love and knowing light as a state of consciousness according to Yahweh and Id's intention.

Yahweh is our loving creator. Id is our light-bearing father, who brought us to life by enspiriting us into an ideal that acts independently. Jehovah is that which brought us fear as an ideal to aspire to and apply through conquering, enslaving, and destroying others. This leaves God as the great unknown. Yahweh can also be thought of as our form of divinity, and Id can be thought of as our form of deity, making us the image and likeness of God according to their ideal. Notice that the first chapter of Genesis tells us, "Let us make man in our image after our likeness, male and female created he them." Notice the plural and the emphasis upon our. More than one 'thing' was involved. This is a mistake many make in failing to realize there is more to us than we understand as to who and what we are. God and universe are two aspects of who and what we are, and divinity and deity are also two aspects of who and what we are.

What we find is, negative service polarity requires us to believe in the fictions of perpetrator and victim. This leads to each of us to becoming co-dependent on something or someone to 'protect us' from what is going to get us eventually. Notice also that we rely on the very traditions and institutions instilling us with what we believe, but are in fact the 'real' perpetrators making us their victims by our deciding what they state is real and true. We believe we are victims of Satan, God, evil, or some other monstrosity.

This is in fact impossible, and not the way it works.

Truly serving others entails knowing God's is-ness as our own. This means we must return our attention, our conscious awareness, to remembering God's originality that foundates all creation, and life as we know it and live it.

This is why it is so important to meditate, for this is the way and means available to remember and return to God as God is, forever. How one does this is by sitting quietly, focusing on the breath, and opening his or her life to being and knowing what these are as something personal and real. Not easy to accomplish in that all ideas, emotions, thoughts, and behaviors must be addressed, healed, and understood. Then one needs to understand the meaning and purpose of experience so that the self will be accepted and recognized as God before God can, and will enter into an equal partnership with itself as each of us.

When one becomes fully conscious, one brings God to life, and it is this that makes one born again. It is God as the self, centered within the self, that is brought to life again when one enters into God's realness. The meaning of being born again is that it is God and the life we are living, being re-birthed into something living, rather than dying. This requires us getting away from always relying upon an outer-based agency of some kind. It also requires our getting away from placing our faith in impersonal man-made things like books.

Love and fear are the foundations that tension holographic structure into existing as an ongoing ideal. Love pulls while fear pushes, so that the entire universe stands as an ongoing ideal, giving God being and knowing what it is to exist as an infinitude of ideas that apply both love and fear in creations representing God's I am-ness. It is application that gives being-ness its ability to be and know the self according to what is applied. The universe is God's will applied. What also must be kept in mind is, everything is an extension of time and an expansion of space of God's will to be and know specified ideals demonstrating God's I am-ness as an infinite uniqueness. This uniqueness then downsizes into divinity and deity, creativity and manifestation, and finally as us through what we experience and express. We also discover there are many binary gestalts like joy and pain, love and fear, light and dark, positive and negative, awareness and understanding, principle and condition, universality and specific-ness, male and female, connection and integration, and so forth.

Service polarity requires consciously choosing love or fear as the basis for personal evolution. This then becomes an applied statement, giving testimony to what one feels and thinks is the way it is. Negative service polarity will state openly that creation is absence, nothingness, illusion, chaos, void, and erroneousness through the I am-not-ness of the self, from the conviction the self is an absolute. Positive service polarity knows that reality and life is presence, is-ness, realness, pattern, content, truth, I am-ness, all-ness, and God-hood. Both are accurate according to the path each walks and encompasses.

Service polarity is the purpose evolution serves, not the

development of the species over and through time. One way of thinking about evolution is, beginning with God, life, humanness, service polarity, oneness, healing, wholeness, and finally ascension. Only those who have chosen service polarity are harvested, due to this being harvested from third into fourth density. Negative polarity is harvested and taken elsewhere (RA Material 1984), while positive polarity becomes the 'wheat' that remains, furthering the evolution of the species until it collectively ascends as an ongoing reality that is an infinite, eternal, complete, and total ideal that is self-sustaining, self-regenerative, and self-perpetuating. Those who remain stuck and steeped in the belief of good versus evil are not evolved enough to transition into the reality that comes as fourth density. Division does not exist as a conflict, or opposites in conflict reality, within the reality that becomes life on this planet. The greater truths always remain as what evolves into the new reality. Lesser truths become extinct. This is why it is important to be and know those truths pertaining to and involving life as it will be when earth becomes a fourth density planet. We do this first on a personal level, then relational level, then social level, then global level, and finally a universal level.

Joy and pain, love and fear, light and dark, positive and negative, awareness and understanding, and principle and condition are binary vibrancies existing as awareness, and give each of us the ability to exist in a unique way. This is due to what each aspect does as an ongoing realness. This begins with presence and absence - presence of something means the absence of everything else. Existence then moves into is-ness and nothingness, requiring everything else to become nothingness, from the perspective of that is-ness that exists as an ideal. This gestalt becomes reality and illusion, given a certain reality requiring everything else to become an illusion, so it can exist as that reality it is. These evolve into pattern and chaos, the pattern of a given requires all else be in a state of chaos. Evolution works as content and void, in that what one is contented with requires all else be a void, as to not interfere with what contents one's character. This evolves into truth and erroneousness, so that what is true requires all else to be erroneous according to and in relationship with that truth one embodies.

The important idea to remember: It is we, not God or Satan, who chooses what the nature of the self is, and what is utilized as our chosen path of service.

Serving others is internal. Serving the self is external. The internal path leads to serving others, while the external path leads to serving the self. Both paths have equal merit in the developmental evolution of God, for each path assists the other by their very natures. It is wise to keep in mind what love and fear become as a third state of realness. Love inversely reverses into fear that vibrates as an altogether different reality than either love or fear. This reality will exist as both simultaneously, just as each person is the simultaneity of their parents existing as a third distinct state of being that differs from either.

If a given aspect of God is truly built and based upon division, it will self-destruct and fade away. Death can be thought of this way. People are separated causing conflict between two states of being, unifying into a third that is completely different than the two states. This is what makes this density what it is as three-dimensional. This includes everything that exists at third density. Healing only pertains to division conflicted with itself, as this is the evolutionary realness of oneness, which gives rise to it. All evolution is and does is heal division into a state of oneness once again through the process of growth. Everything that exists is healing into becoming one again. The evolutionary path, or process of the universe, is that each aspect seeks to become one state of existence and experience. Each aspect composing the universe knows it was originally one state. It's like a drop of the ocean seeking to become the ocean again. The two ultimates sought are union and oneness. The positive and negative unify into the neutral. At our level of existence, the neutral seeks to become service polarized. This is the path and purpose of evolution.

Love and fear are the two building blocks of God giving this its is-ness. This leads to positive and negative service. When these are personified, it is how one relates to all else, and how one perceives everyone, and how one relates to her or his environment. What we also do is attribute these qualities to God, life, and others. When love and fear are construed as opposites, they become good versus evil, leading the self to divide against itself, creating disease, conflict, violence, and death. While on a larger scale, this leads to the misguided ideas of hell, Satan, and a God that destroys.

Love and fear unify into any ideal created. Love is positive and fear negative that unifies into what is neutral. Neutrality is being-ness. Being-ness exists holographically due to the equality, balance, relationship, purpose, and harmony between love and fear. These determine and define the entire creation. As forces, they exist as holographic structure, giving what is the ability to exist as all that is. Love and fear exist as the universe, and as everything composing the universe, demonstrating how these work together in the context of all ideals; while leading to the relationships pursuant between all aspects of the creation by and through service polarity.

Service involves God or the self. We are serving God, serving ourselves, or serving nothing at all. Serving God requires love, and serving the self involves fear. A problem arises, in that love lacking fear is fiction, and fear lacking love is foolish. The denial of one for the other renders both incomplete and invalid. Creation exists through love and fear, standing holographically, forever. All other matrixes that potentiates catalyst into experience evolve through love and fear. What is referred to as densification is love and fear, as they evolve into greater levels of existence. Evolution is overlaid by each successive density, and can be understood as entering into a new reality as the previous one fades away. This is like entering and exiting a room in a house. Love and fear and everything existent are versions of this, and more comprehensive renditions of these two realities. Each serves the purpose they do, and when we understand this we will then align ourselves in like-minded fashion. We evolve into the bias of polarization through choosing service. This determines our path as purpose humanly.

Love and fear combine into is-ness or nothingness, depending upon which path is chosen. Negative polarity is convinced nothingness beginning the process called evolution. Positive polarity knows that something, an is-ness, precedes the creation. God is an idea used to assist people in understanding what oneness is and does. If God is all that is, one will act accordingly from a place of reverence, showing respect for everyone and everything. This hinges upon the premise that one comes from God, or the self being an absolute, giving rise to everything that follows from this state. People are given the option of believing who gave rise to them.

Absoluteness requires law, dogmatism, blind obedience, control, manipulation, mistrust, and having an agenda that is hidden and deceptive that followers will never question. The belief that one is chosen or a group is chosen points to a negatively polarized teaching and path, particularly when the underlying tenet of the teaching or teacher is that 'it' is the only way and a given group is 'it.' This is impossible and untrue. Each of us is our own path to God. How one finds God is seeking within until God is seen, accepted, owned, and then entered into. God is only entered into by consciously choosing to do so, and going within the heart, as God is centered there waiting for our life to become its life.

Going within is a strictly personal activity. The fact that no two people are identical means that no two people will ever enter into identical states of being and knowing. Nuance is the game of infinity and the universe. God wants diversity above all else, and it is this that intention's all of creation through God's desire to be and know.

The fact is, everything is its own path, from the smallest particle to clusters of galaxies. Everyone is his or her own path to God, and whatever other adventure one chooses to be and know. Everyone is creating and manifesting her or his ideal as a personal experience and expression. Within every idea existent is the original essence of God that we experience and express as is-ness or nothingness, when love and fear are a manifested representation that we choose to be and know as either oneness or division. The problem each of us faces is deciding what is 'it.' Is it God as the self or something other than, contrary, and foreign to ourselves? Our outer sense of self is neutral. Being centered in our heart makes this positive. Being focused in our head makes this negative. The positive path is heart-centered. The negative path is head-centered.

The fundamental quest people have searched for is the 'one' thing making creation what it is. An 'it' if you will. What people fail to realize is that it is God's will to be and know that created the universe and all aspects composing it. It is this that one must seek and find to answer what began creation. The will of God is the 'smallest particle' within the self. Superimposed around this are all the other components composing not only the self, but the entire creation as the planet and universe we live upon and observe. Service polarity is how God's will is used. Negative service polarity uses God's will to control and manipulate. Positive service polarity uses God's will to create and manifest, as well as heal and inspire others. Self-service needs fear, denial, and guilt to be successful. Serving others requires people being love and knowing light as the self, and then sharing these with others through acts of kindness. This will make the server a way-shower, deliverer, and healer, rather than one who conquers, enslaves, and destroys.

Love is accepting everything. Fear is judging everything. When service is chosen, we either love or fear everything. Self-service evolves through war, greed, and slavery. Serving others evolves through kindness, sharing, and doing what's socially conducive to humanity as a whole. Negative service polarity requires one group being chosen and all others damned or condemned, stemming from fear, judgment, and persecution based upon good versus evil.

The universe is built and based upon extension and expansion, which we call time and space. Love and fear are a single reality of God's is-ness as something specific we grasp as infinity, given all the variables and varieties we embrace here on earth and throughout the cosmos. The extension and expansion of love and fear, positive and negative, evolve into male and female as path of service, utilizing truth to create that ideal, which encompasses the service polarity one has chosen. Each path will understand and utilize what's available in altering and opposing ways.

Self-service requires division to work. This leads to the social behaviors of conquering, enslaving, and destroying others under the guise of either God or entitlement. Serving others understands union and unity, leading to social harmony and peacefulness that works toward healing the arbitrary division established between love and fear by the self-serving, as well as teaching people how to truly be creative in their experience. Self-service lives according to exclusion of God, negation of life, and aversion to others, while serving others lives according to inclusion of God, affirmation of life, and involvement with others for the sake of the common good. Negative polarity isolates, while positive polarity integrates, so that according to each path, one antagonizes, while the other blesses. The content of our character determines where and what our inclinations aspire to.

Love unifies what fear dissipates; it is this tension that maintains the universe as an ideal. The dynamic tension between love and fear as an equality and balance keeps the structure of the universe intact. Love and fear are the right and left hands of God. When love and fear are concepted into good versus evil this cancels them both into what we experience as conflict and disease, leading to war and death.

Opposites in conflict also keep us in an ongoing state of pain and anxiety, leading to all of our dramas. Never is there a time God is in conflict with itself. Love and fear are equal in the roles each plays. When regulated to service, fear evolves into science as that which isolates, defining reality as strictly relative, mechanistic, and predictable, while love evolves into connection and integration of seemingly dissimilar aspects into a harmonistic wholesomeness. Fear perspectives the part into an absolute, whereas love unifies disparity into all-ness. Love is common, whereas fear is elitist. The conflict between absolutism and all-ness only exists in the mind that holds to absolutist ideals. Where is conflict when observing the stars? Where is conflict when observing the orbits of the planets? Where is conflict when standing amidst the peacefulness, serenity, and tranquility of nature? Conflict is only in the hearts and heads of those who are afraid. Fear, when lived as an absolute, convinces us that life is death and love is unreal. Notice how many people are convinced that fear is an absolute, so they die never knowing love as a personal reality. So we continue to die and reincarnate over and over and over again.

Do we serve what 'parts' the universe or what unifies it?

Love binds us all to each other and everything else here and elsewhere. Love and fear are the 'twins' of God's will that inversely reverses into the forces that represent the personal, relational, social, and global that we experience and express as distance and distinction, that we then construe as time and space that feels and thinks within a present or now here. There is only now as being and here as knowing, giving each of us the notion we are our humanity on a planet within the universe. In the context of wave becoming particle, it is fear that perceives itself apart from the underlying all encompassing-ness of love that radiates, like the wave. Fear individualizes all encompassing-ness, so God can be and know individuality as a uniqueness contrasted from its originality. Fear gives God infinitude by segmenting God into smaller versions of itself. All parts then have awareness of the self, something other than and differing from God and all else as a state of consciousness ideated into self-autonomy. It is this each aspect recognizes by contrasted light, refracting variables of wave as part. When observation is made, it is the whole recognizing itself as the part making the observation.

Which 'hand' of God is chosen determines how the part experiences and expresses, as well as what it accepts and recognizes as true and real, it is this that becomes what is served. Our history, the days of our lives as social development, evolve along the ideals and ideologies humanity subscribe to personally from the 'voices' we choose to listen to. Everything has a voice we can hear if we know how to listen to it.

God as-is has a voice. The universe as-is has a voice. This planet as-is has a voice. All aspects of life have a voice. When we are afraid, all the voices will be heard as threatening. When we are loving, all the voices will be heard as encouraging. When the only voices we hear are outer-based, the perspective we come from stems from denial and fear. When we begin listening to those voices inherent, we are accepting and loving of what is within that guides our life. In truth, we live a binary vibrancy, which exists on one level as love and fear, simultaneously binding us to everything, while maintaining our individuality. This gives God, as love and fear existing as the universe, an infinitude of experiences and expressions that are the prime directive of existence. Everything that exists within the universe gives God experience and expresses God in an endless array of ways.

We are called to be God and know the universe as the self as who and what we serve. We are given God's will to be and know to freely create and canvas our personal landscape with love and fear, until we choose to serve either love and God as our life, or fear and the self as our legacy. Both compliment each other. Love offers fear the opportunity to express itself as-is. Fear offers love the opportunity to express itself as-is. Fear lonifies our experience, while love fulfills it. By lonify, I mean that which convinces us we are utterly alone. Fear isolates us into what we are as individuals. Love unifies everything we are into a synchronistic whole. Both remain constant, because this is how each works independently. Love and fear are fulfilled aloneness as the individualization of God's all encompassing-ness. This gestalt, in turn, is being and knowing both as an equality, balance, relationship, purpose, and harmony of love and fear simultaneously existing as a single state or condition called personalized is-ness.

Service polarity is focusing on either the self exclusively, or others as an extension of the self (What must be discerned about the self is who and what we are. Negative polarity focuses upon the self by denying, rejecting, ignoring, and condemning most of what makes the self what it is). Self-service denies the existence of God, life, others, and all else. Serving others acknowledges God, life, others as the self, sharing love and light with them. Self-service always draws attention to that ideal deemed 'it' for the one living that ideal, and demands through expectation everyone else aspire to be and know in an identical way through identical means. If God is construed as something outside the self, or if God is completely denied, this informs us those ideas come from negative service polarity.

Negative service polarity always states 'it' is the 'only' way. Impossible, given anything that exists is its own path to whatever is intended and desired as that reality, stating whatever truths are experienced and expressed. Self-service controls and manipulates to ensure that its ideal is followed, so that those following will empower the one disseminating ideas others agree upon. This is done through co-dependency and addiction. People must feel that without the outer they will perish, or face certain doom, or become the 'victim' of horrible deeds. People often choose negative paths to avoid facing and feeling pain and fear. This is impossible, because pain and fear come with the territory of the self and work in tandem with joy and love. Fear and darkness work together with love and light, as it is these that make us our humanity and life the reality it is (When my heart chakra opened completely the vision I was given was love and light shaking hands with fear and darkness).

What is essential to understand is that will is positive, light is negative, and these combine into love, which is neutral. Will is the mind, love is our embodiment, light is our spirituality existing as identity, and our soul is our conscious awareness.

What must exist for self-service to work is followers denying God, fearing what is true, and hating blindly anything and everyone who disagrees with their dogmatic ideology. Hatred is the base that fuels negative service polarity. The clue to whether an entity or person is negative or positive is what one chooses to feel and think as a type of worship - are anger, hatred, and any other negative act expected as a type of behavior? Only the negative use and justify anger and hatred, culminating in acts of violence. If the gods depicted in our so-called 'holy works' get angry or deemed something unacceptable and worthy of being destroyed, this tells us that that 'god' is only something that is serving itself, not others. Positive polarity will accept wherever people are on their journey, because love accepts before it does anything else. Acceptance renders forgiveness unnecessary. Forgiveness is 'positive' judgment from one who feels he or she is a 'victim' of some perpetrator, stemming from denial about what one has in fact created for him or herself. If good hates evil and evil hates good then hatred is the conflict, not good and evil. Hatred is the attribute of those who despise God, creation, what created us, and what we are as the image and likeness of God.

It is important to know the difference between those who serve themselves and those who serve others. For many a naïve soul empowers many a dark soul, due to lack of discernment.

Also important is to ask, if a given idea engenders one to feeling positive or negative about him or herself through the idea shared. Those serving themselves will state ideas making followers feel pained, afraid, guilty, and angry. Those who serve others will state ideas making people feel joyous, loving, innocent, and humble. Another thing to know is, that those who serve themselves are very arrogant and deceptive, while those who serve others are humble and transparent. Those who serve themselves demand and require blind obedience, while those who serve others require only that one understand what is true and conducive to everyone and everything. Self-service requires followers. Those who serve others only seek to assist people in ways kind and harmonious leading them away from what enslaves people and keeps them dysfunctional. Notice how most of what we consider tradition are systems based on self-serving ideologies.

Essentially, what service polarity accomplishes is that either the individual is empowered through others, or everyone is empowered through the ideology taught. Also, ascension is accomplished individually through negative polarity, or collectively through positive polarity, due to emphasis being placed upon the self or others. This requires seekers, students, or adepts living according to the teaching empowering either the teacher to ascend or the entire collective to ascend. Solitary ascension usually shows a total lack of love, in that individuality exists due to light individualizing into differing states of existence. Love does not exist as an individuality. It exists due to connection and integration. Love (when felt) establishes God relationally within the self that is then shared with others, making it larger and more encompassing.

Those who serve themselves rarely feel love. Those who serve others feel love all the time.

How does one know if a given truth is true? Only if it pertains to all that is. Truth is real when it pertains to and involves everything and everyone. This is what makes it true. Understand that truth is relative, relational, social, global, and universal. Also, truth will come according to one's level of comprehension and according to one's experience.

It is wise for each of us to turn away from always looking

for only outer-based sources to guide us. Fear convinces us all to live as isolationists. As long as we continue looking outwardly for solace or answers, those who serve themselves will continue to convince us the inner is nothingness, illusion, chaos, and void. The inner has equal merit, and is coupled with the outer for our sense of self. Love remains unknown if we ignore the inner, for it is here it exists, resides, and where we find it. The torso is love as a manifested ideal giving it the sense it is real physically.

Self-service maintains fear, guilt, arrogance, and denial as psychological constants (This path strives to replace what is real and true with something artificial and false. For us, this means our biological nature is replaced with something arbitrary and artificial. What replace our humanness are clones and robots). Something or someone is always perceived as a threat. Serving others instills and inspires one to feel love, innocence, humility, and acceptance about the self as a form of humanness. Each path seeks for others to either love or fear all the time. Life is construed as something to fear and deny or love and accept. Each path then goes one step further in that the negative seeks to destroy life, while the positive seeks to create life. How this is done is through war or understanding how to use God's will. The negative path requires drama, stress, and uncertainty to remain constants. The positive path knows that life exists harmoniously without drama, stress, or anxiety due to clarity and certainty. The negative path is convinced of the past as a present that becomes a future, while the positive knows the now here becomes whatever one desires and intends. Also, fear keeps individuality distanced and isolated, so that God's will to be and know, coupled with love and light as consciousness will exist to experience and express in a unique and autonomous way. This is why fear is essential to God's infinitude. Fear disperses love's unity. In order for love and light to exist independently, individually, and uniquely, fear and darkness isolate them into those states of being and knowing.

Every activity we experience is designed to assist us in choosing whom we will serve. Just as there are never mistakes made, neither is there any judgment about which path of service is chosen. God never judges us for the choices we make, because each of us is the image and likeness of God. God does not stand in judgment of itself. Acceptance is what God's love does. Anyone lacking love will either condemn or forgive others. And everything composing the universe is an aspect of God, giving God the experience of infinity and the expression of infinity. Our life is a testimony to God's humanity as our humanness. This is why it is so important to conduct our affairs accordingly, for God is in equal partnership with each of us inwardly, as well as outwardly. The only reason we observe something as outer-based is because it is showing us what is non-physical and more evolved than what we are right now (Fifth, sixth, and seventh densities are non-physical and are only observed as 'something out there').

Can we live our lives where there is equality, balance, relationship, purpose, and harmony between the inner and outer, and can we humans create life as joy, peace, and freedom?

Chosen service accelerates the process of evolution. Those who consciously serve either the self or others are given the opportunity to continue onto the next level. Those who are not harvested repeat third density. Fourth density is that level each path of service is harvested into to further the evolution of both the negative and the positive according to this specific creation (RA Material 1984). Those who serve others are harvested and remain to continue the evolutionary development of the creator and the father's ideal of God as a human being. Those who serve themselves are removed to an environment consistent with and conducive to that path of service. Those who do not survive will continue as-is until another planet is either created or found that matches the earth's biology, and these individuals will pick up where they left off. As it stands now, less than one percent of humanity is harvestable out of seven billion people. Humanity is not working towards resolving the fiction of good versus evil as a social consciousness or social more.

When thinking of service, think in terms of the relationships between the self and others. What effects do the ideas shared engender us to feel, think, and act upon? Do the central tenets focus upon fear, guilt, denial, and self-glorification? Do they organize around control and elitist absoluteness? If this is the case, then those who share in this way are only serving themselves. It is not easy to discern between those who serve themselves using fear and negativity to empower themselves, or those who use love and the positive to empower others. We all must answer the question who do we serve. Serving others is the basis for who remains to continue the process of social evolution until it collectively ascends from this planet. Individuality is negative and collective consciousness positive.

Those who assert that accepting Jesus as God and 'savior' is enough to survive the changes are in for a very rude awakening, as this idea has nothing to do with the harvesting of souls. Those who believe that those 'left behind' are doomed to God's destructive and destroying hand are also very misguided, and very mistaken. Notice that both God and Satan are very negative conceptions, with little difference between them in what each seeks to accomplish with humanity. Service polarity or polarization only has relevance and meaning regarding fourth density, as it pertains to human evolution according to what one chooses to serve. This is why it is so important for everyone to choose to be and know acceptance, responsibility, and kindness, as it is this that serving others is based upon and works through. Service polarity precedes all other wisdom and understanding as a form of ongoing evolution after harvesting. It is needed, so that as we evolve as one people united together for each other, we then embrace love and light willfully, so that eventually we all ascend as one unified consciousness existing as a single state of being and knowing. This is love and light that has greater mass and magnitude than just individuality. Collective ascension is only possible when the mass and magnitude of love and light are greater than gravity. Self-service lives what is detrimental to all else, while those who serve others live what is conducive to all else.

Self-service is built upon division and hierarchy, whereas serving others is built upon unity and oneness. The psychological perception needed to truly serve others is inner oneness and outer perfection. Oneness is an inner state of being, coupled with knowing that everything 'out there' is perfect as is now, and the seeker is at one with everything and everyone. Look upon something and see it as perfect right now, then feel at one with such right now. This entails not seeking to change or alter the outer in any way.

Self-service views everyone and everything as different and distinct from what it thinks of as the self. Everything is viewed as separated and distanced from the self, holding what is a 'threat' to it, then seeking to change into something it can control and manipulate to a given or desired end as an enslaving ideal. This demonstrates what superiority is as a ruling elitist. Society is then constructed according to a 'caste' system, whereby class distinction is made, embellishing those in the upper levels of power and economics according to what hierarchy deems fit for those who rule. Slavery becomes the principle means self-service utilizes to control and manipulate to empower the self at the expense of the unchosen many.

With self-service, those in positions of power as the ruling elite are the only aspects considered worthwhile in institutions like politics, business, military, education, religion, law, and medicine. The technique used to insure people remain loyal and faithful is by creating a methodology of co-dependency or addiction through fear, guilt, arrogance, and denial, reward, and punishment. The effectiveness of threat is to ensure loyal and faithful followers generation after generation works very well. This ensures strict adherence and maintains the involvement with those agendas implemented to empower the few by the many. Wealth and control are the two primary elements created to insure self-service remains successful. The only purpose involvement serves is, as long as we are involved with a given ideology, it empowers those who created it and those who maintain it. This is true of any and every ideology built and based upon fear, guilt, arrogance, and denial.

Almost everyone is enslaved in many, many, many ways. Greed enslaves more people than any other psychology save fear. Fear, greed, and control are the primary catalysts used by the self-serving, thereby creating an arbitrary greater than and lesser than schism. When examining these behaviorally, few people work towards healing these on a personal and perceptual level. So, fear, greed, and control remains constant, and not without grave consequences to us all. Unless we actively and consciously seek to change these, there will come a time environmentally when the issue will force our hand, as the planet evolves into greater life intelligence.

Extinction is the result of what transpires on a planetary body when its evolution outgrows the life forms on its surface. We are very close to finding ourselves in exactly the same place. Most of what we do currently is not conducive to or pertinent to the health and welfare of the planet. Self-service only cares about and is only concerned with world domination, politically and economically. Slowly the agendas needed and necessary come together, so that the vast majority is enslaved and controlled through fear and greed.

The threat of death by weaponry is always a technique used by the self-serving, to maintain and ensure that fear remains as high as possible within the psychology of those convinced good versus evil is real and true. Competition and conflict insure that the ideology of good versus evil thrives.

The time comes when reality, premised by truth, undoes all the fallacious ideologies, and only those that correspond and pertain to what comes will remain intact and left standing. Great changes come. Life returns to simplicity. Civilization as we know it ends. Those who remain faithful to fear, greed, and control will find themselves no longer amongst the living. Life returns to an indigenous way of living. Service is what fourth density harvests. This is why it is so important to choose whom you will serve.

Service polarity divides between exclusion, negation, and aversion, or inclusion, affirmation, and involvement with God, life, and others. This is the level of awareness that comes forth when third density ends and fourth density begins. Unfortunately, most will be caught unaware, as everything untenable will cease to exist. Only those who serve others will continue the evolution of the species on this planet.

Humanity will discover that oil and electricity will cease to be viable energy sources within the next five years, due to the vibrational rate of the planet rising above the parameters of their existence when the earth changes its polarity. This means every machine will cease to function, and we will be left with our hands, heart, and heads to do the work. This will be a time of getting back to the land, and living life self-sufficiently as farmers do, according to our design as an indigenous people.

Service polarity is based upon fear or love as an applied state of being. From this, we engage and conduct ourselves according to what each entails and encompasses. Pain, fear, and anger are the three basic or primary catalysts we experience individually, complimented by joy, love, and peace. What we feel, sense, think, and envision determines whether we are serving ourselves or others. Keep in mind that knowing the self develops into service polarity, which culminates positively into collective ascension. Collective ascension is the pinnacle achievement of a social group from a planetary body, requiring positive polarity as a path of service by everyone composing the collective. Everyone must live the ideal for it to become a social reality.

Fundamental to serving others is being the oneness of God, for this precedes all else. Everyone must have an experience of just what this is personally. The natural path of oneness is healing into wholeness what ascends. This is the ideal each member seeks to be and know if we hope to experience and express this as a social reality. The idea that hinders and prevents this from becoming an actuality is the belief in good versus evil that divides the self into being and knowing disease, conflict, violence, and death. It is the belief in good versus evil, as a personal ideology, that leads to the cessation of the body as our own crucifixion and death experience. Good versus evil creates the fiction of gender disparity and personal disenfranchisement from life, God, and the universe. You'll notice that these are the very 'ideals' used by the self-serving to empower themselves and disempower others.

Before service to others can become truly effective, knowing the self as source-centered within content, structure, intention, development, understanding, insight, and wisdom as a state of being establishing one's ethics, integrity, and morality as an implied and applied state of realness is required. Serving the self states that agenda, ritual, organization based upon greater and lesser, reward and punishment, obedience, ignorance, dogma, and blind faith establishes the social order that always 'promises' an end that never becomes the reality one seeks to find. This is the art of the carrot always dangled in front of the eyes that never see or get the prize promised. The promises made never materialize in life or after we have passed on.

Invariably, self-service and its ideological approach lead to division for the chosen who must conquer others by convincing them their ideal (a 'savoir') will protect them against personal demons and the ill will of others. This enslaves people to an ideal that promises something that never materializes. However, the end result is the demise of the adherent, as well as the organization as a whole when third density ends and fourth density begins.

The nature of the self must be resolved. Issues must be faced and healed. There are three schools of thought pertaining to this. There is the path of the outer, the inner, and the balance of both. Most of humanity chooses to ignore everything except appetites, addictions, distractions, and dramas.

Service development evolves with what concept of God is revered. Unfortunately, each major religion falls down when it comes to ideas revered about God due to not taking enough into consideration. God is more than bliss, nirvana, perfection, and those ideas we consider absolute and beyond approach or reproach. The problem each of us faces is that we are striving to become our own absolute. This keeps us locked in a state of individuality that is personal, but not relational or binary. We have completely missed the point about what inverse reversal is as a binary vibrancy.

As it stands now, very little of our 'civilized' culture has any relevance to the larger community beyond this planet. We are destroying ourselves and each other through our fear, arrogance, ignorance, indifference, and greed. Life lived does not need to be expressed this way. When an area is infected with rampant disease and violence, what is done? The areas so infected are avoided and possibly kept off-limits to those who live a more appropriate, safe, and sane way of being. This is why the cosmic community leaves us alone. We are the hope and inspiration of the universe, and hopefully we will resolve disease, poverty, gender disparity, greed, selfishness, and war. It is up to each of us to decide that these are no longer going to be our reality. We are the ones who choose for life to be as it is as us and for us. We decide what is real and true. Life as we each live it is our "make believe." We give something the only meaning it has.

Every solution to every problem lies within each of us. I personally doubt humanity will do anything to return life to its natural garden state. We only change when we are forced to, and even then do so very stubbornly when faced with disease, disaster, or some other malady. Disease is a personal creation to the one afflicted. Disaster on a mass scale is the collective creation of all those involved (Seth, 'The Individual and the Nature of Mass Events" 1981). What we hold to socially is our collective experience.

How we conduct our affairs determines what we experience personally and collectively. Sadly, we are determined to destroy this planet through fear, greed, and self-empowerment. The race is on as to which activity will actually destroy this planet: pollution or nuclear weapons, our great legacies. The health of this planet and the diseases afflicting us are identical in that our body and the planet are the same ideal. Who seeks to heal? Who seeks for life to return to the garden state again? Unabated, we will either poison this planet to death or blow it up. Eventually, a device will be created that will be powerful enough to destroy this planet. Eventually, pollution will prevent this planet from regenerating itself and it will cease to exist as a viable biology. Who cares enough about God as a living ensoulment to relinquish the fear and all the other psychologies maintaining the insanities we call 'civilized?'

Fortunately, for those of us who serve others, all is not lost. Fourth density comes and the insanity will stop, but not before great changes alter the surface. I recommend everyone read Mary Summer Rain's "Phoenix Rising", John White's "Pole Shift", "The RA Material", "OAHSPE", and listen to Ramtha's Jehovah tape. Seek to serve others, for it is this that precedes collective ascension.

Service polarity establishes the relationships one has with everything else through how one conducts his or her affairs with the opposite sex, humanity as a whole or single family, and the planet. What are we doing with others? Whose rules do we follow and live by? How tied are we to the dictates of law, science, religion, politics, family, business, education, and anything else making tradition what it is? When do we begin to truly get in touch with who and what we are, and the natural extension and expansion that ensues when the physical and spiritual are truly understood and lived, then shared to enhance the quality of both? We are so far away from living this intended design as implied and applied. We are still convinced we are alone in the universe, that we are the only intelligence in existence, that we are advanced and evolved with our fears, our greediness, our chemicals, and our weapons of mass destruction.

There are intelligences in existence that dwarf us. Realities remain hidden by the fear and darkness we hold dear to our hearts. Depth of being and scope of knowing remain an illusion because of our petty foolishness. The magnitude of change coming is proportional to our fear and ignorance about God, life, the self, and how these triunifically evolve. As with most lessons, we insist upon learning the hard way. And no, we will not solve our demise in the final hour. Most would rather die and be right, rather than change and admit they were wrong. Our attitude is, I am right and I'll take my rightness to the grave.

Service brings to the surface one's intention and basic psychology, seeing the authenticity of the self viewed as shadow and costume. God and universe are the truest authenticity we personify. Actually, those who serve others know the self as God and universe, while those who serve themselves deny God, treating the universe in a completely impersonal way, as a strictly mechanical medium that one seeks to control. Both views have equal value. One loves while the other fears, leading to how service is shared with others.

Both paths compliment each other and act as catalysts for each other. Self-service uses part of the brain, while serving others requires full use of the brain. Serving others requires entering into the center of the heart and bringing God's realness to life. Self-service requires the heart be filled with pain; the body lived as fear, the head known as darkness, making one's experience negative. Denial, irresponsibility, rejection, and projection lead us all into following the dictates of those who serve themselves, culminating in our death experience. Religion convinces us we will go to heaven, but heaven only exists for those who refused to live life according to God's will to be and know. God incarnated into my heart, and I ascend this actuality when I am living God as my personal and human realness that's true.

The higher-self is that aspect of existence that is non-physical, knowing everything, and is our guidance, if given the opportunity to do so. Also, as manifested representations, the body is divinity and the spirit is deity. We live these as an embodied spirituality.

Reality comes regardless of where we are in evolution. Humanity is wise to choose ideals that assist them in becoming what ascends. The inharmonious and detrimental soon fade away, and humanity will face itself stark naked without distractions. Mechanical distractions will cease to function. Humanity will be left with itself, and the opportunity to tend the garden once again.

One day the purity of love and light will be our reality as our humanity. These will remain forever as our eternal legacy; the entire universe will recognize and honor this through collective ascension. Collective ascension means becoming a permanent social reality no longer bound to the physical. Ascension means to take with, rise above, and integrate into a greater medium of involvement that is the observed universe. Collective ascension means taking our physical bodies with us when we evolve into an eternal rendition of what humanity personifies as an infinite and eternal state of existence. Then humanity discovers there are many, many, many, many collectives in the universe that have ascended. All are fourth density or higher. Several fifth and sixth density collectives interact with us as channeled sources sharing ideas to assist us in choosing to serve others. The universe or soul of God is a collection of ideas and ideals that either assist or confound creation.

Humanity is wise to choose to serve others if it hopes to evolve beyond its current state of affairs. It is left to each of us to discern what is real and true, whom we are, what we are, why we are here, what God is, what purpose is, what life is, where we are from, and where we are going.

Each moment we move closer to our awakening. Choose wisely my friends, as fourth density births, and humanity evolves until it collectively ascends.

Collective Ascension

Part 3

Collective Ascension

So where does knowing the self and serving others lead? It leads to collective ascension. Now, just what is collective ascension? It is the culminated fulfillment and achievement a human population accomplishes by transitioning from a temporal state into an eternal ongoing-ness. It is how humanity evolves from a planetary state of being into a universal state of existence. It is society moving from impermanence into that which remains constant. It is the unified integration of individualized consciousness, existing as the connection between all souls, composing the collective that ascends into a useful correspondence with the larger universal community. It is what positive social polarity becomes as a larger version of a unified whole, willed into a reality that is only accessed through collective ascension. It is the integration and connection that consciousness attains. This becomes the new reality for those composing it; that transitions into a state representing collective actualization of God's will, the living-ness of the creator's love, and the personification of the father's light as a single and unified state of consciousness. These exist as the personal, relational, and social unions, representing a single state that corresponds to and is in accordance with the greater whole as a state of consciousness.

Consciousness begins with the self. It is this point of reference we find ourselves aware of, giving each of us the notion we are as a form of God's I am-ness. This awareness pertains to the reality we find ourselves in, and as all the conditions pertaining to our psychology. On an individual level, this is the nature of relativity, from the inherency of self-awareness involving emotions, thoughts, and behaviors. This awareness extends and expands through our personal and social relationships, and how these touch the lives of others. As the planet evolves from third density into fourth density, those individuals who have chosen positive service polarity transition, as the harvest, into the density this planet births into as the 'new age.' This will mean those people who remain will again choose to live as we were intentionally created to live as humanly as an indigenous people, rather than an invader culture.

Collective ascension is not an 'ism' of some kind like communism, socialism, or capitalism. It is the communified gathering of souls who live God, planet, and universe as their conduct of character. It is built upon through faith that God is inherent within each and everyone of us, and that we are all the image and likeness of God through Yahweh's love and Id's light, and that the realness of the self is universal. It is living, knowing the self as God and universe.

Each of us has the opportunity to address what we give life to. What do we embody? Is it the Christ, or self-glorification, disease, or some other sand-like quality giving us fame, fortune, or power over others? Collective ascension is the aspiration humanity individually and socially works toward. All activity engaged in must facilitate what humanity becomes. This is no different than desire and intention becoming one's experience. One must have an idea before any outcome will transpire. Reality corresponds to and conforms itself to what we intend, as intention activates God's will into those experiences we embrace.

The entire premise of this medium called earth, and the medium of the universe, entails self-conscious awareness of God as I am-ness. From God, all else comes into being and knowing creativity as a manifested realness. Some choose to live a life seemingly devoid of God, contrary to God, and antithetical to life, however, this is never the case, as God is all that is. Understanding the difference between God and what we are as the image and likeness of God is important. God is all encompassing, and we are will, love, light, and consciousness.

Each of us is responsible for affirming our life, and accepting responsibility for everything that we feel, think, and do. Each of us is responsible for the content of our character, and how this affects everything else upon the planet. The planet is a miniature universe we get to test our applied intentions toward, then experience first-hand how effective we are in our creativity. The two areas we are wise to address are remembering God, and becoming conscious of all that is, while living a life that is a biology on a planet. This requires meditation to accomplish. We are wise to heal into wholeness, as it is this that ascends. Think in terms of oneness ascending into oneness, and this being done by knowing oneness as our state of being. We are each perfect in our uniqueness and our creation of God as human beings. We are wise to value and revere ourselves as sacred, honoring all of life as it lives. We are wise to accept ourselves as is choosing to live life joyously, peacefully, harmoniously, and contentedly, solely by the fact we are alive.

We need to recognize the inherent shortcoming of ideas as ideologies of tradition that don't work, and cease creating institutions and social conditions that perpetuate shortsightedness. This is done on the personal level first, then extends and expands until it becomes a social realness, and then conducive to the entire planet. Each of us is responsible for healing those qualities that hinder life on this planet, like greed, war, violence, and poverty. Greed creates the balance of poverty. When greed ceases, poverty ceases. Poverty and greed are the same state of existence. The nature of balance ensures both exist within a medium where either is lived as a state of being. Ending poverty only happens when greed is stopped. Peace only happens when war and conflict cease. Freedom is only possible when peace is lived personally.

Collective ascension hinges upon three areas of discipline, as development according to personal truth. These areas are God, life, and universe as the self. I personally affirm I am being God, knowing life, and becoming conscious of the universe as and through the fact that I am a living human being. I take this idea one step further by including the ideas of doing unto others by serving them and becoming ascendant. Words only mirror our self-imposed attitudes, or our self-affirming truth and realness. We are wise to choose to know the self, choose to serve others, and choose to ascend. All that is needed will come to assist us once the decisions are made. It does not matter if others choose to hold the left hand of God, or remain ignorant about their self beyond body and behavior. The fact I am is sufficient humanly.

We are each other. I am everyone. I am everyone who has lived, is living, and will live. My humanity is humanity. This idea works positively, negatively, or neutrally depending on how I choose to react to my holographic creations. Is my life one of joy or pain, love or fear, light or dark, or positive or negative? What am I choosing to feel, sense, think, and envision? How long will I continually fund institutions that are misguided and mistaken ideologically?

Collective ascension is foreign to this place because of our fear, ignorance, and arrogance. Our indifference to living is reprehensible, for it prevents us from living life in honorable ways. We fail to honor and respect our divinity and deity. The over-emphasis we place upon individuality prevents us from being and knowing what oneness is as a collective state of existence.

Collective ascension requires intunement and involvement, consciously with the pre-physical and non-physical, before the opportunity avails itself to us to ascend and live eternally within the universe as a contributing member as a post-physical realness. We must be it and know it before we ascend it. Faith requires holding to an idea and or ideal before it becomes an environmental manifestation we participate with sensually. For those of us who serve others, this means holding faithfully to the truth God is within, we are within God, and the soul of each of us is the universe. We become these consciously, collectively, as these are what humanity ascends. God incarnates into all aspects composing the universe, then each aspect reintegrates into God through ascension. Collective ascension is everyone doing this together. Collective ascension for a group means, it becomes a new member adding to the cultural diversity of the universe.

We begin where we stand. We need to remember that God centered within our heart is sourcing our life. We need to recognize the outer does not define or evolve us, it merely shows who and what we are, through our desired intentions as where we are in our becoming-ness. Outer-based teachings and teachers prevent us from going within to access what is inherent. Books do not define, explain, or make us who and what we are. It is God as universe that makes us human.

Ascension is living and becoming these in a larger and more comprehensive format. Time and space are the extension and expansion of God. Collective ascension is an expanded version of this as an ongoing reality.

Holographic structure informs us what any given part or aspect is, and contains all that is. Love unifies itself. Fear breaks itself down. When we are loving unconditionally; this will unify us into a single social order that ascends when oneness, healing, and wholeness is what we are all being and knowing as a shared kindness by every member of humanity.

This is not a utopian ideal. It is the pinnacle achievement of humanity as it graduates from a planetary biology into a non-physical and post-physical ensoulment.

By far, the most intelligent material we receive comes from collectives that have ascended. Seth is one. The RA is another. If you are involved with channeling, ask if it is a communal collective or hierarchical order. If you are listening to a channeled source, ask it if it has collectively ascended. I have found the depth and scope of channeled material from a collective that has ascended greatly outweighs anything a solitary source has to offer, or a hierarchical source has to offer. My favorite source is the "RA Material" also called "The Law Of One." I also really liked Seth's, "The Nature Of Personal Reality." There is a process that takes place collectively that never does individually. This is the increasing of love's mass and light's magnitude exponentially. Hierarchies develop, like a pyramid, whereas collectives develop, like a globe or sun. Hierarchies focus upon individuals as it, whereas collectives understand that everyone is an integral part of the whole, making the organization complete.

The soul houses or retains the memory of every life we have lived since the beginning. The soul is composed of every experience since the universe began. The soul is the collective consciousness of hundreds or possibly thousands of selves, depending upon how many lifetimes one has lived. Ensoulment is adding to what already is. Think of this like pieces of a puzzle that are put together, making a new state of being. This continues to take place until nothing is left out or missed, and one moves on. The importance of loving, forgiving, and doing unto others are those people we react to negatively are those individualities ensouled we have not yet healed. Also, any time we react strongly to someone's behavior this shows us that their attitude is still an unresolved issue we need to address and heal by owning and letting it go. Every cell composing the body pertains to a type of experience making us who and what we are. The soul is a tapestry composed of many differing states that we become conscious of and then forget about over, and over, and over again.

What is interesting about this process of ensoulment is that we are aware of now as our humanity, but it also encompasses all other experiences up to this present moment. The mosaic of the soul is like a personalized version of the universe. The paradox of this is that everyone's soul is the universe, and it is also a very personal reality as well. All we are doing is making a decision about something. Eventually, this becomes service polarity, then collective ascension.

This requires a working knowledge of what each path entails. With collective ascension, we are coming into being and knowing outwardly oneness, healing, and wholeness that ascends, by our choosing to live this way with all aspects we perceive as being outside our self. We only recognize outwardly all the people composing our own soul. Those people we fear, hate, mistrust, or are co-dependent with are those lives ensouled that we have not learned to love, forgive, and release. Reacting to a given catalyst only shows us what issues we still need to resolve, particularly ones we get really upset over. When we re-act with an emotion, we are letting ourselves know that an issue is still alive and well as us. When I accept myself as what I fear, hate, and dislike these cease to act as catalysts for me to heal and evolve beyond.

Every quality, truth, and aspect of all that is must be lived to have any relevance or personal reality. Life then becomes what we choose to be and know that becomes ensouled through experience, making it our personal reality. We have all lived as many, many others. If we haven't lived it or don't live it, it does not exist as our own reality. Everything exists now. We remember ourselves as all and everything, then we choose whether we live love or fear, light or dark, or positive or negative by serving our self or others.

What we find is that we become conscious of something, forgetting everything else. This happens over and over again, as we continue to refine our abilities to create and manifest ideals, demonstrating our ideas about God, life, self, and what we do with these. When we conduct our affairs consciously, we will engage God in a deeper, truer, and more conducive manner. We are the ones who choose how we are going to live our lives as who and what we are humanly. The universe waits for us to ascend as a God-conscious existence that is as ongoing as the universe.

It is useful to have an idea about God as it is, and what the universe opportunes. God assists itself through those who choose to be and know the nature of the self as it exists. Contrasted to this, are those who intentionally live antithetical to God. There are those whose sole purpose for existing is being contrary to God's design.

Collective ascension requires a working knowledge of what's involved with the self as it is designed. God becomes creator, that becomes mind, that becomes the embodiment of. Universe becomes father, that becomes the ensoulment of, that becomes the spirituality as. These combine into us making each of us the image and likeness of God as our humanity. Body is God as the specific, and spirit is universe as the specific, giving God the experience and expression of what it is and means to be and know humanly. If we continually focus upon what we are not, the realness of the self remains fictitious and foreign to our personal and social development. This is why 94% of the brain is dormant, as we are not living our design as intended, so what we are ignorant of remains non-existent as an experience. Most of the self remains unknown, and does not exist as an available involvement. Sleeping clues us to this. The 94% of the brain we do not use involves aspects of the self we deny, ignore, and fear. The 6% we do use is all we allow ourselves to be and know humanly. Our attention is focused upon 6% of what we are. The other 94% pertains to and involves our collective nature.

Intunement is moving our attention from strictly thinking of ourselves as only our psychology and our body. Part of the path is becoming conscious of our own mind, and doing conscious out-of-body experiences. This is returning to those states of being that incarnated into this embodiment and ascends. These are God and soul. The problem we all face is that we do not think of ourselves as other than or beyond our current physical being. We deny, reject, ignore, and even condemn the notions that we are more than our physical body. We then claim what is does not exist within, so we become dependent upon outside sources for what is real and true. This prevents us from truly discovering for ourselves what is inherent as the self by seeking only what the master, guru, or teacher stipulates is 'it' as her or his form of enlightenment. What humanity misses is the infinite nature of existence. God became the entire universe. The universe is God's identity and God's ensoulment, giving each us the ability and opportunity to be and know as we choose to. The essential idea to understand is diversity, in that this is what God desires above and beyond all else. The universe gives God variable and variety contrasted to its all encompassing-ness. This is the only binary vibrancy that truly exists. This is the pulse of God, and this pulse exists on many, many, many levels as demonstrated through all the differing states of existence people discover when they become conscious leaving their body.

Leaving the body consciously informs us about the larger community of universe within the contexts of spirit and soul. Intuning within the body informs us to states of mind that precede creation, as an ongoing differentiation within the context of embodiment that is self-aware within a specific medium that for each of us is planet earth. This medium of biology we find ourselves within and amidst gives all that is involved the opportunity to apply will, love, and light consciously or unconsciously, as that state of consciousness each of us is, equaling all the experiences we embrace as our personal forms of expression. We discover for ourselves what a given feeling, sensation, or thought is as it pertains to our identity. We see first-hand what a given quality is and how it works. Refinement leads to effective and consistent creativity of what we desire to be and know, and this is what the work in consciousness accomplishes for everyone who applies it.

What do we truly desire and intend our lives to embody?

We are more than meets the eye, and are wise to become conscious of the self as all it is. This requires moving the attention beyond limitations self-imposed by outside sources. What I do is envision my heart radiating just like the sun, my body absorbing just like the planet, my head illuminating just like the full moon, and my conscious awareness, encompassing all that is as a unified and single state of being. This can also be thought of as the purity of mind, the distortion of body, the refinement of spirit, and crystalization of soul. Terminology is not as important as understanding what is implied and applied by each of us. This requires focusing on an idea that becomes our personal ideal, and is what we actualize and demonstrate.

Everyone within the planetary culture is wise to embrace similar states of being without sacrificing him or herself in the process. By similar, I mean feeling joy in the heart, love as the body, light as the spirit, and becoming conscious of the soul and what it entails and encompasses. Then we move this into an ideal that includes the opposite sex, humanity as a single family, and the planet as a whole.

To do this effectively, certain ideals we hold about ourselves, humanity, and life must be released. The first ideal we need to cease personifying is self-glorification and self-importance, leading to the entire psychology that certain people are greater than others who are treated as less than. Then we are wise to release the entire notion of gender disparity, as this is an arbitrary fiction we have devised to keep us feeling inadequate and at odds with each other, as well as convincing us one gender is superior to another. This is flatly untrue, as everyone is the equality, balance, relationship, purpose, and harmony of both genders. It takes both to create us into the humanity we personify as and through gender. The sperm is not greater than the egg. Each is an aspect that combines into who and what we are as humans being gender. The real significance of this is that it gives specific-ness to divinity and deity as an embodied state. Creation only exists due to the equality, balance, relationship, purpose, and harmony of love and light as an ideal that is ongoing.

The entire notion of 'good versus evil' is something someone decided long ago that light was in opposition to love and this created war. This created the entire process leading to social groups conquering, enslaving, and destroying others through hatred, and the fiction God had chosen them to do just that. Gender disparity is our holding to the fictions that love is fear that must be hated and light is darkness that must be destroyed. Gender disparity also shows us what humanity feels and thinks through ignorance and arrogance that God and universe are at war with each other, or that divinity and deity are at war with each other. This is impossible, given the nature of creativity and manifestation, which is the extension and expansion of God into universe.

Another area humanity is wise to heal is the ridiculousness it holds about sexuality as an involvement. Sexuality is God and universe as gender, in that it is through sexuality that everyone, including Jesus, comes into being. Everyone living is a sexual being. Sexuality is essential to collective ascension. Lacking a positive sexuality that is shared honestly and openly with others, humanity will not collectively ascend. Sexuality is love shared, and makes love a relational realness between God, universe, divinity, and deity. Celibacy is love denied a personalized sharing of itself. Love is shared physically and relationally through sexuality. These are the experiences of union, oneness, and sameness, and increase the mass of love through continued practice. Sexuality also shows us we are both genders by creating new life through engaging in the behavior regularly. Sexuality is the desired intentions of love and light seeking the experiences of union and oneness. These are accomplished through conception and orgasm.

What humanity fails to realize is, those who serve themselves have turned love into fear, celibacy, pornography, gender disparity, conflict, and war. Loved shared physically is always and only done sexually. Everyone advocating and practicing celibacy does not realize social evolution is impossible without love shared sexually. Love, as a sexual experience, is the sharing of God humanly. Guru's, monks, priests, nuns, masters, teachers, and anyone else who refuses to engage in the activity of sexual conduct does not grasp God as a shared realness and experience. This is why few of them ascend. Sexuality is the experience and expression of union and oneness between two states considered different and other than what one is. Sexuality shows us that the differences we observe between male and female do not exist. Sexuality demonstrates gender is only oneness and union that is biased by catalysts.

Besides self-glorification, gender disparity, and sexual inhibition, another area needing a complete change is the entire psychology of nation state (Neal Donald Walsch, "Conversations with God" 1995). Humanity also needs to evolve beyond the attitude of race distinction. There is only the family of humanity that is given daily the opportunity to get along. There is only one of us, and each of us is that one. Each person living is an aspect and quality of the Christ. What we do in relationship with others is demonstrate how Christ-like we are. Christ is and means the collective consciousness of humanity as a single state of being, or family. Those individuals who choose to live selfishly shows us all they live as is the anti-christ. The anti-christ is anyone who is selfish, who serves themselves, contributing to self-glorification, gender disparity, negative sexual practices, and maintaining the social fictions of race and nationality.

God is not a respecter of persons we are told, and we are all wise to begin treating everyone as they are as the image and likeness of God. For some, this is impossible to do, due to their fear and hatred used to create an ideal that empowers them through enslaving others, using business or politics to accomplish their agenda. Science and religion also enslave billions.

The world today shows us what happens historically to the present when nationality, gender, and race are considered different and a threat. History, as humanity tells it, is who went to war, the outcome, and where humanity stands today as a result of what transpired then and remains a potential threat now. True enough, there are those who are ensuring this process of nations warring remains until the very end. People do not see or understand what is actually going on, because they lack the ability to discern the intentions of others. The political arena worldwide shows how dismal humanity is in moving beyond shortsighted and misguided goals and ideals of great political corruption and unconscionable greed, leading to violence, war, and slavery as the 'great' accomplishments of humanity today.

Retention of the nation state as a racial ideal, coupled with the belief in good versus evil, creates a nation where few get along, men and women live without equality, and everyone else on the planet is considered inferior or a terrorist, worthy of exploitation and destruction. Only the self-serving conquers through agenda or might. The propaganda shared as dogmatic ideology becomes what enslaves people when they subscribe to that as doctrine of some kind. This leads to the eventual destruction of the individual as the death experience, or the destruction of the entire culture.

We have seen, first-hand, how the role of nation state plays with indigenous cultures worldwide. 'Civilized' nations have almost exterminated every tribe living indigenously on this planet. We also see first-hand what religion and science have done under the guise of God and progress historically and currently. Billions have lost their lives due to the callousness of both religion and science, because of their mistaken and misguided beliefs in what humanity is and does as our biology. Little has changed humanly in 10,000 years. Science denies the existence of God. Religion only teaches false doctrines about God.

Does an idea promote attitudes of respect or disrespect for people, places, and things? This clues us to the agendas fostered by the proponents of any given ideology. Do the ideas we live culturally engender us to feel positively or negatively toward ourselves, the opposite sex, sexuality, and cultures worldwide?

Each of us is responsible for creating an ideal that works conducively for humanity. This requires looking honestly at everything we feel, think, and act upon. This leads to our feeling, thinking, and acting those qualities that are conducive to life humanly portrayed. Collective ascension requires humanity living an ideal that is conducive to everyone and everything. People are wise to feel what is real, sense what is true, intuit what is involved, speak what is pertinent, and meet the need in the moment. People are wise to look for opportunities to assist others in their time of need. This is like Jesus healing someone, and rather than getting paid for services rendered, he asks them to do for another something of equal significance when the opportunity presents itself. Doing kind acts for others is not difficult. Getting along is not difficult. It only requires an attitude that one is making a contribution to themselves in serving others.

Our current world affairs promote thinking in terms of getting, rather than giving. This is like a child doing what it needs to get his or her needs met. Humanity lives like an infant, demanding that mommy or daddy meet its needs and satisfy its desires. Society acts according to this modality in every aspect of its culture. Religion treats God as both a rewarding and punishing parent. Humanity has not matured into owning its biology, and accepting life as it is created to exist.

This is why meditation and personal work are so important, as it is through these methodologies that love and wisdom are learned and lived. When one lives his or her life with joy, peace, harmony, kindness, humor, and contentedness through just being (without outer-based motivations) they are living life according to its biology. This is not easy, given all of the distractions pulling us in so many directions. People are wise to let go of and center their attention on what makes them feel good about themselves, all the time. This requires putting one's attention into a state of rest, for it is here one discovers within the self those qualities making one's life what it is. Meditation is how like mindedness finds like mindedness. If we are always focused on activity or movement, we will never come to know what gives rise to it. Love radiates and attracts, while fear disperses and repulses. Both forces are necessary for holographic structure to exist and stand as the universe or any other holographic body.

Darkness works very assiduously at maintaining pain and fear as the primary and secondary involvement humanity faces on a daily basis. This is accomplished through disease and violence on a personal level, and hatred and war on a social level. In this context, nothing has changed, for humanity continues to experience and express disease, hatred, violence, and war as constants people face everyday. People have this attitude that cultural institutions and traditions through ritual are just the way it is, and few work beyond what hinders humanity's growth. This is demonstrated by all the rituals people engage in since the culture began. If one goes back far enough, one will discover that rituals are designed to appease angry gods and bring about good fortune. The problem humanity faces is that pain and fear create every social discord, not gods who enjoy tormenting us. This ties our psychology and experience to those who thrive upon conflict designed to empower themselves at our expense.

Converting love and fear into good versus evil divides the binary vibrancy of both into disease, disharmony, conflict, competition, violence, and war, as those ideas and ideals darkness deems necessary to enslave humanity and empower itself. As long as humanity holds to greater and lesser, and either/or, darkness remains the governing 'force' ensuring nothing changes socially, except which nation is the next chosen one.

Notice how history favors one nation above any other, until it falls from grace and another rises to claim it is the next form of elitism and superiority. Notice also, nations rise and fall because of holding onto justified doctrines, re-enacting the ideals darkness needs to empower itself, maintaining its organization at the expense of life itself. Life on a planet is manipulated into maintaining pain within the surface of the planet, and fear within the majority of people inhabiting the surface. Always some threat exists to ensure people remain afraid constantly. Acts of violence are always perpetrated to ensure people's fear is warranted. What people fail to realize is that those subscribing to the ideals of darkness are in fact the very perpetrators of acts of violence. Warranting an attitude, creating the conditions, justifying the attitude held, and ensuring the threat is real and expressed; this is what terrorism is really all about. This leads the perpetrators enacting violence as an engagement from intended consent. Those who serve themselves will create a circumstance, giving them the opportunity to do their ill will at the request of those who are fooled and afraid.

Positive evolution is becoming the personalized state of oneness felt as joy, peace, harmony, and contentment. Negative evolution becomes division felt as pain, anxiety, discord, and emptiness. Contentment radiates itself, while emptiness continually needs something or someone to fill its sense of void or lack, hence the roles slavery and control play. Social evolution involves is-ness, realness, pattern, and purpose as the foundation of social well being, or nothingness, illusion, chaos, and hidden agenda as conditions needing control and enforcement.

We are always faced with our desires and intentions involving the choices we make. This maintains what remains as the affairs of humanity. Has any institution vanished or faded from view due to our evolving beyond it? No. Humanity is as plagued today by disease, poverty, discontent, and war, as it was 10,000 years ago. This is because of darkness, and under the guise of promise and rule through ideology, like religion and science, maintains the conditions by keeping us in pain and afraid of some nebulous evil that is out there somewhere just waiting to get us. Dogmatic superstitions are the perpetrators that keep us steeped in fear and the anxiety of something getting us.

Darkness then plays upon our rituals by creating 'ghosts' that depict and act out what we fear is real. Humanity faces the same social conditions now as then. Each of us is wise to change what causes us pain and instills us with fear. Humanity is wise to change those conditional catalysts represented as the institutions directing our lives. It is we who define social evolution. Institutions stand as a reminder of personal and collective ideologies renditioning what we feel and think is real and true about God, life, and this human ideal. As long as humanity holds to an emotion and thought as behavior, it becomes the culminated fruition of what is held by a given society as the way it is. This then defines the culture and its people as a whole. Everyone in the culture must examine and question the validity of any idea the society holds, shaping its development and relationships.

The path is where a given idea or ideal takes us mindfully, spiritually, and behaviorally, culminating in ensoulment and ascension. Ensoulment began with the instantaneous, spontaneous, and simultaneous creation of the universe. This means, every soul is the same age universally. However, there are those of us who have had a longer involvement with this planet, so we are called "old souls." Some people have had many, many, many incarnations, making them an old soul. Some people are new to this planet and some have only incarnated a few times. This is why it is important to remember where we have come from, in the context of God as our originator, the creation of the universe, and where we have come from within the context of the universe as our basic spirituality. Billions of people come from differing star systems and can remember where that is and what they belong to as an ongoing reality. This requires doing a conscious out-of-body experience. What this also avails us to is understanding our purpose for being here now. Everyone is more than just her or his body and his or her humanness. Each of us is a collective of some kind called human being. Collective ascension is what happens when people live life joyously and kindly.

As with any collective, we are all given the opportunity of creating a new ideal composed of those people who are living. Everyone adds to the overall mix composing humanity. Collective ascension ensures that the newly created reality corresponds to all the other aspects composing the new ideal. Everyone consciously aware of what she or he belongs to becomes a new reality that is ongoing when working together, for what is envisioned. The more added, the greater the levels of experience and expression. The only way love's mass and light's magnitude are increased is when people decide to be and know these as their true state of being and knowing.

What comes to mind with this is that our biology is specific to this planet, and our spirituality specific to what part of the universe we belong. These combine into the contribution we make, unless we refuse to remember what our purpose is by subscribing to an ideology that ignores, denies, rejects, and hates our true reality and reason for being here now. When one intunes into his or her own mind he or she will remember God as it is. When he or she becomes conscious of his or her own soul, he or she becomes aware of the self as all that is making the self all encompassing and infinite. Darkness no longer can control the individual for he and she knows the self is all powerful, and nothing can adversely affect God and universe self aware. This is why it is important for humanity to heal its differences and begin getting along.

This requires unifying disparities and inequalities, so that a new collective consciousness will emerge, establishing a global community similar to that of the universe here on earth. Humanity now faces the opportunity of integrating and representing as one state a social ideal that harmonizes the myriad of perspectives from all over the universe as a single galactic family.

Before this happens, everyone must know that he or she comes from some place else and will return there when they pass on. Each of us is actually two beings as one. There is our physical embodiment and there is our spirituality. These unify into us as our humanity. Actually, we are four beings in one - God, universe, biological, and spiritual. These are called mind, body, spirit, and soul. Collective ascension requires a working knowledge of what each aspect is and what purpose each serves. Each of us can think of this in terms of a myriad of universes combining into an expanded version through all of us.

This is done when humanity heals division and social discord, getting along through love and kindness. This is what serving others does. When serving others is our purpose for being, this establishes the foundational catalysts that culminate in collective ascension, which is graduating or transitioning from a planetary state of existence into a permanent ongoing-ness, by evolving from a finite state into one that is eternal.

Love unifies what fear disperses when love is chosen as one's content of character. Love and light through consciousness willed increases personal mass and magnitude. Just as fear and darkness decrease or extinguish personal mass and magnitude, so that it ceases to exist within and upon a given medium, like earth. How do we become larger than the infinitesimal? By unifying our individuality into a collective that emulates will, love, and light consciously. It is this that banishes darkness and all it entails, so that humanity will evolve as what it chooses to be and know, sharing collectively. Darkness will do whatever it can to prevent this from happening. It will go so far as to destroy the entire planet if given the chance to do so. This has happened in the past with many planets throughout the universe. Asteroids are the fragmented remnants of planets destroyed by darkness.

Think of darkness and fear as catalysts, used to assist each of us in choosing whom we will serve as God's will to be and know love and light as a state of consciousness, that assists others in becoming as we are being, knowing, and doing. Many fall prey to the darkness, thinking it has real power and significance through hierarchy and elitism, giving the aspirant the conviction it is superior to all else. This is the basis for religious faith and idolatry. Ritual, symbols, and nation states are aspects darkness uses to ensure compliance with an ideology that maintains this as the status quo for humanity on this planet.

Darkness sends emissaries of deceit, like Jehovah, to select and then bewilder its chosen by implementing into social consciousness an ideal of chosen-ness. Ideas are used stating its people are superior to others and are entitled to destroy others and take possession of their land in a manner similar to how the emissary took possession of its chosen people. As long as people subscribe to the ideology disseminated through their faith and dogmatic adherence, this empowers what introduced the idea to begin with. This is something people are unfamiliar with, and few question the real intent of what is posited as God's way. It is energy alone that funds both paths. The majority of people fund an array of 'dark' sources due to denial, fear, and superstition that is projected, establishing the relationships these self-serving entities have with humanity. There are many light sources sharing their love and wisdom with those who seek to be and know such. This gives everyone the opportunity to choose whom he or she will serve.

Those who choose to serve themselves and those who deny, reject, abandon, fear, and remain indifferent to personal evolution are given the opportunity to continue as-is elsewhere. The earth's coming change means service polarity is evolving into service development, until humanity exists as what ascends as a single state of being. Those who serve themselves and those who serve others are the harvesting of souls. Those who serve others remain to continue the evolution of the species. Each of us has had plenty of time to choose whom we will serve, and most of us have had many incarnations. There is never any judgment or condemnation for our refusal and unwillingness to choose service polarity.

Judgment only comes from ideas that are self-serving and exclusionary, and is done with any idea or anyone who disagrees with the doctrine established as 'it.' Judgment stems from fear, culminating in intolerance, leading to persecution. This is not what Jesus taught or emulated during his life. How can one take another life if love, forgiveness, and doing unto others is lived? One who loves cannot take the life of another. Love never does violence unto another, never judges another, and never takes advantage of another. Those who love unconditionally always get along, seeking for harmony and happiness for everyone. Love and light are the path of the way-shower, who delivers others by healing anyone seeking to be and know God as his or her self. Countless millions have died at the hands of those who are fearful.

Collective ascension requires individual choices, and a personal willingness to embrace, as a personal realness, those qualities that are ongoing. Jesus taught the basics of this subject two thousand years ago, and nothing has changed, so our hand will be forced, not by God, but through densified evolution that we are oblivious to.

It is curious so many people are convinced that God destroys. I do not know of any loving parent who desires and seeks to destroy their children for disobedience, given love unifies and creates life. Fear is the culprit and the destroyer of life in all cases, not God. Fear's role in creation is dispersing and separating energy, while love unifies and bonds. A truly loving parent will hope and wish for nothing but the best for his or her children, it is no different with God. The notion God would create the universe giving everything within it freewill, then create a place of eternal punishment, is as absurd as it gets. This would make God insane for doing so. All aspects inherent within the universe are God, and it is impossible for God to wish or seek to destroy parts of itself.

Look at how people create death for themselves. We know people are the culprit behind what actually destroys life. Humanity knows everyone is destroying him or herself, so it automatically transposes this onto God, making God the destroyer through denial and projection, stemming from fear and guilt. The notion of God destroying is like me deciding to destroy an organ in my body, a muscle, or tissue composing my body. People do this to themselves and then blame God. God only loves us as-is. This goes for everyone, regardless of whom they are, what they believe in, and what they choose to do and become. Humanity is never judged. God's will, the creator's love, and the father's light only bestow upon us what we desire and ask for. I cannot find it in my psyche to injure or kill anything, and I know God is identical to this way of living. God does not create and then destroy. Those who insist otherwise are misguided and mistaken.

If everyone seeks to be and know joy, peace, freedom, and adventure as his and her personal and social reality, eventually this will be our collective experience. Nothing ever really ends. Aspects of creation change form. The idea that God returns to destroy and condemn us to hell is ridiculous, and informs us we know nothing about God as this life.

Energy patterns itself according to what we feel, think, and do as our intended desires. If our psychology involves pain and fear, then energy will conform itself into a holographic representation that is our experience and expression of what we believe is the way it is. Victimization shows us how energy as experience one meets mirrors one's relationship with the inner and outer that are, in fact, identical. Randomness, chaos, chance, luck, fate, and coincidence are ideas helplessness uses to explain what denial and projection are as an impersonal attitude, when people refuse to accept their self-created ideals embraced. These ideas reinforce the idea we are powerless to affect change environmentally.

Notice how everything represents and corresponds to someone's idea about what is observed, both in the context of the self and that that is non-physical. It is always someone's representative ideation about that we see as a three dimensional reality. There is never a time, circumstance, or condition that is not self-created. Disease, violence, poverty, greed, fear, pain, and the like are attitudes we choose to embody and perform.

Humanity is wise to grasp that any quality we are born with is what we either share as a gift, or heal as an issue. Each of us chooses what to fear, hate, deny, or compete and go to war against. Jehovah of the Old Testament is our decision that God is this way.

Fourth density comes ushering in the 'new age' of being, knowing, doing, and becoming. Incompatible ideas as ideals will fade away and become extinct. The earth will heal and become a garden state once again. Humanity will remember God and become conscious of the universe as the self that is ensouled.

Humanity will once again live this design gloriously and graciously. Humanity is wise to be kind, for we are each other, and doing acts of compassion lifts the burdens of others and heals their wounded souls.

Know that humanity is God as the Christ, and it is this that collectively ascends when everyone is living this as a way of life. The opportunity comes very soon when each of us will be presented with the opportunity to live as the Christ or not, and what will you choose. Always, God extends both hands, and we choose which to hold and which to serve.

Inclusion and exclusion co-exist, we decide which works for us as an application. Casting out by disenfranchising crucifies us all, for humanity is all that is humanly and otherwise. Stop and think about this idea: People come from many, many, many parts of the universe, as well as being homegrown. When humanity collectively ascends, all of the differing aspects of the universe as our humanity unify into one state of being, thereby adding an entirely new gestalt to the universe, composed of those people who represent what God and universe are as their humanity. This is the point and purpose of what collective ascension is and does for God and universe. The day soon dawns when humanity returns to its divine inherency, and our countenanced radiance will shine wondrously again, and humanity will live amidst the garden smelling roses and drinking green tea after passionate erotic orgasmically satisfying sex. Life will become a truly profound experience again. Humanity returns to living who and what it is as the humanness of God and universe and all these entail.

Let us pray for deliverance from our own shortcomings and

erroneous ways of living. Soon the pain, fear, darkness, and negativity fade in prominence, replaced by joy, love, light, and positive modalities representing peace and harmony. Soon humanity lives at its communal best. Soon each of us will be living as and according to God's will, Yahweh's love, and Id's light according to all that is. Humanity soon lives the intentions of the creator and father. I bless you all with the love and the light of God, universally portrayed by and through everything that exists. I wish you all joy, peace, freedom, and adventure now.

Humanity is wise to know its being-ness and choose whom it will serve, aspiring and intending to collectively ascend. Each of us is wise to choose what will help us all heal. God is the oneness that serves purposefully. Humanity will return to God, as God, for God, through God, and by God. There is only God as all that is each of us humanly portrays through what we feel, sense, think, and envision. Smile please. Enjoy the moment. Relax. Drink fine wine. Eat delicious food. Wear comfortable clothes. Dance naked. Breathe peace and harmony. Make your life truly an act of humanly portraying God in all your activities by rejoicing in the moment, and giving thanks for this blessing in being-ness that creates whatever it desires in the moment.

History as we know it ends, abruptly. Life on this planet returns to the garden in the forest amidst the communities of God's children. This place we inhabit is but one aspect of God's ideal. Soon the adventure becomes another type of 'exodus' (or is it exit us) when we collectively ascend.

Humanity chooses what is real and true as a personal and collective experience and everything corresponds accordingly. Joy and pain, love and fear, light and dark, and positive and negative stand as our personal and collective testimonials demonstrated as our environmental representations showcasing our faith, desires, and intentions.

Each of us is faced with knowing the self, choosing who and what we will serve, and aspiring to ascend individually or collectively. This determines our ideas about the self, what our purpose is, and what we become eventually. Be what is loving and wise, my friends. Know that all is one and all is perfect now as it is. May your lives be filled with fullness bursting forth, blessing the lives of others. Shall we dance promenading love's kindness? God is having a shoe sale now just for this occasion, and I personally know God only offers what looks great and fits perfectly for you to dance the cha, cha, cha. Socks are optional and the evening wear handsome and lovely. The band is excellent and the food delicious. See you soon. By the way, the ballroom is spectacular.

Appendix A
The Second Coming ...

The Second Coming ...

I have often wondered about what 'the second coming' is and entails. For traditional Christianity, this idea is interpreted as Jesus' return. According to the Bible, Jesus returned immediately after his resurrection, so it has already taken place. I am fairly certain God does not do instant replay. The irony of this speculation is the intent and purpose of Jesus coming the first time was missed, and basically rejected by most of those who met him. I will share with the reader in this Appendix seven ideas of what 'the second coming' is and entails.

1st Idea: My first idea concerning 'the second coming' deals with each of us returning to living our life as it is designed. This requires a working knowledge of will, love, light, and consciousness as our physical and spiritual make up, or composition. What is God humanly and personally? What is life humanly and personally? What is humanity as a single state of being? What are will, love, light, and consciousness as an application? What do these become? Lacking experience, that gives one insight and understanding, these remain beliefs about that are misguided and mistaken. 'The second coming,' on a personal level, is our returning to applying God's will through love and light consciously for the enhancement of all of creation.

God is humanly applied through faith, desire, and intention, using God's will to create all aspects of one's experience. Life is humanly love and light as an individuation that knows itself as someone. Humanity, as a single state of being that knows, is the Christ. Will, love, light, and consciousness, as an application, are humanness at its basic or fundamental level. Also, these are what compose the universe. Will, love, light, and consciousness when applied create all that is. What these become are collectives unifying divergences into single states. These single states in turn reintegrate back into God's all encompassing-ness. Before doing this, these collectives assist evolving consciousness into becoming conscious of the self as what it is on all levels of existence, and evolving beyond individuality existing exclusively for itself. Only collective states ascend back into God. The reason is God is not an entity unto itself, so individuality will forever remain within the context of the universe. This is why individuals fail to know what true ascension is. Ascension from a planet is only part of the process. According to the RA Material, individuality cannot go beyond the 3rd octave of 6th density, because the 4th octave requires a balance between love and light. Individual ascension means the unification of love and light as a single state is lacking. One is wise to remember love is the relationship between God and ideation, and ideation's relationship with all else. Love is a state of being. Light is a state of knowing. Consciousness is a state of becoming or evolving. Will is a state of perpetual creativity. Humanity becomes a collective that ascends when will, love, light, and consciousness are lived humanly by each person choosing to be and know these as his or her true nature.

2nd Idea: The second idea concerning 'the second coming' involves man and woman as equals through balance. It is imperative that humanity return to living gender as an equality that is the balance of love and light. This requires each of us knowing we are both genders, and neither is greater or lesser than the other. Each of us is as much the opposite sex as the gender we portray. Our inner sense of self is our opposite sex, and it is this we actually have a relationship with, and our attitudes about our inner being is demonstrated as whom we are involved with as spouse, lover, and friends. When there is dysfunction and disparity between feminine love and masculine light, one is always considered greater than the other. Love and light are divinity and deity that we portray as female and male. When fear and darkness hold sway, life becomes one of disease and conflict, ending in death. At our present level of awareness, love and light operate as the relational and shared state of existence.

3rd Idea: The third idea pertaining to 'the second coming' encompasses humanity as a single state of being. In its truest context, humanity forms the Christ as a collective state of consciousness, consisting of people living as a whole or single state of existence. This requires ridding ourselves of the notions of nationality, gender, race, and psychology convincing us we are not each other, and that we are other than each other. The Christ is humanity living as a single whole. It is also a state of unification, whereby humanity lives one ideal inclusive of everyone. The Christ as an ideal works when there is equality, balance, relationship, purpose, harmony, peace, serenity, and tranquility within and between all peoples. When humanity consciously chooses to return to living as one family, the Christ has then returned. Each of us has the option of choosing to live as Jesus did. This makes us the Christ on a personal level. When humanity lives God's will, coupled with love and light consciously, then it lives as the Christ. The Christ is the collective consciousness of people who live their lives according to and based on God's will to be and know love and light as a state of consciousness. When accomplished, this state of collective consciousness ascends into the larger community of universe.

4th Idea: My fourth idea centers upon the literal return of Jesus. Christians are convinced Jesus will return as a man. I personally doubt this due to God does not do instant replay. Plus, almost everyone living during Jesus' incarnation missed the intent and purpose of his life, which in part was healing the Jewish notion that they alone are God's chosen people. This is impossible, because each person living is the image and likeness of God. The assumption made by traditional Christians is that Jesus will come and destroy the wicked, saving all true believers in the final hour. The irony of this is there is nothing we need to be saved from, ever. It is only our denial, fear, and guilt that convince us otherwise. It is God's will to be and know that creates all aspects of the creation and all of our experiences. The societal expectation placed upon us all is denying our true self for an outer-based ideology instilled through pain, fear, guilt, arrogance, ignorance, indifference, and intolerance, leading to what composes modern day civilization. People are expected to conform to the demands of others through obedience and self-sacrifice. The ultimate sacrifice is death, stemming from denial and fear becoming projection. Jesus served his purpose and has moved on to greater levels of service. Returning only means us doing so as the Christ, when we choose to live God's will as love and light consciously as one humanity.

Does this mean Jesus will never return? No. I am of the opinion Jesus has used the same medium as his return that conveys and teaches us about his existence now through three books (under one title). The Bible tells us about Jesus' life and his teachings. It is fitting that he would choose this type of medium as his return. I am convinced the books are, "A Course in Miracles," channeled by Helen Schucman in 1975. The 'Course' is composed of three volumes: Text, Workbook for Students, and Manual for Teachers. I have personally studied these three books for over 25 years, a truly stunning work that is challenging, insightful, and clarifying of many Bible versus. Jesus returned in 1975 as, 'A Course in Miracles.' The literal return of Jesus a second time was right after he left this planet 2,000 years ago.

5th Idea: My fifth idea entertains the notion that 'the second coming' involves Jehovah of the Old Testament, and Id the father of man. According to Ramtha, "The last great battle fought will be between the war-lord God Jehovah and Id. They will battle in the heavens for seven days, not seven years." It is this that is referred to as 'the battle of Armageddon.' So who and what are Jehovah and Id? Jehovah is a 'war-lord god' that came to this planet around 9,000 B.C., taking possession of the Jews as his chosen people. Id is the father of man, who imparted his spirit bringing to life what Yahweh created as our human ideal. Jehovah introduced the philosophy and psychology of hierarchy, elitism, superiority, chosen-ness, and good versus evil, leading to the social behaviors of conquering, enslaving, and destroying others through a 'select' group of people. Jehovah is to the universe what Hitler was to Germany. Jehovah is the anti-thesis of our creator Yahweh and father Id. Jehovah replaced Yahweh as our creator God. Since that time, humanity has evolved as a warring people. War has remained a social endeavor since Jehovah. Jehovah's legacies are the social behaviors of war, greed, and slavery that are perpetrated by people choosing to conquer, enslave, and destroy others through the mistaken belief that this is what God demands of his faithful as the "holy war."

History is marked by who warred against who and who won. Our entire sense of culture is based upon one group of people destroying another. So-called "advanced" civilized cultures destroy so called "primitive" pagan cultures, under the guise "it is God's will." Good versus evil is a way of justifying invading cultures warring against indigenous people and taking possession of their land. The true legacy of Jehovah is the continual annihilation of Yahweh's people who live indigenously. Indigenous people live according to the ideal Yahweh created as a human state of existence. Jehovah established the psychology and philosophy of the invader culture mindset, as the good that considers Yahweh's creation an evil needing to be completely destroyed. This practice began with the Jews destroying all the other tribes living nearby. This legacy of Jehovah continues unabated to this day. The real addressment needing resolution is between taking possession of people, places, and things, or being in possession of what makes us the image and likeness of God. It is the practices of war, greed, and slavery that end as social arrogance.

The nature of Id's spirit is light without bias, which is why Id remains unknown to us. Id's spirit conforms itself to our ideal. This gives us the ability to live as we choose to. The spirit works according to our intention through faith and desire. It is the love of Yahweh and light of Id that makes us human. These are without bias and have no agenda. Jehovah replaced love and light with fear and darkness. Anyone holding to fear and darkness as his or her true nature belongs to Jehovah. Everyone living fear and darkness are whom Jehovah comes for in the end times.

It is each of us that give love and light meaning and purpose. This is why Yahweh and Id remain a mystery to us. Love and light are unified as us. They are equal and balanced. These are what make us "the image and likeness" of God. The Bible verse that states: "Let us make man in our image after our likeness after our likeness, male and female created he them" explains this on two levels. Ours means a collective state created us, and ours means more than one aspect of God was involved with our creation through Yahweh and Id using God's will to create us and bring us to life. According to three different sources, Yahweh is a collective of thirteen beings existing as one state of being. The sources used are Ramtha, the Ra Material, and Seth.

I predict Jehovah and Id will return on December 14, 2012.

It is interesting to me the belief many hold that planet earth will be destroyed. This is not the case, as God does not destroy what's created. The end only pertains to those individuals and institutions that live according to the fictions imparted as Jehovah's truth and way. The war between Jehovah and Id pertains to Id preventing Jehovah from destroying this planet. This last battle will end Jehovah's influence. Humanity will begin living what love and light are and do. The end of the world is the ending of the world based upon pain, fear, darkness, and negativity as personal and social mores. Negativity is the overemphasis upon individuality that denies collective states existence and freedom of expression.

Jehovah 'conquered' the Jews and claimed them as his own by taking possession of them and then 'enslaved' them through an ideology practiced as a theology called Judaism. According to the Seth Material, Jehovah will return due to the retention of the Star of David and recreation of the state of Israel. Jehovah will then destroy the Jews and everyone else living according to the invader culture mindset. It is this that's 'promised' by Jehovah for his chosen.

What people fail to realize is, Jesus taught love, forgiveness, and doing unto others in the hopes this teaching would end the personal psychologies of fear, hatred, and selfishness and the social practices of war, greed, and slavery. John's vision recorded as the Revelation was a warning to us all that continuing these behaviors of war, greed, and slavery will end by being destroyed by the very source that gave them to us. The Book of Revelation is a warning to the Jews that maintaining the Star of David, recreating the state of Israel, and maintaining their faith results in this by the year 2012. Anyone subscribing to and supporting the behaviors of conquering, enslaving, and destroying others will become extinct. This is accomplished by the same agency and means that instilled us with choosing to live by those ideals. Jehovah can only undo what 'he' established using the same means of application.

6th Idea: My sixth idea entertains the notion 'the second coming' is earth returning to a garden state again. This requires people accepting the responsibility of involved evolution that collectively ascends, and appreciating their biological physical-ness, as well as honoring and respecting the planet itself. These two types of acceptance insures the health and welfare of everyone and all of life from a place of peace and harmony. This requires people living peacefully. This requires people understanding and knowing what equality and balance are. The garden returns when contrariness is released, leading to healing. Healing means the release of negative attitudes that create disease, conflict, and death. The return of the garden state requires an end to everything and everyone who lives a life that is contrary to love and light by personifying detriments of intention.

Everything and everyone who is inharmonious will cease to exist, they'll become extinct. Life will return to its original and natural state of being. People who choose to live a life of simple elegance will remain as those harvested. The harvesting of souls only involves those who have chosen to serve others. Serving others requires letting go of self-importance, and understanding that the whole has greater relevance and significance than personality and individuality. Each person must let go of the notion his or her identity has greater value than the whole of humanity and the planet.

Change is our responsibility, and only requires changing our minds about fictions that kill us. The physical is love made manifest. Biology is how love and fear are physically expressed. Acceptance of our biology, as love and fear unified and all other forms of love, is what returns, as the garden state is populated by those who consciously love what is physically expressed. Life is sacred. When we return to living indigenously, the garden will become re-established.

The return of the garden is that state of existence between people and planet where there is peace, not war; kindness, not cruelty; harmony, not conflict; equality, not elitism; balance, not bias, through people choosing to live joy, love, and light.

7th Idea: The seventh idea touches upon 'the second coming' as the return of those 'sources' making a contribution of some kind to our evolution from the 'historical' past. Also, humanity will remember where they have come from within the universe.

If one studies the 'historical' past from a non-traditional point of view, one discovers many, many, many, many, many 'sources' have come leaving a legacy of some kind. The RA left us the Great pyramid. The Mayans left their calendars. Every 'source' has returned in some capacity in the last one hundred years. The return of these 'sources' usually entails channeling, books, and visitations such as U.F.O sightings and 'abductions.' 'Sources' contributing to our evolution serve both hands of God; some negative, some positive, and some neutral. Information is shared to assist us in our personal, relational, and social evolution.

The imparting of information establishes a responsibility for those sharing 'their' wisdom with us. This was done in the past as a distant observer. When a teaching became corrupt, the 'source' responsible had an obligation to correct by healing the corruption. Sometimes this would take centuries to accomplish.

The legacies left behind by 'visitors' tells us more is going on than meets the eye. Expanding our awareness and horizons is important. Remembering whom we are and where we come from is essential at this time. Many are oblivious to the obvious. The days ahead are our 'second coming' into our own magnificence again.

Our wandering in the wildernesses of our own creation comes to an end soon. People are wise to begin focusing upon ideals that are based upon joy and love that demonstrate truth as a personal artistry and social kindness that endear us to each other, and enhance the quality of life for all life forms, not just the chosen few. Much comes to an end. Humanity was given 2,000 years to heal and mature. Humanity has refused to do so.

Jose Arguelles stated: "Time plus energy = Art." When a culture has attained a level of artistry on all levels of being with all aspects of their culture, they ascend as one 'state of being.' This is the true 'second coming,' and a time when humanity will create a world where art is the ideal that testifies to our living life as and according to those qualities that have an eternal value. This will then be 'added' to the universe through ascension, our birthing into a larger context, because we are conducive to it. This is what collective ascension accomplishes when people live as the Christ.

Appendix B
Taken to Task

Taken to Task

I personally do not think there is an odder statement than: "Nothing personal, it's just business." Actually this statement is ridiculous, and only demonstrates the callous disregard business holds about God, life, and humanity.

Business is the attitude selfishness holds as a negative application of God's will. The human drama is the application of what each of us feels and thinks about ourselves that we share with others. This is the basis for bartering. Something of value that is personal is given in exchange for something of value that is wanted or needed. Within the context of business, these are construed negatively leading to what we now have as economic theory. The current ideal is people denying and neglecting what they feel and think for an ideal that only takes them to the grave. This leads to the callous disregard of indifference on the part of the person who perpetrates a great fiction that others are expected to follow and aspire to. This is why businessmen state, "nothing personal" as emotions are denied, and money and status are the only ideals of importance. Money only exists as a form of exchange to establish class distinction, and the social aberration of slavery. Slavery is nothing more than the socially acceptable fiction that greed warrants and justifies as 'man's inhumanity to man' under the guise of good economics and that it is God's will. Also coupled with this, is the social fiction one aspect of humanity is God's chosen and all the rest of humanity worthy of being enslaved and destroyed.

I remember when I was told the invention of money coincided with the creation of slavery. The fact is, you cannot have one without the other. The fact that money still exists as a form of exchange shows us humanity is socially retarded and spiritually inept.

Class distinction only exists due to hierarchy that insists upon establishing an 'elite' that creates the fiction of superiority, living the false doctrine of being God's chosen few. The fiction of chosen-ness is a form of social coercion. It is also a form of psychological slavery, as well as a form of manipulation designed to control others into keeping the faith. There is only the family of humanity that all people are members of. Money only exists to glorify the ego and make it a false god. It also is the basis for what taking possession of is all about. It is the false god of the self-serving. Money is one form of giving value to something that is meaningless. In order to take possession of something or someone, a value has to be given to it. People lacking content of character will place value on all sorts of outer-based things.

Hierarchy works when God, life, and humanness are denied, and people believe it is other than and less than what it is as the image and likeness of God. This creates the scenario of a ruling elite and an enslaved populace, under the guise that this is "divinely sanctioned" as God's will, leading to those who have and those who do not. Everyone is in possession of what is real and true right now and right here. Being in possession of means one can share these qualities without an agenda of any kind, or having an expectation of any kind. This is truly giving of the spirit for the enhancement of that given to. Gifts of the spirit are freely given to the individual, and sharing them with others is true service.

The irony is, money as a system of exchange is totally unnecessary. When looked at from the point of energy, it is freely given and the 'exchange' is one of development through applied intention leading to the betterment of humanity as a whole. Our failure to move beyond money as slavery binds humanity to a level of existence that only becomes extinct over time. Extinction is the result from our holding to what is less evolved than what reality is, entails, and develops into. Greed is spiritual bankruptcy. In a medium of balance, which this planet is, greed here is 'balanced' by extreme poverty there.

When society is looked upon as a single state of existence, then God and life must be lived humanly. The lack of personalizing God and life humanly leads to all the social ills humanity embraces, like disease, conflict, crime, poverty, war, and death.

The measure by which a population is viewed as evolved

involves what issues of hindrance and struggle are healed and eliminated from people's experience. Has disease, gender disparity, social animosity, selfishness, poverty, greed, the need for controlling others, competition, and war been eliminated from the social cultures existing on a planet? Lacking the healing of such, humanity will have to repeat third density until it does so. Each one of us is responsible for healing everything discordant in our lives. Social evolution requires outgrowing issues of hindrance that maintains personal and social retardation and traditional stuck-ness.

Modern man is still very, very, very primitive in its social intercourse, given the fact that humanity has not evolved beyond disease, slavery, greed, violence, war, and death. These great fictions people perpetuate stem from denial, fear, guilt, arrogance, ignorance, and indifference through subscribing to the propaganda of hierarchy, convincing us that elitism makes one superior to others, and are chosen by God as a favored son or daughter. People then live according to the great lie of good versus evil, necessitating the behaviors of conquering, enslaving and destroying others. This leads to 'nothing personal' and the entire composition of politics as business and economic theory. The hand maidens of economic theory are greed, poverty, crime, slavery, and ultimately, war. Wars are only fought to empower those who go to war. War is the vehicle of greed. Anyone who decides to go to war only does so to empower him or herself to become exceedingly rich. World domination is the ultimate goal of war. The elimination of money as a medium of exchange ends poverty, slavery, crime, and war as social behaviors. The irony of this ignorance is, humanity evolves in a completely different way. Human evolution evolves through each member living God's will as love and light that is conscious of itself as all that is. Money only exists to establish class distinction and substantiate and sustain the ideas some are chosen and superior to others.

Humanity, through tradition, holds to the erroneous fiction that life is as it is, and there is nothing anyone can do to change it. Anyone attempting to is deemed a 'terrorist' and then put to death for daring to actualize and demonstrate what is real and true humanly. When looked at from the point of individual intention, everything comes down to one's desire for life to be as intended. Many are so afraid they insist upon life remaining those insanities composing 'civilized' life. Each person living decides through agreement how life is. Life humanly is our 'make believe' through applied intention and blind belief.

The irony of humanness is whose rules do we follow and live by.

When examining the ideal of taxation, it is a premise based upon the insistence someone in power has of getting something for nothing. Taxation is the ultimate form of greed. It is the assumption what is gained equals power. Taxation connotes one's 'right to life' is contingent upon another granting us that right by our giving them something for nothing.

The irony of life lived this way is that people discover at death–they never lived a day in their life.

Hierarchy, in all its fabricated insanity, creates our modern day civilization, and the monstrosities of nation state, greed, slavery, disparity, and war, leading ultimately to complete and total economic collapse. These are great fictions keeping humanity unevolved, socially retarded, and heading for extinction.

The universe and life work according to a simple format, the free exchange of energy for the overall health and welfare of what makes the universe God's ideal of itself as something specific. We demonstrate this truth in action by understanding how life gives of itself freely, so the species will continue on. I refer to this as life giving of itself to life. Each of us is wise to follow this example. God gives to me, so I can give to the rest of the creation piece by piece and moment by moment. One day humanity will again live according to bartering from a heart that is generous, kind, and very joyous.

Appendix C
The Meaning of God
as an Idea and Ideal

The Meaning of God as an Idea and Ideal

It is a curious observation seeing the world as it is now. Humanity has not done a very good job of getting along. It is fairly easy and accurate to state humanity lives dysfunctionally. The dysfunctionalism of people show their lack of understanding of what the Christ is. The Christ is the collective consciousness of people living as one family or ideal. The irony of this is, the idea of "one God" mirrors how people choose to live. One God was introduced thousands of years ago. The original idea of one God was negative and based upon exclusion, negation, and aversion to anything involving our creator and other beings more evolved than we are. The idea was also conveyed as "the oneness of God" involving inclusion, affirmation, and involvement with others and conscious aspects of the creation not of or from this world.

The introduction of the concept of "one God" arose due to people believing in many, many gods. People believe these to be powers of affliction or benevolence through faith, or the lack thereof. Many people today perform rituals paying homage to their version of God or gods, in the hopes of appeasing their wrath. Rituals, all of them, are simply fear and denial, existing as projected superstition used as a form of appeasement, avoiding punishment, and getting a reward of some kind. The concept of the one and only true God arose out Jehovah's conquering and enslaving the Jews to living out his decrees of war and slavery. This made Jehovah the "one true God" of the Jews. Jehovah however, is a war-lord god that first conquers and enslaves his chosen people, converting them into a warring group of individuals. Jehovah then returns, destroying his chosen for maintaining their faith in war, greed, and slavery.

First and foremost, the concept of one God was taught as a unifying idea. Then it was taught as an idea that humanness is "the image and likeness of God." Then it was taught as an idea that life is an aspect of God. Unity and oneness are the reality that exists as an eternal truth. A secondary concept involved with one God involves marauding war-lords that consider themselves "the one and only true god."

With any idea that encompasses all that is or the universe, people need to let go of ideas that are less evolved and less encompassing. Not easy to do as we see with most cultures new ideas are combined with the superstitions and rituals of old. This usually prevents the new idea from becoming truly effective in assisting people with their own empowerment, outgrowing fear and denial creating dysfunction, ineffectiveness, and the fiction that one is a victim of some perpetrator. Denial and fear become projection, leading many to think God is 'out there' somewhere.

When we look at the cultures of India, the Middle East, Europe, Asia, South America, North America, and Australia, one sees billions of people believing in one God, yet few cultures get along as one people. The irony is people use the idea of one God to war against one another. Wayne Dyer stated a few years ago that he was told: "One billion people have been killed in the name of Christ." People use the idea of one God to war, maintain gender disparity, enslave people, and maintain fear and guilt, keeping people steeped in ideologies that lead to crucifixion and death.

Another irony is, Christianity is divided into thousands of differing teachings and factions, making unity impossible. There are more versions of Christianity and interpretations of the Bible than all other religions and holy works combined. People have made one God into whatever version suits their intention. As it stands now, one God does not exist, for humanity worships thousands and thousands of gods. Christianity fails to realize that neither Jehovah of the Old Testament or Jesus of the New Testament are God. The Bible does not address God's oneness as it is and exists. Every religion fails to grasp what the oneness of God is and encompasses. So far beyond us is this truth, that few people have humanly embraced and lived what God is. The collective consciousness of an individual makes them a Christed one.

The truth of one God only works if everything is an aspect of that. The idea of God is designed to instill reverence toward, and respect for, honoring aspects of God. One God means there is always and only equality and balance between differing aspects of this one being (Within the context of a continuum, it is impossible one aspect to be greater than another, given everything makes this one being what it is).

People need to stop projecting their pain, fear, guilt, and arrogance into a 'god' that exists exactly like these. As long as people insist upon living qualities that are contrary to God's life humanly portrayed, social dysfunction will continue unabated.

Just as there is only one God, so it is there is only one life, one humanity, and one universe existing as all that is.

Each one of us is responsible for doing whatever it takes to heal our issues of hindrance that make our lives dysfunctional. This requires doing the work to the point where one lives a life of equality and balance as even-minded-ness. People do not realize that everything is allowed and accepted by God. If God truly had an attitude about something deemed unfavorable, God would eliminate it by making it disappear. Obviously God does not do this. Each person is responsible for addressing and resolving all the conditions composing his or her life. Anything taking place humanly is due to that state existing as the mind of those involved as an experience. It is impossible for something truly foreign to one's mindset to be affected by that which is other than or contrary to the individual. Victims experience mindated perpetrations of their own making.

Healing is important if we hope to evolve into living life as an equality and balance showcasing unity. This means eliminating the fictions of greater and lesser, that men are superior to women, that one race is greater than another, that one truth or tradition is chosen as God's own, that one aspect of life has greater significance than another, that 'cultures' more evolved than ours are 'it.' Humanity needs to address the truth that all aspects of life are an aspect of God, and that making a contribution to that that is conducive, is the point and purpose of the entire creation. We do this by not allowing ourselves to get bogged down in figments that only perpetuate fictions of insanity. Essential to the truths of oneness and unity are acceptance and even-mindedness.

What do we feel, think, and share with God's differing

aspects making life what it is? Do we choose to fear it, judge it, and destroy it? Do we love it, accept it, and seek to enhance the quality of life for all involved?

I had an experience a few months ago that informed me the universe is one being, the being-ness of God. Everything in the universe is God stating I am. Everything composing the universe is God's I am-ness. The universe is an idea held in the mind of God informing such that it is. From the smallest particle to the largest cluster of galaxies, this is so. Everything is an aspect of God. Do we choose to love it or fear it? We choose which of these we feel that either unifies us with God as joy and peace, or keeps us at war with God as pain and violence.

Experiences are real and true, based on what each of us chooses to feel and think, making life into what these are for each of us personally, relationally, socially, globally, and ultimately universally as a shared state. Conflict only exists when one is divided against him or herself. Your experience defines your truth as your personal reality.

The universe shows us ongoing harmonious order. The idea of one God educates us into eliminating those ideals that are contrary to peacefulness and compassionate kindness bestowed. Love, acceptance, kindness, and even-mindedness are the highest ideals humans can aspire to and live. When these are shared, then God's oneness is lived humanly as an ideal that is ongoing forever.

Appendix D
The Missing Link

The Missing Link

Unusual isn't it, the 'gap' that exists between early man and our type of humanity? Modern science has not figured it out yet. Why the differences in types? Of course science is stuck in its insistence as to what reality is and what is the determiner of truth. It is stuck to such an extent it misses entirely the point and purpose of life as 'proof' of the existence of God.

Evolution explains nothing. Humanity convinces itself natural selection weeds out 'inferior' life forms by 'favoring' what is considered more evolved.

The best science has is a doctrine of faith based and built upon absence, nothingness, illusion, chaos, void, erroneousness, and I am-not-ness. Its entire history of humanity is only 6,000 years old. True enough, science claims the first type of man came into existence four million years ago, and the universe is about fifteen billion years old, but these dates tell us nothing in that ideals of existence are 'missing.' There are levels of intelligence that exist that we are ignorant about and trillions of them exist within and throughout the cosmos.

Our ignorance is so total we are clueless about the hundreds, possibly thousands, maybe even millions of 'entities' who have come to earth over the eons of time.

According to the Ra Material, humanity began 75,000 years ago, created by Yahweh (who is a collective of thirteen beings). As I understand it, a second entity was involved with our creation named Id. Yahweh created us, and Id brought us to life. Yahweh created our body that Id brought to life by imparting its spirit. This is divinity as our embodiment of love, and deity as our spirituality, living as human beings upon a planet. The original human design is indigenous people. They have remained true to their ideal according to how they are created to live humanly. The rest of us live according to false doctrines of some kind existing as dogmatic traditions, like religion, or science, or some ism. According to Edgar Cayce, seven root races were created at the same time. The Bible gives two differing accounts about the creation of human beings. One is a true account of our creation, and the other is false as it does not involve how humans were created.

According to the Ra Material, biological robots are created that do not have a soul. They are also called soulless ones. I call them cellular biological constructs that exist solely to do the bidding of those who constructed them. These drone-like creatures are constructed cell by cell until a functioning organism exists. According to Zachariah Sitchin, these early constructs were created to dig for gold. According to the Adam and Eve myth recorded in the Bible, the male was created first and then the female. What is lacking from information shared is how we were created. Only our creator Yahweh knows. True creation of a human being requires four elements: will, love, light, and consciousness. These exist personally as mind, body, spirit, and soul. Soulless ones are used to disseminate propaganda. The main purpose of a soulless one is ensuring war, greed, and slavery remain unabated upon this planet.

When looking at the expression of early man, we see something primitive, a type of rudimental functionality. The Bible gives us two versions of creation because two types of beings exist currently. There is our creation as human beings, and there is the construction of soulless ones.

The missing link is the difference between the construction of a soulless one, and the creation of our type of human being.

To understand this, one needs to be aware of who and what constructed the soulless one, and the purpose it served those. A hierarchical level of intelligence came along and discovered our creation, and then decided to conquer one tribe and convert it into living according to its dictates of intention. It is very possible that Jehovah of the Old Testament created soulless ones to do its bidding here on earth. The intention of Jehovah was replacing Yahweh's ideal with its own using soulless ones to deceive those enslaved converting them to a warring faction based on hierarchy, elitism, and superiority.

The missing link is the 'source' between the existence of soulless ones and our creation 75,000 years ago. This can also be thought of as what created the soulless one, and what created us as its image and likeness. To truly understand who and what we are as human requires a working knowledge of love's creativity and light's manifestation. Love and light were imparted to us, making us the image and likeness of God. This was accomplished according to Yahweh's love and Id's light, manifested as our ideal.

The missing link is the organizational scheme between two differing types of intelligence. One is hierarchical, the other a unified state that singularizes differences into one being. The creator of the soulless one exists as a hierarchy, instilling the notions of elitism, superiority, and chosen-ness based on the ideology of good versus evil, leading to the perpetration of conquering, enslaving, and destroying others. The other is based on equality demonstrating balance, relationship, and purpose, based upon the truth of harmony that instills peace, serenity, and tranquility through meditation and kindness. Depending on which aspect one aspires to, will determine whether one becomes extinct or ascends.

Jehovah of the Old Testament is a hierarchical intelligence that conquered and enslaved those chosen, thereby destroying their relationship with their true God. Is one's idea of God outer-based or inner realization? Any idea or ideal that holds to God as an outer source or force does not know what God is or where it is. This process is one of love and light being replaced with fear and darkness, leading those conquered to believe unto death, they are the chosen ones of God. His chosen then become the ones implementing war and money upon the planet leading to the wealthy elite and the enslaved and impoverished.

The missing link is the difference ideologically between the creation of a slave drone, and the creation of what we are humanly. One lives as a biological robot only existing to do the bidding of what created it, and us as the image and likeness of God. What exactly is it that makes us God's image and likeness? Almost everyone is God's will, Yahweh's love, Id's light, and the consciousness of all that is. These four qualities are what each of us evolves in our own way, in our own time, and according to our faith, desire, and intention. Humanity's failure to grasp this stems from an either/or mentality. Plus, humanity has not figured out there are two aspects to our type of expression. What I refer to as Yahweh and Id.

The real culprit is people relying upon their five senses to 'know it all' rather than remembering and intuiting by embracing through experience directly those truths that define our reality as human beings. The missing link also explains why there are two types of cultures existing indigenously and as invaders.

What these two cultures show us is how each aspect of creation works as social ideals. Humanity will return to living indigenously in the years ahead. People will remember their true natures of living life as it is designed to exist.

The missing link is the ideological difference between warring intelligence and peaceful intelligence. We, in our ignorance, choose which aspect to aspire to ideologically. Most people do not realize these two ideals evolve hand and hand throughout third density. There are those who aspire to the 'left' hand of God, and there are those who aspire to the 'right' hand of God. There are those who seek to control others while becoming very rich, and there are those who seek to enlighten others from as loving a place as possible.

Humanity does not do a very good job with understanding and grasping creation as it is designed, and what it evolves into.

To truly grasp why there is a missing link requires a fundamental knowledge of the self as it is according to and involving both paths that evolve. This is easily understood as doing the bidding of another, or using God's will to create effectively enhancements to all that is.

The fundamental problem science faces is that it rejects completely the notion of 'sources,' creating ideals that are self-evolving, leading to ideas considered 'it' that fail to address what is actually going on and involved with what is observed. This inevitably leads to conclusions that completely miss the point about intentions rendered as an ongoing ideal.

The entire universe is a medium of applied intention. The application requires intention and utilization of those components, making the medium what it is. Intelligence is one aspect giving structure to something that exists. Feeling gives structure content. Intention gives contented structure the ability to become something. God's will creates everything into an existence that evolves over time through space as a durated placement of some kind.

Within the context of our humanity now, the missing link is our failure to understand our roots according to who created us and why. This is the development of God's will to be love and know light as a state of ongoing consciousness. This is only done by and through the will of another, fear, darkness, and unconsciousness, or what is not. What this accomplishes is that it makes what is infinite and eternal into something specific. The existence of something only exists, as long as it is held as an ideal. When this is changed, what it was becomes extinct, like the dinosaurs. Soulless ones lack the ability to self-evolve. This is why they became extinct. The flaw was in their design. People have been following this example by choosing to die. God's will is a constant, as is the universe. Within these are love and light that alone evolve into differing states of being that know. The missing link is love and light were lacking as the basic makeup of a soulless one, because what created that was lacking that as their basic nature. Any aspect of the creation can only create what they are consciously being and knowing. Just as people will only create ideals based upon what each feels and thinks is him or her self.

The missing link is not taking into consideration what's actually involved with what created us, and the construction of a soulless one.

Making an observation and then trying to figure it out and piece things into something sensible rarely works very well, and is almost never accurate about they way things are in the overall scheme of things. Action at a distance tells us nothing of what's actually going on right here, right now.

Making the correct connections requires knowing what's involved with those aspects one chooses to work with. In the cases of humanity, this requires a working knowledge of service polarity, and what it does as a function of the larger universe. Almost nothing points this out to us, so most of humanity is clueless as to what's actually happening here and why.

The missing link is the time and space between one reality and another. The construction of a soulless one is a type of cloning, making it a type of biological robot used to do the bidding of that which created it.

Our type of creation has free will, giving each of us the ability to choose what we feel, sense, think, and envision is our reality and truth. The reason we have parents is because of who created us and what brought us to life. When one becomes conscious of love and light as his or her humanity, one will become conscious of Yahweh and Id as that which made us their image and likeness.

What we can understand through the missing link is one ideal is eternal by nature and design, while the other is not. Soulless ones can only die. Human beings can ascend individually or collectively.

What purpose does an aspect of creation serve? The missing link is our not taking into consideration those elements involved with why soulless ones exist as they do, and why we exist as we do.

Nothing in the Universe
is an Absolute—
Not Even God!

Nothing in the Universe is an Absolute – Not Even God!

It is a curiosity to me that Hinduism has its bliss consciousness, Buddhism has its attainment of nirvana, and Christianity has as its ideal perfection. Each teaching feels that its state of consciousness attained is 'it' and an absolute. The problem existent is that nothing within and composing the universe is 'it' as an absolute. The universe as a whole is not an absolute, so why do we humans insist upon making an aspect of awareness an 'it?' What people fail to address is, everything one becomes conscious of within is the union between differing states. Bliss consciousness is the union of will and love we feel as joy that fills our heart. Our entire existence is the union of many differing states of being we come to know through meditation and experience.

I have discovered the idea of evolution explains how ideals become from one state of existence to another. I have found God's will to be and know evolved into love, then light, then consciousness that learn how to apply these as a personal creativity. Creativity is the process of God's will, applied to everything composing the universe, which is an applied state of existence demonstrating infinity, eternity, completeness, and totality. Creativity is the artistry of oneness. Creativity precedes evolution that is the ongoing-ness of God's willingness to be and know eternally.

Curiously, people have decided aspects existent within the universe are 'it.' This poses a problem for God, universe, and everything that exists that is other than what the 'it' is. Another problem arises, the process of change, which is what creativity does as evolution. People confuse the idea of oneness with single states exclusive of all else. I remember Jack B. telling me one afternoon that oneness invalidated yin and yang. I was not quick enough to ask him how his idea of oneness worked with the states of male and female. Femaleness is divinity existing as love personified. Maleness is deity existing as light personified. The irony is, our male bias focuses upon light and completely ignores love. This is why there is gender bias. Love and light are equal and balanced making the entire creation an infinitude. The only reason why time and space exist is due to love and light becoming individualized states we live as male and female.

If the seeker wishes to be and know God that is great, but there are also life, humanness, differing life forms, the planet, and those ideals composing the universe that all have their place, point, and purpose for being. People do not do a very good job of accounting for diversity as infinity. Infinity can also be thought of as variable, variety, or differentiation, making oneness look like it is composed of many different states of consciousness. People then get hung up trying to find a single state and make that their 'it.' People also have difficulty in knowing everything surrounding them, to the farthest reaches of the universe, are aspects of their self. The entire point or purpose we exist as is seeing what attributes we hold about difference, or variable, and what we do through contribution to anything we feel differs from us. What contribution do we make to others and differing life forms we observe as the biology of this planet? Do we love or fear what differs from us, and are we kind or cruel to life as a whole?

It is interesting to me there are so many aspects to God's I am-ness we observe as ourselves, others, this planet, and the universe informing us that God is real. Interesting also how some aspects of God remain as-is for billions of years and some change quickly over time, through space.

Anything attained, retained, realized, or understood is merely a 'grain of sand' in the overall scheme of God. True there is depth of being and scope of knowing, but also contrast and purpose. These all exist as a relationship through sharing that contributes to the development and enhancement of what is by what is contributed as a state of being that knows itself as its creation. Intelligence organizes and then manifests ideals into any and all life forms composing the universe. This is something science has missed due to not understanding or experiencing what God is, or what divinity and deity are, that created us long ago. Even if one enters into and becomes conscious of God as it is, this state is not an absolute as it is an aspect of the self. Never is there a time a given state is absolute.

Humans are curious in their quest for an absolute that excludes everything except that state attained. God's original state is all encompassing, so nothing is excluded, and everything is an aspect that contributes to God's ideal of itself. This only shows people do not grasp what infinity is and does. People do not realize that one aspect of the creation holds to exclusion, negation, and aversion to anything other than self-idolization, while another aspect holds to inclusion, affirmation, and involvement with anything that differs from its state of being. It is only the self that seeks for absolutes of some kind when the collective nature of the self is denied and rejected. Nothing existent within the universe is "an entity unto itself." It is true humans like the idea or notion of an 'it' being 'it.' This usually means one seeks to be 'it,' and one can create a state of mind that is 'it' to the seeker. However, doing this fails to grasp that everything is in relationship with all else, making the entire universe a relational state of being. Love is the relationship between what God is as God, and what God is not as all aspects of the creation. The mistake we humans make is in thinking that a specific state is 'it' to the exclusion, negation, and aversion to all else. This mistake stems from egocentricity. People fail to grasp and recognize two processes taking place making creation what it is. This is the extension and expansion of God's will to be and know into everything composing the universe.

Consciousness is the soul existing as an awareness of something specific coming into existence through God's will to be and know. This differs from all encompassing-ness existent within any medium in the universe. It is this specific-ness that lead some to seeking a specific state as an absolute that for them is 'it.' People will notice that in their seeking they desire, through faith and intention, to attain and become conscious of a state that is other than and contrary to their ideal as created. It's like we state that we wish to be anything other than human. Each tradition holds to a notion that being human is illusion, suffering, or sin. By this, we state that God did not know what it was doing, and we are correct in telling God 'you are mistaken' and we are right in our ignorance and arrogance. Becoming is the key word. God became the universe, which in turn becomes self-conscious as everything composing the universe. Every aspect composing the universe gives God the ability to state I am. Self-consciousness then seeks to unify disparity. Actually, love seeks to unify itself through living the qualities of joy, peace, and freedom, giving love the experience it is at one with all else. Fear breaks energy down by dispersing it into a myriad-ness. When consciousness is self-aware of such qualities as love and light, the natural course of events is to assist others in becoming like-minded. All great teachers do this. When enough people are conscious of those states making them human, then the possibility exists for those aware to ascend as one being.

Everything in the universe differs by design. The importance of this is no two aspects of the universe will experience and express identically. No two people, places, or things will experience or express a given state of awareness in the same manner or way. Uniqueness prevents any two expressions from being identical. No two states will attain or embrace the same state in an identical way, as difference in ideal makes it impossible to do so. Anyone who seeks a given state of awareness will do so differently and according to one's natural way of being. Differentiation ensures nothing is the same. If people become aware of God within each person will do so from a different perspective due to the difference of each person. The notion that one person's attainment is 'it' fails to account for variables in and with the design. I challenge anyone to prove to me that a given ideal is 'it,' within or as the creation that is infinite by intention and design. Once one decides upon his or her answer what does everything else pertain to? This is no different than someone trying to decide upon one idea as 'the' truth. Then there is the problem of people seeking to become 'the Buddha' or 'Jesus' or some other master from the past. Ill-advised due to our truth and reality differs from theirs, and it is not meant design-wise for people to be identical or even live as others have lived. I am unique as is everyone else. My path will differ from everyone else's.

In the Seth book, "The Nature Of Personal Reality," Seth

demonstrates to an audience how no two people view or see life in the same way or manner, and how everyone experiences life in a unique and personal way. Very important to know and understand. People assume erroneously that their way is 'it,' expecting everyone to see life the same way. The irony of this assumption is life, truth, and reality differs from person to person. Plus, people exist for differing purposes. Interesting to me how, the experience of some, have become traditions others follow, like Hinduism, Buddhism, Islam, Christianity, or the like.

What is lacking, as an understanding, is a working knowledge of the universe as an applied state of existence. According to the Ra Material, the universe we observe is composed of seven densities each containing eight octaves, like musical scales. Having a working knowledge of this requires being and knowing each density and each octave as a single collective or state of existence. The problem pursuant of this is part of the universe is pre-physical, non-physical, and post-physical. One way of understanding the universe is studying the chakras, as each corresponds to a given density. Trying to explain this by the past is an approach that is not only misguided, but impossible, given each aspect trying to do so differs from any other, so each explanation will differ accordingly. Plus, most of us 'originated' in differing ways, so what we touch upon will correspond to that.

Bliss, nirvana, and perfection are not God's originality. Primary states, like will, love, light, and consciousness give rise to secondary states and then tertiary states, etc. Never is there a time a given state is absolute. Not even God is an absolute within the universe. All encompassing-ness, as a state of being that knows, requires depth of being and scope of knowing from an understanding of equality, balance, relationship, purpose, and harmony between what is and what is not. Coupled with this, one must resolve the entire notion of opposites in conflict. Also useful is learning to feel what a given idea is and means to the self as it lives humanly.

In "Conversations with God" by Neale Donald Walsch, we are told: "In the absence of that which is not, that which is, is not." Individuality is impossible without opposites as it is contrast that gives God's all encompassing-ness its ability to exist as differing states of being that know giving God its ability to state I am.

This is akin to becoming aware of the sun, earth, moon, and personality as a self-awareness that understands function, as well as purpose as an applied state of existence.

There is that which is within its context of being, establishing the relationship between it as it is and what it is not, as what it became as an expression of everything composing the universe. This is the extension and expansion of God's will into ideals that are ongoing, because God's realness is inherent within everything.

The path is the contribution made as an applied intention that is either conducive or contrary to creation. We can ask ourselves if we are living that which is conducive to or contrary to our life and the life surrounding us. Is our intention killing us or ascending us? For most, death is the applied outcome of a life unlived. This is due to agreeing one ideal is 'it,' rather than understanding what's involved making the self who and what it is here ad now.

Specific-ness is important to be and know, as that is what we are humanly. We are God and universe unified into a specific ideal, but not as an absoluteness exclusive of all else. Humanness is the embodiment of God, and the ensoulment of the universe as a state of being and knowing existing as the body and spirit. It is from a state that is specific we exist as and move from as we meditate upon depth of being and scope of knowing. Specific-ness gives God and universe perspective and purpose. It also gives love and light context and nuance. It is impossible to state one person's love and light are 'it' rather than anyone else's, or that one person's path is it.

The mistake made by those who feel they have attained 'it' is what does everything else correspond to and represent. The traps one finds oneself imprisoned within are absence, nothingness, illusion, chaos, void, erroneousness, and I am-not-ness. These convince the seeker they have attained 'it' to the exclusion, negation, and aversion of all else. This prevents the seeker from polarizing into that path of service assisting the development of not only humanity as a whole, but the infinite, eternal, complete, and total as well.

There is that which is specific to the self. This becomes the relational and then collective. Absolute states prevent the seeker from moving from an 'it' into balance between, and the relationship between other than and differing aspects of the self. This is shown and demonstrated by gurus, monks, and mystics never entering into male/female gestalts, then communities that extend and expand the relational into a reciprocating ongoing-ness including all aspects of the environment one lives within.

I have met aspirants who subscribe to the notion of an absoluteness being 'it' that few attain. This merely makes them an entity unto themselves. Everything and everyone is kept at a distance, making personal and social evolution impossible. This is akin to how we observe the stars at night, as tiny specks of light with nothing but darkness between them. The physical is love as a created ideal, just as the spirit is light as something specific.

God states I am as the specific that is also a relationship between ideals that are ultimately the entire creation. If one holds to the notions of bliss, nirvana, or perfection as 'it,' the seeker is prevented from truly being God, and knowing the universe as him or her self. Then applying God's will through love and light consciously into ongoing states that represent God as a workable ideal that are larger versions of the self as the specific. This requires living connection and integration. One way of being and knowing is experiencing how will becomes love, and these becoming peace, and harmony, then oneness, wholeness, and completion that reintegrates with God. One arena needing resolution exists between individuality as a state and collective-ness that exists as a state of being. People who are stuck upon their individuality will always seek for an absolute of some kind through an outer-based source of some kind.

My mind, body, spirit, and soul are all differing collective states existing as one ideal I share with the rest of creation. My trying to make one aspect of the creation an 'it' prevents me from being and knowing who I am as all that is in conjunction with the realness of God. This requires being God and knowing the universe as a unified and single state of existence. If I state God is 'it' as an all encompassing-ness centered within my heart I disallow for everything that is not that state. This means I disallow the universe and everything existing within the universe the right to be and know, as each is created and manifested to exist as.

This can be visualized as a sub-atomic particle, atom, molecule, life form, planet, solar system, galaxy, and universe. Notice how none of these is an absolute, ever. Notice how each is a larger version of the same reality and truth.

I am reminded of the scientist studying quantum physics seeking to find the smallest particle in existence. Smaller and smaller and smaller they get. The truth is there are an infinite number of smallest particles. Science will never find 'it,' because 'it' does not exist. Likewise the seeker seeking for that absolute state considered 'it.' 'It' will never be found or attained, and there will always be other states to be and know.

People fail to grasp that collective states exist outside and beyond self-awareness from a specific point of view or reference. Just as there are relational states, what I call binary vibrancy, which exists as a larger more comprehensive state of being. The will of God is not an absolute from the perspective of individuality. Neither is joy, or love, or light, or any other quality or state of being. When the seeker makes an aspect of God absolute, this makes all else a fiction from that perspective, and prevents the seeker from becoming conscious of him or her self comprehensively.

The entire creation does at its level what God does. Each of us and each aspect of creation extend and expand consciously through experience that expresses the intentional purpose of being. God seeks, from the point of it's I am-ness, to be and know all encompassing-ness again. Ascension is this one aspect of the self when known as God and universe that is connected and integrated.

The first type of ascension is evolving from the planetary state into the larger community of universe, due to being and knowing that which is infinite, eternal, complete, and total as the self as it is this that is integrating into when connected to it. The second type of ascension that takes place is when that which is universal ascends into all encompassing-ness surrounding the universe. In order to ascend into the universe, all that is must be known and lived as the self as one's ensoulment. The universe must be known as one's own soul.

The mind is God's will as something specific and personal, the body is love manifested into an ideal we think of and live as the body, which is the embodiment of love made real. The spirit is light that brings to life the will of God as love, making our life our spirituality. The universe, when personal, is our soul. Ensoulment is all that exists as a specific state or ideal. Notice how none of these aspects of God is an absolute in and of themselves. Each is an aspect of giving differing experiences within a state that is the oneness of them, namely our humanity. The personality of God's will is our mind. The love of the creator as something personal is our body, making us something physical. The light of the father as something personal is our spirituality. The universe as something personal is our own soul. God, life, humanness, and universe are terms used for will, love, light, and consciousness, that when lived as something personal, are the mind, body, spirit, and soul. None of these is an absolute existing as an entity unto itself.

The work we do in consciousness is moving, by healing our notions of something being 'it.' 'It' in any form or manner is only the ego based upon selfishness convinced it is 'it' seeking to enslave others as a justification that it is correct and true. This is the basis for all outer-based teachings and teachers.

Denial of the self forces one to seek outside of the self for an 'it' of some kind that one then worships as a false god. People do this religiously, scientifically, politically, socially, and economically. The 'false gods' of humanity are numerous. Many an 'entity' clamors making us think it is 'it.' Not even God is an absolute when viewed from the perspective of individuality. All encompassing-ness is not an absolute when viewed from the universe. The universe is not an absolute when viewed from an aspect composing it. Self is not an absolute when observing anything that differs from it.

Only those who serve themselves deem something an absolute to enslave others to their ideals of self-importance. Anyone who assumes he or she is studying an 'it' of some kind, and that his or her way is 'it,' and the "only" way only shows how arrogant and confused he or she is about being, and what purpose it serves God as an ideal that shares and evolves.

God is all encompassing and universal that we portray as the self. No one and nothing is an absolute, not even God when taken into perspective as the self. Bliss, nirvana, and perfection are merely ideas held as ideals due to our refusal to embrace, own, and live our humanity as it is. Bliss, nirvana, and perfection are our unwillingness to live God as life humanly portraying desire and intention based upon will, love, light, and consciousness that are our humanity. Little wonder almost everyone has died only to reincarnate again. Death of the body is reincarnation of the soul. The process is identical for both aspects.

Attainment of an 'it' of some kind does not allow any kind of involved relationship to exist. The question I have for all those who've attained an 'it' of some kind is, how is 'this' shared with others? Given the 'state' attained is mutually exclusive to the self and fails to take into consideration that everything surrounding the self is an aspect of it. Denial states otherwise, and it is denial that seeks to attain an 'it' of some kind due to not being able to address what the self is humanly. So the arguments abound about what 'it' is. On and on and on we carry about notions like God and heaven and some 'other' person who was or is 'it' now.

What is your truth and when are you going to live it?

What is the nature of the self, what does this become, and what do these evolve into? Interesting, it is so many things that make me who I am humanly, like atoms, molecules, cells, tissue, blood, bone, glands, organs, muscles, chakras, and feeling, thinking, and sharing. Now I ask the reader which of these is 'it'? Notice how each is what it is and combine into who and what I am humanly. Oneness only works as an idea when everything is taken into account as values making the self an ongoing ideal.

Appendix F
The Meaning, Significance, and Importance of the Mayan Calendars and Their End Date of 2012

The Meaning, Significance, and Importance of the Mayan Calendars and Their End Date of 2012

I was told during a reading given by Joseph Eric Karagounis my basic nature is Mayan, and that I created the Mayan Calendars during one of my past lives. This rang true for me, as I recalled knowing immediately why the Mayan Calendars ended with the year 2012.

I have never liked astrology. I believe it is a misguided and mistaken approach to divination. I do not believe the movements of the heavens determine intention and outcomes here. I am fairly certain it is denial and fear becoming projection that leads to our rituals, and the notion that the heavens control our fate and destiny. Ritual is the personification of denial and fear as an enactment, testifying to what we deny and fear becoming a projection of some kind that continuously haunts us. Movement never repeats itself, and is never involved with or based upon past, present, and future. There is only now here becoming as what evolves and eventually ascends.

The significance and importance of star systems involves two aspects of life here on earth. One involves 'cultures' that have come introducing ideas for us to implement, and that people actually come from many of the stars we see during the night sky. Sources of intent, or aliens, have come from other planets throughout our galaxy and other galaxies. There are literally thousands of artifacts showing us 'other' cultures have come leaving their mark. Billions of people actually belong to cultures existing elsewhere in the universe.

The Mayans originated from the Pleiades and collectively ascended back there when their work was completed. The Mayan Calendars are a series of pictographs left to remind, inform, and foretell. Those who think these calendars are primarily concerned with time as movement of the constellations over aeons are mistaken and misguided. The Mayan Calendars involve the evolution of this planet, and the evolution of our species. They also show us who were involved with our creation, and what we will develop into when we begin living who and what we are humanly. The Mayan Calendars remind us our soul comes from somewhere in the universe. They inform us about what evolution and collective ascension is. They foretell of a time when changes occur and endings take place.

One detail missed by everyone is once the Mayans had achieved artistry socially, it was time for them to leave, and they left by collectively ascending. Honesty, artistry, and kindness are the measures that allow a culture to ascend collectively. The Mayan Calendars show us this as a series of pictographs. They also show what God is and where, what life is and the purpose it serves, what humanity is and does, and what these become as an ongoing state of being that knows.

Everything composing the universe is and works according to relationship. This can be thought of as community involvement and social evolution. Outer-based influences do not determine intention or evolution. God's will creates experience taking place during the evolution of consciousness through space and over time. Experience is the unfolding or blossoming of one's personal ideal manifested. That which is ideally suited to one's desired intentions becomes that reality one finds oneself in. People who believe that conception or time of birth determines one's fate or destiny fails to take into consideration that which is actually evolving within. God's will creates every experience we embrace. The movements of the heavens have nothing to do with our evolution, beyond the relationships we have with those planets we are involved with. The Mayan Calendars tell us where sources came from that have influenced this planet, either negatively or positively. The two calendars show us human and planetary evolution. They also show us invader culture and indigenous people evolving side by side. They also show us how the male and female evolve side by side.

The Mayan Calendars detail earth's relationship with those 'sources' contributing to this planet in major ways. Part of their focus details possibilities, probabilities, and outcomes. There is that source which built the Great Pyramid in Egypt, the stone faces on Easter Island, the step pyramids in Mexico and Central America, the Sphinx, Stonehenge, and many, many more. There are also those sources imparting ideologies that have become the various traditions and social mores practiced by most of humanity.

People are wise to remember where they have come from and why they are here. Not easy to do as family, tradition, gender, peer pressure, and social upbringing usually prevent one from remembering these.

I remember reading in The RA Material that this planet is under quarantine due to 'foreign' sources influencing us negatively. Now most sources can only contact us through dreams, channeling, or books. The Mayans left us pictographs to remind us of our past, and inform us about our future, as well as to show us whom we are and what we are by those sources responsible for our creation that we are now here being.

I have read a few sources that speak about the Mayan Calendars according to astrology, but this misses the point entirely of what they are actually a representation of. The Mayan Calendars and the surrounding symbology actually show us the nature of the self and our social evolution beyond the fictions of false doctrine. This is shown as both indigenous cultures and invading cultures. The numbers 13 and 20 are the numerology of love and light as they exist as Yahweh and Id.

Third density ends and fourth density begins in the year 2012. Third density is that state of existence where people choose service polarity, either positive or negative. Free will exists solely for the purpose of choosing. Service polarity is the only aspect of humanness that evolves and continues on through the harvesting of souls. Everyone lacking harvestability repeats third density, elsewhere (RA Material 1984). Service polarity is a measured gradient. Only two types of people are harvested during the harvesting of souls: those who serve themselves and those who serve others. What is measured is God's will, love, and light consciously lived as serving others, and that that is contrary to these as fear, darkness, and total allegiance to a doctrine focused upon war, greed, and enslavement of others. Everyone I have read speaks of the end times. No one posits what ends; 2012 is that time when all aspects of self-service ends, and war, greed, and slavery will cease to be the social activities personified. Anyone engaged in such activities will cease to be a part of the continuing social evolution that remains to eventually collectively ascend.

For humanity, this involves teachings 'sent' that instill and instruct us to live what eventually polarizes the self as that service shared with others. Coupled with this are the two primary cultures composing human evolution: indigenous and invading, or what we call primitive cultures and advanced or 'civilized' cultures (What people fail to realize is invader cultures live according to false doctrines and artificiality. Our artificial cultural trends are cloning and robotics. These will replace humanness with ideals that are only designed to exist according to mechanical function).

Our current arrogance convinces us that the industrial world is 'advanced' and that indigenous cultures are primitive. I offer the argument the Native Americans were here before the arrival of the Europeans to teach them how to live a life that was culturally conducive to the planet. In this, we obviously failed to get it. By 2012, technology will cease to be viable; electricity and oil will cease to exist as energy sources. This is why the idea of the end of the world is posited.

Examining cultures worldwide, we see ideals making traditions what they are. The assumption is, tradition is the way it is for a given culture. However, every idea agreed upon is only an idea someone decided was 'it' at that time. People usually fail to grasp the mechanics behind what eventually becomes a social more. Philosophies abound as traditional social standards. Sources for this are usually relegated to individuals. Each of us is responsible for determining being, knowing, application, and development of the self. Each of us decides what is important to us, and what our life is and becomes. Each of us is responsible for accepting personal involvement in human evolution. Evolution is the development of consciousness through experience and understanding.

There are two ideals that evolve here on earth as the polarization of the negative and the positive as a human ideal through service. The ending of service polarization and the beginning of human evolution of that polarity will remain from what is harvested in 2012. It marks the end of all aspects of negative polarization on this planet. War, greed, slavery, and technology become extinct. It also marks the end for everyone who has not worked at polarizing. This is why the concept of 'the end of the world' is stated. It begins the journey of life here on earth evolving positive service. The Mayan Calendars are a depiction of the evolutionary process, and what was involved with the creation of the species. The serpent represents Jehovah as an outer-based negativity. God centered within is also depicted. Those who serve the self will incorrectly interpret the symbology.

It is the end of hierarchy, elitism, superiority, chosenness, and good versus evil leading to the social behaviors of conquering, enslaving, and destroying others. The year begins life as the equality, balance, relationship, purpose, and harmony of people, leading to life that is based upon peace, serenity, and tranquility, making life what it actually is. All institutions based on hierarchy and using money and law as mediums to enslave and control will become extinct.

The number 13 of the Mayan Calendars show us through each pictograph what composes the creator of humanity and what love is composed of as an actuality. The creator is a collective of 13 beings existing as one state of consciousness (RA Material). The name of the creator is Yahweh. Each pictograph is a quality of being. These in part make us whom we are humanly. The number 20 of the Mayan Calendars shows us through pictograph what composes the father of humanity and what light is composed of as an actuality. The father is a collective of 20 knowings, existing as one state of consciousness. The name of the father is Id. Each pictograph is a quality of knowing. These in part make us what we are humanly. Our true parents are Yahweh and Id. This means our basic composition is the 13 states of being of Yahweh and 20 states of knowing of Id. The significance of 20 for the Mayans was the five senses coupled with the four phases of the moon. The new moon shows us negative polarity. The full moon shows us positive polarity. The two quarter phases of the moon show us male and female before any polarization takes place. When looking at the moon's quarter phase, each represents man and woman. The last quarter phase is feminine, and the first quarter phase is masculine. It is our biology as our five senses coupled with the phases of the moon as our spirituality that determines what our polarity becomes as a state of ongoing assistance to the universe.

What does the moon show us? It shows us our spiritual development. Each human being works at becoming that which serves either the dark or the light through discipline and development. The actual path involves four areas of study. This can be delineated as sun, earth, moon, and universe. The Mayan Calendars put these into a system of study.

These calendars show how God and universe unify into life humanly portrayed. The number or symbol of completion is 360. When coupled with the five senses makes for our current year. The significance of 13 moons is how they correspond to our creator's collective consciousness as it develops into what eventually serves. This is why there are two calendars. One depicts Yahweh and Id and the other our development over time through space as that contribution made to the universe. That point when those harvested begin the journey that eventually culminates in collective ascension is 2012.

The Mayan Calendars are reminders. They remind us of who created us and what brought us to life. They remind us of where we are from and where we are going. They remind us of what work needs be done. They tell us what lies ahead and why two cultures exist. They inform us as to why there are two genders and what roles each plays in the ascension process. The Mayan Calendars show us what God is and where, what life is and why, what humanness is and what it becomes, and they show us the role the universe plays as an ongoing development that is eternal. Ascension is the outcome when what is eternal and what is not are lived as a healed reality.

A common mistake made by many regarding the Mayan Calendars is that they attribute the 'heavens' with power. Constellations do nothing. They show us where we are from and where we go. The only active force in the universe is God's will. It is this that creates all aspects of experience and creation. God's will to be and know is ceaseless in creating experience. Being-ness is joy and love coupled with pain and fear. Knowing-ness is light and consciousness coupled with darkness and unconsciousness. Joy and love are God lived. Light and consciousness is the universe known. When these four states are unified and in harmony with what they are not, they exist as humanness that ascends.

I have read three different authors who make the statement that the galactic center plays a role. This is erroneous. God exists within the center of all aspects composing the universe. The Mayan Calendars inform us of this. It is the center within that plays a role. People are wise to go within and discover God centered within. Not easy as one must live those qualities that make life, human-ness, and the universe what they are as aspects of God's ongoing-ness existing as our humanness.

This state of God centered within is the only aspect within the entire creation that is always in a state of rest. This is due to everything else in the universe is becoming by returning to that state giving rise to the universe as an expression of itself. Surrounding God's realness centered within is a state that is an exact opposite. When viewed from outside it and beyond it God looks like a small sun surrounded by complete darkness, the absence of anything at all. This microscopic 'sun' is God as it exists within and gives God I am-ness. The size of God differs with each aspect composing the creation. The color is a dark bronze that has a porous-ness to it. When one in-tunes and enters into this, one experiences what God is - a state that is all encompassing. Anyone who becomes conscious of this becomes God humanly portrayed. Few people have become truly God conscious in 75,000 years of human evolution. The search for the smallest particle is actually the search for God. God is the smallest aspect composing the self. The study of the universe is the study of the soul. Both are done from a place of denial and projection.

The Mayan Calendars are pictographs showing us who created us, and what we become over time through space. The Mayan Calendars inform us about the natures of the self, service polarity, and the ascension process.

The primary elements involving the Mayan Calendars are God within, life that surrounds, human-ness that ascends within the medium of the universe, and our place and role in the overall scheme of things.

I caution the reader not to get too distracted by technology, and the fictions of those who serve themselves. These will fade away forever. People are also wise not to get too steeped in tradition or teachings, but rather to go within and discover one's own truth and live that for the benefit of humanity as a whole.

The Mayan Calendars assist us all in going within and finding God as God is, of living life as it is, of living humanly according to our design, and seeking to become conscious of the universe as your own soul. Then each of us who does this has the opportunity to share with others what these are as a personal realness and truth.

The Mayan Calendars are not so much concerned with time and space as they are connection, integration, and development of our humanity into something that is ongoing and contributory. These calendars are pictographs of the self according to Yahweh and Id existing as four states of being we observe as sun, earth, moon, and universe. That which is centered within the heart is God. That which is depicted as the serpent is that which serves itself.

God is what one feels. Life is what one senses. Spirituality is what one thinks. Service is what one envisions. Combined is the path.

Another way of looking at the Mayan Calendars is, thinking of the number four representing the mind, body, spirit, and soul, coupled with the five senses and what these eventually choose to serve. For some pain, fear, darkness, and negativity are the choice for service. For others joy, love, light, and the positive are the path of service. It is important for people to realize that only service polarity is harvested (RA Material 1984). These two paths involve either God, or what is depicted as the serpent. Everyone who has refused to choose service polarity repeats third density elsewhere as planet earth is evolving beyond the typical scenarios of birth, crucifixion, death, and reincarnation.

The entire universe is an applied state of existence and expression. This is all and only what each aspect does through its evolution; trial and error until a given aspect becomes effective and efficient in the applications of God's will using joy/pain, love/fear, light/dark, and positive/negative.

One can see first hand how four works in conjunction with five, seven, thirteen, and twenty. The mistake many make is in thinking of these only in terms of time, distance, days, months, years, and affectation of solar bodies. People refuse to own up to their inherent and innate creative and manifesting abilities. So we naively blame the heavens for our failures, and thank the heavens for our successes. Also, aspects of the self exist as collective states of consciousness. Think in terms of interlocking circles. One circle has one state of being that knows. Two circles have three states of being. Three circles have seven states of being. Four circles have thirteen states of being. The number of states composing interlocking circles continues as 21, 31, 43, and 57. The numeration making the self what it is in its entirety is: 1, 3, 7, 13, 21, 31, 43, and 57.

Humanity has allowed itself to remain duped by those who convince us we must rely on an outside source for everything that takes place in our life. Many believe God, life, and universe exist outside and beyond. The reverse is the truth and reality. Humanity fails to realize how the universe works when differing aspects work for a common goal.

God's will to be and know seeks to increase its mass and magnitude through cooperation. The only aspects of existence that increases are love and light. This is called the law of doubling. The numeration is 1, 2, 4, 8, 16, 32, 64, 128... This continues for each member added to the whole. The chart one can draw showing this as a graphic is by putting the sequential numbers above those that are doubled. Then one can see what the mass and magnitude of love and light are when there are thousands or millions of like-minded souls working towards the same goal, outcome, or state of existence (RA Material 1984).

The only states that exist in seventh density are collectives, because only these represent what the universe is as one collective. The Mayans came and left by materializing their humanity onto this planet, then dematerializing when their work was finished. Once the Mayan Calendars were in place, it was time for them to leave. When the Mayans entire culture was an art form it was time to leave, as that is the highest ideal attainable humanly. Collective ascension takes place when

God's will is lived as love, peace, and kindness socially, after people have resolved opposites in conflict into the harmony between what is and what is not.

People do not realize both positive and negative 'sources' entice people to fund them. People are naïve when it comes to service polarity and what it is actually seeking to accomplish through agreement. Hierarchy works to enslave, go to war, and glorify greed. Those who live according to the 'Law of One' know equality between all forms of existence, and working towards educating people into what truly is and works eternally. Coupled with this are those embodied qualities that ensure peace and harmony exists between people.

By 2012, this planet will return to its garden state again. This means and requires everyone wishing to remain to become integral in his or her faith, desire, and intention. This is why the Mayan Calendars foretell of the end times. The entire fiction and process of self-service and its war, greed, and slavery will become extinct by 2012.

According to the Mayan Calendars, that which disseminated the propaganda of hierarchy returns for those who subscribe and perpetuate war, greed, and slavery. According to Ramtha, Jehovah of the Old Testament, and Id, the father of man, will battle one last time in the heavens. I believe they will begin this on December 14, 2012, and finish on the Winter Solstice, December 21, 2012. At this time, everything contrary to God, life, humanness, and serving others will be torn asunder. The sources used to perpetuate war, greed, and slavery will cease to exist as viable forms of energy. They will cease to be involved with our continued evolution (The Mayan Calendars depict Jehovah as the serpent, so does the Revelation of John in the Bible).

Then life continues on with those who live life according to God's will, love, and light fully conscious of the universe as the self.

The numeration of the Mayan Calendars is one equals the realness of God. Two equals the basic structure of the universe as a binary vibrancy. Four equals the basic self as mind, body, spirit, and soul. Seven equals the chakras which correspond to the seven densities composing the universe (These can be thought of as is-ness/nothingness, realness/illusion, pattern/chaos, content/emptiness, truth/erroneousness, I am-ness/I-am-not-ness, and specific-ness/universality).

Thirteen equals the number of entities composing the creator of humanity. Twenty equals the number of entities composing the father of humanity.

All heavenly involvement are the relationships that correspond to our life and the 'culture' our soul belongs to. These become more real and true through evolution. Evolution is the development of an ideal as it grows. Growth is evolving from one state of existence into another. Ascension is limitation outgrown.

We only confuse ourselves when we attribute power to that which shows us whom we are, what we are doing, and where we are going, from our points of beginning. God became you and you become from what you apply.

God is the originator of the entire creation. Yahweh and Id refined this into us. We refine it into our ideals of intention. The entire process then collectively ascends into the universe as an ongoing servant that assists the universe in its journey back to God. The Mayan Calendars show us this through pictures. This artwork also shows us what the journey actually entails as an adventure in consciousness.

The Mayan Calendars also show us how movement works harmoniously, as an artistry that contributes and enhances oneness. The Mayan Calendars show us how the creation works, what is involved, and what these become socially and eternally.

Collective ascension requires each of us resolving differences into an integrated synthesis, based on connection and integration, establishing a community involving God, life, people, planet, and universe. These are us as the five senses.

Appendix G
Enlightenment, What is it and What Does it Mean?

Enlightenment, What is it and What Does it Mean?

Enlightenment is an experiential awareness and realization that assists the seeker in depth of being and scope of knowing. It means "in light of." Enlightenment is the sudden realization that a given truth is real for the seeker. Enlightenment puts an idea in a context that is both personal and relevant. There are many different types of enlightenment.

Fundamental to becoming aware of something, one is wise to focus on an idea or ideal until the experience of it comes. This begins the journey and process of the path. It allows the seeker experiential realness involving a state of being, and how it pertains to the self, and the importance it plays in the ongoing-ness of one's experience.

There are two primary aspects to enlightenment, being and knowing. These can be thought of as the being-ness of God and the knowing-ness of the universe, unified into a single state called the self.

A common mistake made by many is, thinking realization of something, as a state of consciousness, is 'it.' This is never the case. Another common mistake is, the assumption a given realization only pertains to the self and nothing else or to God and nothing else. This is impossible, due to all aspects of the creation are being involved with and pertaining to everything else. Another common mistake is, everyone is unique, so no two people have the same identical experience. The path is being real, and knowing what is true, leading to purpose and content of character.

The curious nature of enlightenment is that it comes and goes quickly, lasting only a few seconds. Enlightenment is a profound insight into the nature of the self that sheds light upon a desire or interest. Those who feel their experience is 'it' might have a prolonged realization lasting minutes, hours, days, weeks, months, even years. Enlightenment means understanding and knowing what an insight is and how it pertains to the self. It also means one is being and knowing from a state that touches and encompasses depth and scope.

People, in all walks of life, experience differing types of enlightenment. These types of experiences can take place anywhere. The assumption one must remove themselves from society and live an isolated life in places, like a monastery or cave is erroneous. The existence of a given truth or reality is inherent, and by going within, one will discover whatever one's faith is centered upon.

Nuance is a curious quality. It gives variation to truth, and individualizes reality into something unique, due to the role and nature of the universe. The universe is a state that makes God infinite, and no two aspects of it are identical, ever. The notion two or more people must attain, realize, or be aware of the same idea, state, or ideal is foolish and ill-advised. Movement prevents repetition. It is only stuck-ness and bias that recreates a given state over, and over, and over again.

Enlightenment is open-ended. Key realizations begin the journey of self-discovery and purposefulness. Pre-requisite experiences come until one is ready to embrace and comprehend. Sudden enlightenment is a gradual process. Touching on what an idea or quality is and means requires discipline, diligence, determination, and patience.

Enlightenment is the understanding of what an idea is, how it works, and what a given quality feels like. There are degrees to enlightenment, and some realizations can be very profound.

There are traps to be aware of; one is attachment and another is importance. Enlightenment usually only has relevance to the individual. Anyone lacking similar experience will not grasp or comprehend what took place and what's involved. Explanation at times is pointless.

No two people are identical, so no two people will have the identical experience of a given feeling, or thought, or vision. Each person seeking insight into something will have a differing experience of what is focused on. Each of us individualizes God and universe as a unique state of existence. This is disconcerting for anyone seeking something to be 'it.' Conformity is a form of confusion.

People are wise to be aware that there is nothing to get. Life is not figuring out and explaining movement, composition, or placement.

All work in consciousness is is understanding what works as an applied truth, creating an ideal that is ongoing, and making it an existence of some kind. This requires being love and knowing light consciously, that one willingly creates experience through intention and desire.

Enlightenment works in two specific ways. Knowing what a given quality is, like love or light, and how it works as a sequence. Nothing exists in and of itself and independent from anything else. Everything is interconnected. Everything is sequenced with other qualities and aspects. Nothing works or exists in isolation. The entire universe is the relationships between an ideal and as a community. Symbols represent willed intention. Every aspect of the creation is a combining of many differing elements existing as a unified symbol, stating the existence of as that. A given symbol involves the relationships between all aspects composing it, and all aspects composing the entire creation.

Enlightenment is often confused with taking one aspect and denying all others. One can intune to an endless array of differing states of consciousness, and declare each one 'it' when one is conscious of such. This is like deciding one aspect of the environment is 'it' and everything else false or an illusion.

Enlightenment only means one is aware of a reality or truth as a state of being. Tradition hinders and prevents depth and scope due to conformity and predetermined stipulations that are 'it' now, then, and to come.

Truth, reality, and consciousness are open-ended. Any form of enlightenment requires growth. This allows the seeker and insights the ability to become truer, more real, and more conscious. People make the mistake of thinking only and strictly in terms of their truth and reality.

Enlightenment requires embracing and owning without having prejudices or preconceived notions about "the way it is." Coupled with this is, actualizing acceptance, responsibility, purposefulness, and even-minded-ness. Enlightenment encompasses feeling, sensing, thinking, and envisioning simultaneously. Another trap to be wary of is being too specific about what enlightenment is and entails. The entire universe is a medium of what is and what is not. Everything composing the universe has an exact opposite, even God. Those who claim otherwise have not experienced God within as it exists. Not surprising as only a few people have in 75,000 years.

Any form of enlightenment has an application. This is the purpose it serves and why it exists. Attainment is pointless lacking application. Being and knowing unify into application that evolves. This is the ongoing-ness or continuousness of application. This can also be thought of as the becoming-ness of a given truth's reality. Sharing is a form of application. The path is how conscious one is, and how effective he or she is in his or her creativity.

Application arises from the union of being and knowing as understanding. Personal bias prevents people from truly becoming enlightened, and understanding what purposefulness is. To such an extent, most of the creation remains unknown and non-existent to the self as the self.

I will share some of my enlightening experiences.

Back in the early 1980's, I asked myself what was the constancy of change? I had pondered this for about a year. One afternoon in the Santa Cruz Mountains I was sitting next to an almost dry creek bed surrounded by lots and lots of trees, and as I was observing both the change and constancy of this particular environment, the realization came answering my question. Certainty is the constancy of change. I have since added the question: Of what can one be certain?

I had the opportunity in 1986 of going to Taiwan for 18 days. One afternoon Prof. Chu and I went to Wang, Yang-ming Park for a walking meditation. During our visit, we walked to a waterfall that fell several hundred feet. We were both standing on a bridge at about the mid-point of the falls watching the water's continuous flow. As I stood there watching, I realized that when a given aspect of life serves its purpose, it always returns to that which gave rise to it (Ascension is the returning to what originated us after we have served our purpose for being human).

In November of 1992, I was waiting for my ride to pick me up in Craig, Colorado, and drive me to work in Steamboat Springs, 42 miles due East. It was 5:00 a.m., thirty degrees, with a slight breeze, and a clear view of the heavens. I realized from this that one only observes what is inherent. That any idea we feel or think is within us.

I was sitting on the San Francisco coast meditating upon what was 'the' truth. When I returned to normal consciousness I was asked by a 'voice,' what in my immediate environment was 'the' truth? I began looking around. The 'voice' continued, explaining that if I made the rock 'the' truth everything not the rock was automatically excluded from the truth I had decided upon. The 'voice' went on with this analogy with twenty different aspects of the surrounding area. I realized immediately the insight just shared with me, and was devastated. And I knew right then, right there 'the' truth does not exist. I have come to realize truth is the premise or principle, defining and describing a given state of existence as a specific reality. Truth establishes the reality of as a state that exists, experiences, and creates its identity and ideal.

I am walking through the flat I grew up in and lived for eleven years in the Richmond district of San Francisco, California, for the last time. When I entered the living room I experienced a four-fold realization that was felt, sensed, thought, and visualized simultaneously. This interesting form of enlightenment was that God's will to be and know extends and expands by inversely reversing into a focused becoming. That was it, lasting all of two seconds (It took me twelve years to put into words what inverse reversal is and does). Inverse reversal is binary vibrancy. We experience and express this on four primary, seven secondary, nine tertiary, and fifty-six complimentary levels within a medium that is infinite. The scope of this is vast. I won't go into all the levels in this appendix. The four primary ones are our heartbeat, breathing, waking and sleeping, and incarnation and ascension.

I am sitting on a rocky cliff face bordering one side of China Beach in San Francisco, California, in the afternoon one Summer in the mid 80's. It was a beautiful clear day. My eyes were closed, and I was focusing on my breathing. I began thinking about the nature of light. Suddenly my entire being was pure white light. My arms flew up into a cross position and my body began to undulate. The only thing as my existence in that moment was this white light. This lasted for eleven seconds.

I returned to normal consciousness, and as I walked away I knew the being-ness of light.

I am on a swing swinging back and forth, up and down, in Sacajawea Park in Livingston, Montana. It was a cool and clear August day with a strong wind. As I was swinging observing the Yellowstone River and the surrounding park, woods, and mountains, I suddenly experienced everything as an aspect of myself. Everything outside of myself is part of myself, and my identity is the oneness of all that is environmentally and universally. I am the being-ness of observation, showing me that everything is an aspect of who and what I am. I am the sand, grass, bushes, trees, bugs, birds, wildlife, all of humanity, the whole planet, and the entire universe, all existing as the realness of God made manifest. These are what I identify.

I am sitting in my arm chair meditating on God as my existence, as my I am-ness. I behold a vision of the universe instilling a knowing that it is one state giving God I am-ness; that the entire universe is a unified state of being. I 'knew' in that moment the oneness of the creation as a single state giving God its I am-ness.

I am sitting in my arm chair in Rome, Georgia, meditating on joy, love, light, and consciousness. As I think about joy, it fills my heart. When I thought about love, it fills my body and surrounds my joy-filled heart. When I thought of light, it fills my head surrounding joy and love. When I thought of consciousness, I see the universe surrounding my joy-filled heart, my love-filled body, and my light-filled head.

I am standing observing the sun, earth, and moon one afternoon and realize the sun is my mind, the earth my body, and the moon my spirit.

I am sitting against a tree stump in Colorado at the base of Mt. Elbert. As I sit quietly, I become peace, serenity, tranquility, and harmony. I know that these are the states life exists as. This experience was very profound.

I am wondering about my life humanly, and I realize it centers upon and evolves through feeling, sensing, thinking, and envisioning through my faith, desire, and intention.

I am walking to the store and realize there is only now here as my being and knowing, and that I only remember, actualize, and become conscious of God, life, and the universe. That now is my being-ness and here my knowing-ness that I share with all else in ways positive, neutral, and negative.

I am meditating upon the nature of the self, and I behold myself as the will of God, the love of the creator, and the light of the father as the ensoulment of all that is.

I have always had an interest in God's originality. This desire of mine arose out of an insight I deduced. If something exists as something, then something gave rise to it. The question I asked myself was: What gave rise to the universe? The answer is God. God manifested the universe as a self-created ideal allowing God to state I am. As I spent my time meditating upon this and pondering this year, after year, after year, the realization came to me, knowing that God's originality is a state I call all encompassing, and it is this that surrounds the universe. This state is uniform, constant, and unchanging. What I saw as a vision was the all encompassing-ness of God, surrounding the universe that is the ensoulment of God. The universe is the soul of God. In the beginning, the universe was a 'space' opened within God's all encompassing-ness. God began filling this 'space,' which is an exact opposite of all encompassing-ness, by incarnating into it as individualized states of pure being. This was God willing itself into smaller versions of itself that began as an idea that became distorted, refined, and crystallized. These evolved into everything composing the universe through willed intention desiring to know what it would be like to exist as stars, planets, galaxies, and all other forms composing the universe. Movement is the experiential and expressive journey of God back into its all encompassing-ness over time through space. To do this, all aspects of the universe must grasp they are states of being that know itself as God and universe unified. This requires all aspects of the universe to be and know all and everything as a specific-ness and universality existing as a single state of consciousness. God incarnates into its own creations that ascend when all that is–is owned as an experienced expression.

Enlightenment is a never-ending process, journey, and path. Anything realized leads to deeper levels of being and vaster scopes of knowing, until one is effective and consistent in his or her applications of will, love, and light, adding to God's I am-ness. Life as truth is not passive. It is active, applying, seeking, understanding, and contributory.

I am watching the movie 'The Little Black Book' in Rome, Georgia, at the Martha Berry Cinemas along Hwy. 27. About two-thirds of the way through the movie I have a vision showing me God's originality centered within my heart surrounded by a state that is the exact opposite of this. What I 'see' within is a microscopic sized 'sun' that is porous, bronze, and in a state of complete and total rest surrounded by a blackness, the absence of anything and everything, and is the beginning state of the universe before it became stars, planets, galaxies, or life forms. This is the first state of existence centered within all aspects composing the universe. God's all encompassing-ness rests within what's individualized, surrounded by a state that is its exact opposite. God then willed to be and know all that is that we observe as each other, life, this planet, and the entire universe.

What came with this experiential observation is knowing everything, even God has an exact opposite within the universe. God's realness is centered within the heart. When viewed from outside within the self is seen as a small 'sun' surrounded by a black absence. When the seeker intunes into this small 'sun,' what is experienced is all encompassing-ness. The universe makes this infinite, eternal, complete, and total in and of itself as an individuality. In dividing you have the reality known as the universe. Lacking the state that is the exact opposite of God's all encompassing-ness, God could not and would not exist as something individual, unique, and evolving. The universe is the triunity of God, as it is this that God and God's opposite became. God is all encompassing, while the universe is infinite. God and universe are a binary vibrancy. All encompassing-ness inversely reversed into all that is. This is the pulse of God we enjoy as our heartbeat, love as our breathing, light as our waking and sleeping, and consciousness that incarnated then ascends back into God's realness gifting that with all the experiences embraced.

Enlightenment reveals to us insights that expands our awareness, and moves us from the fictions of untruth.

I caution the reader on always relying on and following the dictates of outer-based sources such as books, teachers, teaching aids, or gurus. These are only needed and necessary until one is willing to finally go it alone to discover the self, let it go, and move into one's purpose for being and knowing. Given the uniqueness of each of us, this differs for everyone. Follow another until you are faithful enough, disciplined enough, and courageous enough to go it alone and finally find out the you of you.

I have discovered we are always and forever, being/knowing, learning/teaching, doing/becoming, and actualizing/demonstrating creativity manifesting our experiential expressions. This extends and expands God's will to be and know love and light consciously through faith, desire, and intention on and in levels that are personal, relational, social, global, and universal.

Enlightenment begins, ends, and continues endlessly. Enlightenment is arriving at a big sign that states: Welcome, good achievement, you are now accomplished in this awareness. After the celebration ends and we get bored with our newfound awareness we become restless and begin to stumble away unsure of what's next for us. We become confused and afraid and looking back for some reassurance we read the back of the sign. It reads: Now get going, you have work to do. Stop relying upon 'this' as 'it.' Your journey as your path is endless.

Enlightenment gives clarity to questions we have through experiences, answering for us what we did not understand being-wise as a form of personal knowing-ness. The beginning of it all started with this question God asked: What am I? The enlightenment that came to God as an answer was I am all that is willed from a state that is all encompassing.

As each of seeks to be and know, the answers come to us as God and universe unified into a single ideal we think of and know as human. Enlightenment is piercing the veil by becoming conscious of whom we are, and what we are as a state that is eternal, specific, and unique. Enlightenment is the 'knowing' that suddenly presents itself to our awareness clueing us to what a given feeling or thought is and what's involved with it as our humanity. Enlightenment is a form of resolution of paradox into understanding and wisdom. Enlightenment is pieces fitting together into a puzzle, picturing for us the natures of God, life, self, and all else as a connected and integrated union of oneness we are as a state of consciousness. Enlightenment is the union of awareness and understanding existing as an individualized ideal that seeks to be and know what's real and true as meaning and purpose that never ceases to evolve. Enlightenment is entering into and out of experience quickly, without becoming attached or addicted to what is embraced. Enlightenment is the clarity that dispels illusions of confusions that hinders and hampers growth and personal well being. It also reveals depth of being and scope of knowing, until nothing is hidden or unknown as the self.

Appendix H
God and Universe as the Self

God and Universe as the Self

It is interesting putting into words experience that encompasses great truth. The gist of experience is depth of being and scope of knowing touching upon God and universe, as these exist perpetually and personally. The average person never touches on these as his or her personal experience. Few humans in the last 75,000 years have touched on and lived God's originality as their humanness. This requires knowing the universe as that which compliments God. Experience is sometimes accompanied with a vision. I recently had such an experience on a very profound level. It's difficult to define using words that confine it, they do not explain it very well. However, I'll attempt to explain what my experience entailed as a realization.

The gist of my vision was a four-part portrayal consisting of God, God individualized, the universe, and this individualized.

Centered within the self is God's original state that remains unchanging forever, as it is all encompassing by nature and design, yet very, very small, like a drop of the ocean. This core self becomes the embodiment that surrounds God on seven levels. These seven levels are like rings, or globes, each having an exact opposite. There is God that is surrounded by an exact opposite. The heart surrounds both of these; that in turn are surrounded by its exact opposite. The torso surrounds all of these; that are surrounded by its exact opposite. Four other states exist that are also the existence of surrounded by an exact opposite. The last state is the universe that is surrounded by its exact opposite; that is the all encompassing-ness of God.

God dwells within the center of our being, within the heart. This becomes the embodiment of something and everything, composing the universe is a version of this. The natural tendency of embodiment is rest, because God's realness within remains in a state of rest forever. God is forever unchanging as a state of rest.

When the universe becomes something specific, it exists as that which is spiritual. God is the embodiment of and the universe is spirituality, unified into expressions filling space for a duration of time, giving both an experience that is specific, rather than all encompassing and infinite. Spirituality brings to life God's embodiment. This makes everything throughout the creation a binary vibrancy. God becomes specific and the universe becomes particular. All encompassing-ness becomes an embodiment of some kind that gives content to and identifies God as something specific, giving identity to the spirit that makes it something particular. The spirit animates, brings to life, what God becomes as an embodiment, thereby giving this the ability to move and act independently within a state that is one reality. The universe, as a single state of existence, is the soul of God. How soul and spirit differ is that the soul is universal, while the spirit is specific. The spirit assumes the identity of what it brings to life.

God and universe is a tandem as are embodiment and spirituality; what we feel is our embodiment, and what we think is our spirituality. Love is God's embodiment as something specific. Light is the universe as something identifiable. Joy and love exist because these correspond to God's all encompassing-ness on and as a specific level of being that knows. God's originality becomes joy, love, light, and consciousness demonstrating God's all encompassing-ness as something specific.

Embodiment and spirituality evolve through intentional purposefulness, by our willingness to be and know experiences that express truth, defining one's reality. This is true for the entire creation that is in a continuous process, or journey, of becoming conscious and returning to what gave rise to its existence.

Meditation assists the seeker in depth of being and scope of knowing. Depth is entering into God and experiencing all encompassing-ness. Scope is becoming conscious of all that is as a state of knowing. Embodiment and spirituality are the individuations of all encompassing-ness, or God and all that is, or universe into and as specific ideals existing as the one unified state we live as humans.

God individualized is our embodiment. The universe's individuality is our spirituality. Embodiment allows us depth of being and spirituality allows us scope of knowing. This is being God and knowing the universe as the self, as the human portrayal of God and universe existing as what each of us experiences and expresses day by day. Becoming conscious of this is our purpose, serving the entire creation for the sake of assisting in evolving beyond limitations and shortsightedness, moving beyond stuck-ness, attachment, and denial.

God's individuality becomes our embodiment. God's realness remains as-is, as and in a state of perpetual rest centered within us. The universe's individuality becomes our spirituality that animates by bringing to life God's embodiment, so that it can evolve back into itself over time through space. Movement as change only exists because of God's incarnation desiring to ascend back into its originality. Change is the growth of an ideal through experiential embracement, evolving until God as universe reintegrates into all encompassing-ness.

The universe is continual and perpetual movement, while God is a state of permanent and perpetual rest. This establishes binary vibrancy, or what I term inverse reversal.

Embodiment establishes God's I am-ness. Spirituality brings this to life, so that God can act and move as something individual and independent. Spirituality identifies what is as something specific.

Everything existing within the universe has an exact opposite, even God. God's originality centered within is surrounded by a state that is the exact opposite of all encompassing-ness. It is a state that is the absence of anything. This allows God to exist within the creation as an individualized version of itself. This can be thought of as a piece of God leaving its reality, entering into what makes the universe infinite, while remaining what it is within a state that it is not. These not God states are the embodiment of God, and the spirituality of the universe existing as one state. An exact opposite is needed for anything to exist as an individuality that lives and moves independently. Joy is individualized through pain, love through fear, light through darkness, and the positive through the negative (God tells Neale, in "Conversations with God," "In the absence of that which is not, that which is, is not").

The realness of God is only seen, recognized, experienced, and entered into when it is grasped and understood as what it is. One must have a working knowledge of God to become conscious of such as a state of being that knows. One becomes God as a human portrayal within the ensoulment of all that is.

Spirituality is the universe individualized; as us it is our head. When seen as a purity is light uncolored. The process light evolves into and through is purity, distortion, refinement, and crystalization.

Embodiment is God individualized. As us it is our body, when felt is known as a radiance of love. The process of love evolves through radiance, absorption, illumination, and encompassment. The heart is the mind of God and is felt as joyousness. The mind of God, coupled with the embodiment of life, establishes the relationship between what God is and what God is not. We either feel joy and love, or pain and fear. Pain and fear eventually die, whereas joy and love eventually ascend into the universe, then into God's all encompassing-ness gifting this with experience owned.

The Trappings of Fixation
Leading to Spiritual Entropy
and Evolutionary Death

Appendix I

The Trappings of Fixation Leading to Spiritual Entropy and Evolutionary Death

I remember quite vividly the remark Seth made about ideas like bliss, nirvana, and perfection–to run from them as quickly and as far as possible. I was curious as to why, given I was looking for 'that' truth that was 'it.' Also, I held the naïve notion of finding an ideal state of being.

Every culture has its ideal aspired to. Every tradition has an ideal followers aspire to attain. Everyone has something they aspire to in life. Endless the array of aspirations worked for and attained. Many make the common mistake of assuming their ideal is 'it.'

The guru has his bliss consciousness. The monk has his nirvana. The Christian has his perfection. The list is endless as to who aspires to attain an ideal considered 'it,' and rather curious to me, given the nature and role of infinity. There is also the odd notion perfection is 'it' and possible to attain.

People 'suffer' from an either/or mindset, insisting half of existence is real and true, while the other half is an illusion. This creates comedy and tragedy for most. Such is the folly of people stuck upon individuality as 'it.'

Attainment of any 'it' is the entropy and death of one's evolution. This prevents continual development, which is all and only what evolution is and does. Depth of being and scope of knowing is always available to be and know consciously. The truth is, there is always more to the self than we realize. Depth eventually leads to being God and scope to knowing all that is, the entire universe, as a single state we humanize. To assume there is a single state attainable stems from one's individuality failing to grasp what infinity is and does for God's will to be and know.

Illusion is the flip side of reality. Infinity is God; manifested in an endless array of ideals existing within a single medium called the universe, a dance of essence, intention, and developmental outcomes. 'It' is impossible in a medium that is infinite. There will always be deeper states of consciousness to realize and understand. This is the way of the universe as it becomes aware of itself through us.

Hinduism is partially correct, as is Buddhism, Christianity, Islam, and any other systems theory. It is impossible for one aspect of the universe to be and know it all, even though each aspect composing the universe is all that is. Paradox exists with every aspect of the universe.

Everything in existence actualizes a certain truth, demonstrating a given reality or realness. One can move his or her awareness from one state of being into another. This is all and only what evolution is and does. It changes itself into differing states of consciousness at will. We assume this change is birth and death, the entering into and exiting out of states of consciousness we think of as being human.

God's will to be and know ensures there is never a time 'it' is 'it' as a state of conscious awareness, or the existence of God as an absolute aspect of creation. Those who think God 'only' allows itself certain states of existence only fool themselves, for everything is an aspect and quality of God. There is nothing God does not allow itself to become. Isolation, exclusion, negation, and aversion are the downfall of every monk, guru, mystic, and seeker. God allows everything to exist as-is.

The attainment of 'it' only means one's evolution has stopped. Entropy sets in, then one's realness as 'it' becomes unviable, and one's reality as 'that' ceases to exist. Almost every guru, monk, and mystic returns; not having gotten it. This is due specifically to making one state of consciousness 'it' and then rejecting all other states, saying they are illusions.

Eternity is and means no end, ongoing-ness, continuation, and becoming-ness.

Few people know God's realness centered within their heart. Few people know what the universe becomes as a specific ideal. Few people allow themselves to be God and know the universe as their self. Notice how everything as an 'it' changes into something 'it' is not over time and through space.

Who dares to state only one aspect of God is 'it' and all else nothingness, illusion, chaos, or void? If one fails to see God as everything, they do not know God's all encompassing-ness that made the universe a compliment and companion to such.

I have found depth deepens and scope widens the horizons of being and knowing God and universe as the self. There is always more to be and something else to know. What is it to be and know God, life, humanness, and the universe through service, likewise any quality as an experience? One aspect of humanness is being what is felt, knowing what is thought, and then sharing these with others assisting them on their path.

God becomes all that is, that in turn becomes God; this is the path and journey of consciousness.

To state 'this' is 'it' only shows and means one has missed the point entirely of what God is as the entire creation.

Notice also, that one moves his or her awareness from the specific into states that are more encompassing. Ultimately, one will enter into a state that is all encompassing as God, and from here become aware of another state that is infinite as the universe, from a state that is both simultaneously. If one takes into consideration that everything is an aspect and quality of God within the medium of the universe, he or she will understand from this function and purpose.

I find it curious that people speak of love, but fail to mention light. Also odd, people do not discuss or teach what God's will is and what it does. This is due to people not knowing extension and expansion of consciousness through connection and integration.

If someone is going to mention the idea of oneness, they must factor into that truth male and female or yin and yang. How does one resolve oneness and infinity, or presence and absence, or is-ness and nothingness, or realness and illusion, or pattern and chaos, or content and void, or truth and erroneousness, or universality and specific-ness, or constancy and change, or being and knowing, or connection and integration?

Then we enter into another arena where one state gives rise to a second state, that gives rise to a third state, that gives rise to a fourth state, that in turn gives rise to secondary states. Example: will, love, light, and consciousness. These unify into joy, peace, and freedom. These unify into harmony and adventure. These unify into creativity within the artistry of oneness.

Then there are those states composed of joy and pain, love and fear, light and dark, and positive and negative. These are what allow individuation to exist. There are also infinity, eternity, completeness, and totality to contend with. Then one notices their heartbeat, then breathing, then waking and sleeping, and then incarnation and ascension. Then one notices feeling, then sensing, then thinking, then envisioning an ideal of some kind. Then one notices feeling an emotion of some kind, leading to a thought that one acts upon. Then one feels one type of emotion one moment, and then another later on, and then another later on, and then another later on. Then one feels angry, then happy, then sad, and then joyous. Then there are what we experience and express, what creates them, and what purpose they serve. Then there is the personal, the relational, the social, the global, and the universal. I'll stop before you lose your mind.

There are endless addressments that we embrace through experience, only to find something else comes along and then something else eternally. God and universe are more than we take into consideration humanly. All encompassing-ness and universality are difficult to embrace from our human perspective. This is due in part to those limitations we place upon what it is to be and know humanly, and also due in part to those who seek to keep us in the dark about being something real and knowing something true by keeping us steeped in fear and denial. God is never an 'it' as an absolute. God is all that is as that which is infinite, eternal, complete, and total as anything existent within the universe. Limitations are the only ends that end or die. Any time we decide upon an 'it' of some kind it will die giving birth to something truer and more encompassing of what is. People die because of not becoming aware consciously of what the self is in its entirety. They die because they decide an aspect of the self is 'it' rather than just part of being human. How does an 'it' take into consideration everything it is not and the uniqueness factor of everyone? This is impossible. The notion of an 'it' stems from denial leading the denier to seek for what is not denied. The problem pursuant from this is denial cannot discover anything real or true that exists. Given what's denied is the self as God and universe.

It is our idea about the self that dies never being real. Love is our reality that never dies. Light is our truth that never ceases to exist as our identity. God's will to be love and know light consciously is the path. Love and light are then shared with others as a state of consciousness existing as a form of I am-ness. I am-ness is never an absolute of some kind. Everything is an aspect of and quality of a greater whole. The entire universe is an aspect and quality of God's all encompassing-ness.

The path or journey back into God's all encompassing-ness is through making a contribution of some kind to it. Not as an absolute, but as a gracious and kind bestower of some kind.

Appendix J
My Life is Simply the Game of Connecting Dot-To-Dots

My Life is Simply the Game
of Connecting Dot-to-Dots

Dot One. I am watching the pilot for the television series Star Trek in 1963. I am fascinated by what I watch each week while the series lasted. I begin to wonder about aliens.

Dot Two. Ah,yes...I am reminiscing about the movie 'Close Encounters of the Third Kind.' I liked it, and have watched it several times. My favorite scene is Richard Dreyfuss recreating the rock formation where everyone is suppose to meet the U.F.O.

Dot Three. Nora, Cindy, and I are driving South from Livingston, Montana to Eagle, Colorado through Wyoming. It is 9:00 p.m. and pitch black. The Grand Teton Mountains are to our left. We are cruising along in a blue 1976 Ford LTD station wagon with a 400 motor. Nora is driving. Cindy is in the back seat entertaining herself. I am seated next to Nora. Time passes as we mosey along.

I happen to glance to my left and notice gliding along the crest-line of the Grand Tetons a large and luminous U.F.O. There is no mistaking what it is. It is huge given the miles between us and it. We are at least three miles away, and it is three feet long, two feet wide, and a foot tall. It is flat on the bottom, curved on the ends, like half circles, and has an elevated upper surface. It traveled in the opposite direction we did.

Nora becomes terrified and mashes the gas, accelerating our speed to over 90 mph. We are now racing down the road. I want to stop and take some photos. Nora babbles incoherently. I try to take some photos through the windows, but only got reflected flashes.

This is a first for me, seeing an actual Unidentified Flying Object. I do not have a problem about them. I am fairly certain trillions exist throughout the universe. I am fairly certain many have come leaving their cultural reminders in various places, like Egypt, Central America, Easter Island, and most other land masses.

Cindy does something interesting to me. She immediately closes her eyes and puts a finger from each hand on her temples and goes into a trance state. This lasts until the U.F.O disappears. Life and our speed return to normal. I am still upset at Nora for refusing to stop, so I could take some pictures.

We are back to traveling along at 60 m.p.h. Nora is now calm and I am still annoyed. Cindy is attentive. Nora asks her daughter, what she was doing while the U.F.O was in view. Cindy replies she was communicating with the U.F.O. Nora asks what their dialogue was. Cindy replies that 'they' told her 'they' were here for her, but not right now. Cindy adds she belongs with them and one day in the future will rejoin them.

Dot Four. I am dreaming a very vivid dream. I am with a woman I love. We are soul mates. A large U.F.O appears and we run for our lives. The U.F.O hovers above people and they begin dropping dead. The U.F.O hovers above a three-story house and lowers itself busting through the roof. All the people in and around the house fall down dead. The U.F.O moves on until it is gone. My mate and I are terrified, glad to be alive, and confused as to what we just observed. I wake up in a cold sweat. This dream took place over a decade ago.

Dot Five. Many people have speculated about the harvesting of souls from this planet. Some believe it will only be true Christians practicing the correct faith. Others believe it will be a certain, or select few. Some are convinced it will only be 144,000. And on it goes as to who and why. I am fairly certain only those who serve will be harvested. There are two types of service, self and others. Those who serve themselves are harvested and removed to that place that corresponds to their negative biasing (RA Material 1984). This planet is returning to existing as a positively polarized state preventing selfishness from continuing their warring, greedy, and enslaving ways. This will happen when the planet changes its polarity from negative to positive (John White, Pole Shift). Humanity will experience this as earth changes. Those who serve others are harvested and 'left behind' to continue the evolution of humanity until it collectively ascends. Those not harvested will repeat third density upon another planet (RA Material 1984). If people remember where their soul comes from and whom they belong to, they will return home with them when the time is right.

Dot Six.   Back in the early 80's I happened upon a book written by Robert Monroe. The book is titled: "Journeys Out of The Body" published in 1971. The book tells the story of Robert doing spontaneous out-of-body experiences beginning in 1959. This was a process of self-discovery for him.   He wrote two other books: "Far Journeys" in 1982 and "Ultimate Journey" in 1994. He is now dead. He began a process of studying and recorded what he found. He created the Monroe Institute in Farber, Virginia. He posited that everyone can do conscious out-of-body experiences, and needs to do them to evolve. He stated that everyone leaves his or her body during sleep. He felt this was a type of conscious awareness allowing people to remember where they are from and 'what' they belong to. Few people today do conscious out-of-body experiences.

Dot Seven.   Christianity teaches an interesting idea, the rapture. This notion is people disappearing at some point. This is shown in the movie 'Left Behind.' Those who are saved will be taken and those who are 'left behind' will face seven years of trials and tribulation according to traditional Christianity. The fact is people only disappear when they ascend by taking their body with them when they go. The body is left behind by anyone who dies. The soul is that aspect of the self that leaves upon death.   Those who know their own soul will return to that culture they belong to universally.

Connecting dot-to-dots is all we do as our manifested created intention through our faith and desire. This is our determining meaning, value, and purpose of what is as and according to our reality and truth.   Our entire notion of being and knowing is composed of meanings we give, as the values we hold that serve the purpose they do making us feel, think, and act as and what we are and do.   Everyone assumes life, truth, and God are as they are according to what each of us decides is so about them.   The irony is no two people are the same, so no two people perceive or experience these in the same manner or way.   This is what makes all aspects of creation unique, and each views and involves itself with God, life, and truth in a unique way.

Connecting dots simplifies the overview one has about anything and everything. It's our way of saying through experience a + b = c. Few question outer-based sources, so much of what's stated stands pat and remaining unchanged year after year. One purpose life serves is that we get to choose what reality is and what truth is, making these uniquely personal for each of us. Each of us decides what God is and does, what the universe is and does, what life is and does, and what we are and do. Agreed upon ideas create social consciousness and collective experience. Experience validates and reinforces ideas and ideals held through conviction. Social conviction teaches us we belong to a collective of some kind. Understanding diversity is a key to wisdom. Acceptance of diversity, beginning with one self, is the beginning of truly loving.

Dots are pieces of a puzzle we put together through experience and understanding. Eventually all the pieces fit and make sense to us, forming a mosaic or a personal mural or collage. Some do such an outstanding job of connecting their dots they are considered saints, mystics, or masters of some kind, leaving historical footprints followers aspire to. The oxymoron is everyone is unique, and no two people walk or live the same path, live the same truth, or embrace reality in the same manner or way, and God refuses to do instant replay, ever.

This is no different than what Mr. Brown did with his book, The Da Vinci Code. Everyone uses information, like clues, to piece together an ideology lived as her or his personal reality. Reality and truth are self-defined and based on experience.

This particular dot-to-dot has to do with people who belong to 'cultures' existing elsewhere living as humans. There are millions of U.F.O's waiting for the quarantine to be lifted so 'they' can retrieve those souls who belong to them (According to the RA Material, this planet is under quarantine by a council of nine on Saturn). As I understand it, this quarantine will be lifted next year in 2008. People need to know what 'group' they belong to and meet them where 'they' are going to pick them up. Out-of-body experiences are essential for this, as people will leave their bodies behind (as the body is specific to this planet). There will come the day when people from all over will get the urge to go to a certain place. Then the U.F.O of that group will meet them there. To the outside observer, this will look like the U.F.O is killing people because the soul housed within the body is taken and the body is 'left behind,' as it is not longer needed.

It is important for people to understand this now and prepare for this as billions will leave with the millions who have come for them. Many people have the urge to go to specific places they consider holy or spiritually significant due to this. It could very well be that place is their meeting place for 'their' true family.

This process will begin in the year 2008 when quarantine is finally lifted. Most of humanity will leave with 'those' who come for them. Everyone serves the purpose they do just by being and knowing then applying what one does for the entire creation.

People need to remember who and what they actually belong to and where that is. This is done through doing conscious out-of-body experiences. This is leaving the body consciously and returning to that place of origin one came from. Then one will know when and where they will leave from and with 'whom.'

Appendix K
Death is the Ego
Getting Even With Itself

Death is the Ego Getting Even With Itself

I have asked myself, "Why is it that people die?" The answer is, people deny their reality and truth as the image and likeness of God. Death is denial, and going elsewhere is projection. The ultimate cause of death is that individuality does not exist as an actuality. Death is also personal division through denial of what composes identity. Identity is light and one's spirituality. People reject knowing light as their identity. Coupled with light is love, as an embodied state lived as life. People deny and reject love, so it is replaced with fear; just as light denied is replaced by darkness. Also denied is the will of God existing as the mind, and the consciousness of all that is existing as an ensouled state. What ensues from this is, people live according to the dictates of an outer-based ideology, like family, tradition, culture, psychology, or the guru, or some master.

Denial leads to projection creating an outer-based sense of what is real and true. This leads to the beliefs that God, life, humanness, reality, truth, and the universe are 'out there' and are the basis for science, religion, philosophy, law, medicine, and all other institutions.

It is curious how people hold so strongly to their psychology as if it is 'it.' This leads to death. Death is the ego getting even with itself through fear, judgment, and persecution leading to all forms of self-sacrifice.

Death in any form is self-sacrifice. Self-sacrifice is how each of us commits suicide, necessitating the need to reincarnate. Reincarnation is to the soul what death is to the body. They are identical in context. People only reincarnate due to denial and projection. Death of the body equals reincarnation of the soul. The process or path of denial and projection are the beliefs one is born, crucified, dies, and then reincarnates. Death is denial of God, life, the Christ, serving others, oneness, healing, wholeness, and ascension. Death is the end result of individuality failing to embrace its collective nature, and some people have the attitude that being and knowing God personally is the greatest violation possible. Anyone who dares to live as God's will, love, light, and consciousness is isolated, excommunicated, ridiculed, ostracized, treated as crazy, tortured, and put to death. There are forms of expression in existence that deny God, and the universe is considered something to conquer, enslave, and destroy. Living as designed is considered a violation to his or her way of being. This attitude, this arrogance, prevents people from living their life as it is designed and intended to exist.

People are so afraid of being true to themselves they 'sell out' just to fit in, thinking that outer-based acceptance, recognition, and attention is the way it is. Few people have the courage to go it alone to discover what being God is and what knowing the universe is as the self. These require going within through meditation by faith, desire, and intention to embrace and own what God, life, identity, and the universe are as a unified singleness.

The Bible tells us we are the image and likeness of God, but few people actually believe that, so few people live life humanly as God and universe unified into a single state that shares. The best ideals people have come up with are worshipping false idols and graven images, coupled with the insistence the faithful must die before receiving their award. Those who die seek for a projected state called heaven. But we are all informed in the Bible: "As above, so below." Meaning, down here on earth is no different than up there in heaven.

The path delineates between going within and bringing to life God's realness centered within. Remaining focused outwardly upon the 'face' given God, one is fooled by outer-based ideologies convinced God is absent, nothing, illusion, chaos, void, and erroneousness stemming from something existing as an 'I-am-not-ness,' leading people to the grave as their 'reward' for denying themselves completely.

There is not a tradition on this planet that does not require fear, guilt, arrogance, and denial in order to work as an ideal. The basis for death is one must subscribe to an ideal that conquers, then enslaves, and then destroys what's created and then brought to life.

Life is the ongoing-ness of God as an ideal giving God experience. Death is the personal insistence that God and life are not real or true. The Old Testament instructs us about what living is like when it is based upon fear, judgment, and persecution as one's way of life. It's "against 'God's' law" to reframe from blind obedience, making the ultimate self-sacrifice by going to war, lusting for greed, and enslaving others through an ideology established making those covenanted 'God's' chosen ones. Dying is not living and death is not life. These are forms of insanity, a personal form of madness. It's like we are so attached and addicted to our personality that we choose to ignore anything other than this.

Vanity and self-glorification dooms us all. The ego is our false god, our personal graven image we seek others to worship and bow down to. Every culture existent on this planet pays homage to those who have supposedly made it traditionally. The over-emphasis on individuality ensures that nothing changes, and humanity now finds itself face-to-face with its own extinction.

People do a good job at making sure God as life as people remain non-existent. Few people have attained true God consciousness in 75,000 years. A few cultures have come and gone having attained the levels of awareness and realness necessary to ascend collectively. The Mayans were one such culture.

People choose death, not life, due to believing in fictions about what is real and true that insures personal demise rather than ascension. The typical Christian holds to the notion they are "saved" and going to "heaven," but dying is not living, and going to heaven is not ascension. Almost everyone holds to the fictions they are born, crucified in some way, die, then go to heaven. However, if the body is left behind, this requires having to reincarnate again, and again, and again until he or she lives as designed. The path of living requires being love and knowing light as one's life and identity, i.e., one's physicality and spirituality, as these are what we are the humanness of. Our insistence upon acting out dramas that die only shows how insane we are humanly. Complicating this, Christianity completely denies reincarnation. How many people would remain Christians if they knew they were going to come back to die all over again?

If the body dies, the soul will eventually reincarnate. Death of the body is the mock death of God and life denied and ignored. Interesting how people have remade God and life into their image and likeness, and nobody questions that propaganda. Few people address their issues of hindrance, so they remain living the very catalysts needed to heal to evolve into what is eternal by nature and design.

If you die, you will reincarnate again.

One of the reasons reincarnation is denied is people are irresponsible and do not want to own up to all those areas in their life that are selfish. The teaching Jesus left us was doing unto others, as this heals all forms of sin or karma. To truly be effective in assisting others, people must understand we are each other. This is the real meaning of the Christ. The Christ is the collective consciousness of humanity existing and living as and according to one ideal inclusive of everyone. Humanity has failed to establish the Christ ideal as a social state of existence within the time frame allowed. This means those who are not living their life as it was intended and created will become extinct (The number I have for those who will become extinct is 99.3% of the human race). People are given opportunity after opportunity to evolve beyond selfishness and individuality. Death only shows the rest of us living those who have died failed to live a day in his or her life.

Each of us living is accountable for whatever we choose to feel, think, and act upon. Each of us is shown upon passing how we 'measured up' humanly. Anything and everything we have personally portrayed, we are shown as our life. We are shown our attitudes as the person we lived and the effects of these upon the lives of others and this planet. Atonement is what we choose to feel and think that allows us to personally be involved with anything we perpetrated upon others. People usually reincarnate as the victim of what they perpetrated in a past life. This is what the concept of karma or sin is and means (Dannion Brinkley).

Everyone chooses this as a form of balancing to experience what it is like when acts of selfishness are personified.

People are more interested in being right and dead, than living as the image and likeness of God. This is why the Bible states: "Let the dead bury the dead, God is only of the living."

Personal charades are fine, but eventually each of us needs to get with a program that assists us living humanly and then ascending collectively.

The natures of will, love, light, and consciousness are given a mask, so that we can recognize them humanly as something personal. The personality of will, love, light, and consciousness are mind, body, spirit, and soul. The work we do is becoming conscious of these as the self.

This is not easy to do, as we deny these personally, and are only interested in those aspects of the self that are untenable leading to our death experience. True enough, will, love, light, and consciousness cannot be destroyed or die, yet each of us is dying in our own way due to denying these, and fearing these, and subscribing to ideologies that insure death is our greatest achievement.

Interesting, seeing the varying fictions people choose to be and know and die through.

The majority of people living on this planet at this time have lived more than enough lives to get it and ascend. I remember reading somewhere where it took one individual 600 lifetimes to resolve jealousy as an issue. That's 600 lifetimes for just one issue.

People are wise to grasp that just because one billion people believe an idea does not make it real or true. Likewise, even though humanity as a whole believes in death, does not make it real. Also, when something is real and true for one, does not matter or mean anything if everyone chooses to deny it, reject it, ignore it, and condemn it.

I was 'advised' once not to let the folly and foolishness of others concern me in any way, as I am not responsible for how others conduct their affairs. I was also 'advised' to stop carrying the burdens of this world on my shoulders, like Atlas (Church of Amron, San Francisco).

When are people going to begin living life, rather than dying death? When are people going to remember God, and where they have come from, and where they are going? People settle for the 'ways of man' graving their lives. It is little wonder so many face the end of their world.

Death is only a fiction of the mind as is disease and any other malady humanly portrayed. It is curious to me we are more interested in small-minded pursuits than the grander and majesty of God and universe existing as love and light as our humanness. Death only transpires because of our unwillingness to address and become what is infinite and eternal in nature and design. Our insistence on holding to the notions that our personality, psychology, and our past lives are 'it' for us, only show that what we have chosen to live as catalysts resulting in our death experience.

Being and knowing pertain to and involve God and universe making us our humanity. Our small-minded pursuits keep taking us to the grave. It is rather silly, if you ask me, that we keep choosing death, rather than living life and ascending.

Death is an impossibility, yet almost everyone chooses that as his or her end game. People mistake catalysts as the way it is humanly. Catalysts are how each person evolves. Catalysts are issues needing addressment and healing through understanding the purpose each one serves us. Catalysts are what is not. There are many.

Take any issue you struggle with, like fear, pain, anger, jealousy, or hatred, and each path to what each is not. Fear is the path to love. Pain is the path to joy. Darkness is the path to light. This is why opposites exist. It is the only way a given reality is grasped through experiencing what reality is not personally. Death is no different than this process.

Each person chooses what to feel, think, and evolve. Reality and truth are states of existence. I consider them experiential realness to be embraced and understood. Ascension is a choice. Death is a choice. Anything experienced is a type of reality. What is exists through what is not. These make creation what it is on all levels of existence. Love and light only exist individually through fear and darkness. Fear and darkness are our individuality. Love and light only exist as collective states. Becoming conscious of love and light requires letting go of fear and darkness, and the notion that one is only an individual existing as an entity unto itself. Fear and darkness give us the perception that time and space are real (Time is duration and space placement of consciousness that evolves from where it finds itself). Our consciousness is focused upon our humanness. Each of us is faced with the task of not only evolving our self, but also the entire human ideal. Death only means we failed to grasp much of anything. Death is our way of getting even with ourselves for being human. Death in any form is suicide. God, life, and infinity never cease to exist.

People only die due to not living what life is as their reality and truth. Life is God and universe downsized into us as the states of love and light, coupled with will and consciousness. When owned personally and shared socially, then a person is ready to ascend into another opportunity of serving the creation as a master.

Appendix L
Meditation

Meditation

There is nothing more important than meditating as a personal form of discipline. Seeking within is where one finds God. It is also how one discovers what a given quality is and the purpose it serves one's life. Meditation assists the seeker in resolving issues acting as catalysts, like pain, fear, darkness, and anything else needing healing.

Meditation is focusing on an idea or ideal as a state of being. Meditation is also the path for discovering what is within us, making us the image and likeness of God. Meditation is expanding the awareness, so one becomes conscious of what is inherent, then sharing that as one's path of service.

When one's focus is on breathing, one discovers the inner and outer breath is actually one state, existing in two different ways. Focusing on the breath is a way of freeing one self from addictions, attachments, and distractions. Going within helps us to relax and touch on alternative states of being. Seeking within is a way of disengaging from outer-based distractions that keep us ignorant and confused about what is real and true.

Meditation is the path for healing biases. It is the means, whereby wisdom is developed by addressing those traits keeping the individual stuck and dysfunctional. It is also a way of delving into the psyche to see how it works and what needs to be healed, so one can become effective humanly. Meditation is also how people learn to let go of one state of consciousness that is negative for another that is positive.

Meditation is effective for reducing stress and healing negative mindsets. It clarifies confusion and uncertainty. It is the path to authenticity and personal realness. It assists the seeker in freeing him or herself from blind beliefs and traditional interpretations, into knowing what is real and true as a state of being. Meditation is effortless and assists in developing keenness of insight, as well as depth of being and knowing.

Meditation frees the attention from all distractions allowing one to focus on a given state of existence, or what the meaning of an idea is, or what the purpose is behind a given type of experience. Meditation will differ for each of us. Each culture will have several different techniques for going within. Depending on which tradition is studied, will determine what purpose meditation serves and what the desired outcome will be. Every school will have what it considers important. The student will also have what he or she expects to accomplish through the discipline of his or her breath.

Meditation is a way of shutting down the constant barrage of thoughts one entertains, so that something specific will be addressed or embraced. Mindfulness is one aspect of meditating. Healing is another. Effective use of God's will is another function meditation serves. Meditation is the path and practice for discovering what is within. It's understanding what exists, the purpose something serves, and what becoming conscious is all about. Meditation is a way of consciousness letting go of certain types of awareness and entering into alternate and complimentary states of existence.

Meditation is very useful for gaining insight into ideas pondered and emotions felt making life those types of experiences. The art of breathing is an excellent way of solving paradoxes that seem impossible to resolve.

The art of breathing is a type of key for increasing awareness and releasing stress, as it assists the practitioner in relaxing and gaining understanding. Meditation is the willingness to examine catalysts working as personal experiences, so that one addresses what each is and what each is not. Opposites are the path to what each is not. Pain is the path to joy. Fear is the path to love. Darkness is the path to light. One can learn to let go of pain and fear quickly by understanding how they path to what each is not. This is one aspect of meditating; the use of mantra is another.

Mantras are statements of intent pathing the seeker to a given state of awareness. Many teachings use mantras as a way of stilling the intellect.

Meditation is the inner path, and it is a way of being and knowing. Meditation is how faith, desire, and intention come to fruition. Any desired experience is assisted through focusing within, as this is where it is planted. This also makes it something personal. When one can feel what the state is then it is real. Meditation is the means, whereby feeling, thinking, and sharing are honed into one's path of service and purpose. Meditation is discovering the experiential realness of the mind. It is also becoming the awareness of what a desired state is as a form of being.

Here are some ideas to focus upon: sit down in a comfortable position. Make sure nothing will distract you during your inner journey. Focus on your breath. Breathe in through your nose and out through your mouth. Allow yourself to relax into your inner being. Allow your thoughts to subside. Notice what you are feeling now. Now decide what you would like to feel in this moment. Notice anything negative and seek to understand why you feel that way about yourself. Anything felt or thought is an attitude about your self.

Take the idea joy and can you feel it? Take the idea love and can you feel it? Take the idea peace and can you feel it? Take any idea that is positive and can you feel it? Meditation is the path of becoming the being-ness of a given quality as a personal ideal.

Meditation is also a way of creating and then manifesting experiences. This is accomplished through faith, desire, and intention that equal personal reality and one's lifestyle. There are the inner and outer aspects of the self. As you meditate, what would you like your inner being and outer knowing to entail and encompass?

Awareness, understanding, and purpose are the fruits of meditation. Here are some meditations I do. Breathe in oneness and exhale perfection. There is only oneness and the perfection of something as-is. Breathe in is-now-ness and exhale at-one-ment. With any meditation see what comes. Allow enough time for something to come to you. Breathe in being God and exhale knowing the universe. Breathe in joy and peace and then exhale freedom and adventure. Breathe in love and exhale light. What comes to your awareness as you do these?

There are several meditations I do that focus upon sequencing. Breathe in will, love, light, and consciousness and then exhale joy, peace, and freedom. Then inhale the ideas harmony and adventure, exhaling creativity within the artistry of oneness. Breathe in God, life, Christ, and service, exhaling oneness, healing, wholeness, and ascension. Breathe in God, creator, father, and universe, exhaling the infinite, eternal, complete, and total. Breathe in will, love, light, and consciousness, exhaling mind, body, spirit, and soul. Breathe in heartbeat, breathing, waking and sleeping, and incarnation and ascension, then exhale the personal, relational, social, global, and universal.

Another type of meditation I do is combining several ideas into a single intention. I breathe in that I am the will, love, light, and consciousness of God, creator, father, and universe as mind, body, spirit, and soul, making me infinite, eternal, complete, and total as-is. I also breathe in the ideas I am the oneness, healing, wholeness, and ascension of God, life, and Christ through serving others.

I also do a binary type of meditation involving several ideas that co-exist. I begin by breathing in the idea of will, and exhaling the idea of consciousness; breathe in the idea of presence, exhale the idea of absence; breathe in the idea of is-ness, exhale the idea of nothingness; breathe in the idea of realness, exhale the idea of illusion; breathe in the idea of pattern, exhale the idea of chaos; breathe in the idea of content, exhale the idea of void or emptiness; breathe in the idea of truth, exhale the idea of erroneousness; breathe in the idea of I am-ness, exhale the idea I am-not-ness; breathe in the idea of universality, exhale the idea of specific-ness; breathe in the idea of connection, and exhale the idea integration.

There are also taking opposites and breathing the positive idea and exhaling the negative idea, like joy and pain, love and fear, etc. I use to do a meditation taking 60-70 terms breathing in the positive term, then exhaling their negative terms.

The art of meditation is consciously choosing to be and know God and universe as the self or any other state of existence. Edgar Cayce stated, "There are as many ways to meditate as there are people who meditate."

Meditation is the path leading one to go within and discover what God, universe, reality, truth, and life is, and where they are, and what purpose and ascension are. Meditation is very easy to enjoy. Just breathe, and smile, and relax.

Appendix M
Another Personal Muse

Another Personal Muse

Peace is a state of being that exists within as the equality and balance between love and light. The belief in good versus evil negates peace by re-establishing an ongoing conflict 'out there' somewhere. Coupled with this is the argument that what is real and true is either/or, rather than two qualities existing as one ideal. The approach to conflict is trying to fix it, by changing either the appearance of it, or the effects of it. The real problem is the cause of it remains unaddressed, so nothing actually changes; the problem is further compounded by unresolved bias acting as catalyst and misunderstanding what oneness is.

Opposites are never in conflict. They exist as companions, and are no different than male and female. What is lacking is a fundamental knowledge of what binary vibrancy is, and how it works as creation. Another term for binary vibrancy is inverse reversal. This is the technique of converting a single state into a binary vibrancy that is ongoing. Conflict is impossible within anything that is eternal.

There are those who claim the physical is an illusion, that only spirituality exists. However, they both exist as a binary vibrancy. Oneness and union are composed of more than one state of existence. Each of us is the union and oneness of our parents. The idea of conflict is like saying that the egg and sperm are at war with each other, and that is impossible. Each compliments the other, and when unified, creates a state that is the oneness and union of both existing as a state that is peaceful. This is also true of feeling and thinking. Each compliments the other when allowed to exist as-is.

A useful question to ask is: What is the intention and purpose underlying the idea of opposites in conflict, like good versus evil?

Answering this question is not easy, as so many people use this idea for so many different reasons. The main reason for using the idea of good versus evil is because it keeps people ill at ease and afraid by reinforcing deep-seated fears. Fear is part of the problem, so is denial, these become projection, leading to something 'out there' existing as an evil of some kind needing to be destroyed, locked up, or restrained.

The basis for conflict is fundamental and exists between what we feel and think when we are at odds with our self, others, this planet, and just about everything else. Conflict is a type of personal division unhealed through ignorance and selfishness.

Conflict only works through intention and agenda, and the active agency of hatred. The irony of the belief in good versus evil is that each hates the other. The actual conflict is between hatred. Good hatred does not exist. Evil hatred does not exist. Hatred is the belief of disallowing an ideal, emotionalized into an attitude leading to violence and suppression. On a personal level, hatred is expressed as disease and death.

Ultimately, the agenda of conflict facing all of humanity is fear and denial about our true identity as the image and likeness of God. This agenda has replaced what is real, true, and ongoing with what is strictly propaganda and destructive by intention.

Peace is only attained as a state of being when love and light are lived. Peace is only lived when there is equality and balance between the inner and outer.

The inner is where God exists. The outer is the universe. Humanly we are given the opportunities to be and know God and universe as our identity. We must heal our fear. We must heal our denial. We must heal our continual projections. Any act of violence is our hatred of God, life, humanness, and the universe!

Peace is never attained through violence, or attained by trying to make others peaceful. Peace is a state of being owned through healing and understanding. Peace is the acceptance of what is as one's true state of being. Peace is even-minded. Peace is the balance between what is within and what surrounds as the environment. Peace is the state God and universe exists as, as us. Peace requires being God and knowing the universe as the self. Only then does peace exist personally. Be peace, and anger, suffering, dying, violence, and death cease.

Appendix N
We Are Our Own Soul Mate

We Are Our Own Soul Mate

I remember the first time I heard the idea about a soul mate. I didn't like it. I still don't. It was during a Ramtha weekend in July of 1986 held in San Mateo, California. Nothing has changed my opinion about soul mates in 20 years. The fact is, everyone we meet and get involved with in some way is a type of soul mate. The problem for me with the idea of meeting my "soul mate" is, it connotes something is missing from my life, and that I will only find completion through someone outside of myself. This is impossible, as I am complete in and of myself.

The universe exists as a holograph, due to love and light separating into differing and individual states of existence. This creates the illusion of time and space (Love and light seek union and oneness). The problem with the entire notion of two differing states existing independently is the possibility of each evolving at different rates of development. One aspect would then outgrow the other, developing more quickly. This would create the problem of retarding the development of that ideal as a single state of existence, meaning half of the self would have to wait until the other evolved, which could take thousands of years, or not happen at all.

The problem with the idea of soul mate is that people are convinced something is missing from their lives, thinking they will find it outside of themselves. What is missing is remembering God centered within, and becoming conscious of love and light as one's true identity. There is also the problem of one failing to remember where he or she has come from as his or her own soul.

Everything existent is inherent within anything that exists. Nothing that exists lacks will, love, light, or consciousness. These are veiled by biases, acting as catalysts. This allows for the developmental evolution of all aspects existing within the universe and upon a planet like ours. The work we do in consciousness is becoming aware of both love and light as an equality and balance, making us the ideal we are living humanly. This requires healing fear and darkness acting as catalysts veiling love and light from our awareness. Fear and darkness assist us in our personal evolution.

Pain, fear, darkness, and unconsciousness are all types of soul mates. Many people we meet and become involved with personify these four traits. They assist each of us in understanding what these are, healing them, and evolving beyond what these non-states are and the purpose they serve. They assist the soul on its journey back to God.

When we tire of the charades masquerading as our life, assistance comes to aid us and guide us on our way. The role catalysts play as experience we see first-hand, shedding light on what we are doing to ourselves through what we feel and think. Feeling and thinking are a kind of soul mate. Soul mates mirror back to us what we feel and think is who and what we are living as human beings. We see humanly what we are feeling and thinking as an attitude that everyone mirrors back to us. Those we get involved with relationally mirror us perfectly, so that we can see our self blatantly. Involvement that is both positive and negative shows us what is applied through willed intention.

I have pondered the idea of soul mate for twenty years, seeking to understand what it really is as an ideal and involvement. I recently awoke realizing that the soul incarnates into the body, and it is this mating, or union, that is the only "soul mate" that is real for us, and as us. My soul is mated within my body making my life the only soul mate I will ever truly be involved with humanly. Involvement with others is my sharing these personally as my reality and truth.

The wisdom of this is, man and woman are inversely reversed ideals that are both in possession of love and light. Each gender has the opposite as a latency. When love is active then light is latent and vice versa. This can be thought of as love/light and light/love as both female and male. The role the opposite sex plays is not completing us. Each gender shows us what is latent within us that we can become conscious of and share if we desire to be and know love and light as our true identity.

The universe exists as a holograph, through this veiling

process establishing time and space as a durated placement that evolves, i.e., moves by incremental change.

Soul mates only make sense when each aspect pertains to the same state of existence, and are composed of and involved with the ideas and ideals as function and purpose. If two people are part of the same collective existing within the universe, they will meet in life and become soul mates, unless the biasing is too difficult to move beyond. Biasing is any catalyst acting as a condition of life needing resolution and healing. This is the role soul mate play for each of us. Soul mates are a type of assisted involvement with issues and purpose. The truest roles soul mates play is assisting us in our becoming conscious of love and light as our physical and spiritual natures.

The male is active light and latent love. The female is active love and latent light. Gender shows us how the veiling works and exists humanly. These two ideals seek union and oneness and are why movement is constant within the universe. People mistakenly think union and oneness take place with someone or something outside their life. This can also be thought of love and light being active when their opposite is in a state of rest. The path is how an individual becomes the oneness of love and light within consciously. Every relationship between male and female is designed to assist each other in this remembering. Eventually, what is remembered is God, and universe is the self as a soul-mated ideal. The soul is mated to God. When the soul consciously enters into God, God is brought to life as a human ideal that assists others in becoming as conscious.

This is done in the identical manner of sexual intercourse and the same process occurs between the soul and God as does the egg and sperm.

Sexuality is the desire of love and light to unify into a single state. This is done with each offspring birthed. Each person is the union and oneness of love and light. The work we do in consciousness is becoming aware of love and light as our embodied spirituality. The mistake we all make is feeling something is missing, then looking for it outside our self. This is why the idea of soul mate originally came into existence.

The primary path for women is personifying love. The primary path for men is personifying light. Secondary to this is becoming conscious of the self as the equality, balance, relationship, purpose, and harmony of what is latent, as the opposite of love and light, and what we are the active agency of as male and female. The truest form of soul mate exists between the soul and the mind. Second to this is the intercourse between love and light as the body and spirit, i.e., the embodiment of love and the spirituality of light personally shared. This is my body as love and my spirit as light existing as my humanness. Relationally this is my light/love shared with her love/light, and this can be anybody I choose to get involved with.

There are three types of relationships we exist as, and they are: the mind/body; the body/spirit; and the spirit/soul. These three kinds of soul mates are God as the self, life as the self, and the universe as the self.

Another way of understanding this is by thinking of the head and heart as a soul mate involvement.

The problem we face humanly is that women do not aspire to be love and men do not aspire to know light, both personally and relationally.

All we accomplish personally is what dies.

The soul becomes light and the mind becomes love that we personify as our humanness. Love is the content of what light structures.

Birthing is my self, unified with myself, making my self into a new version of myself. This makes parent and child a type of soul mate.

The problem with our ideas of soul mate show how uninvolved we are with our own humanness through self-denial. This necessitates looking for outer-based sources to make us feel complete, loved, and whole. This also shows our lack of going within to discover and bring to life what is inherent. It is like trying to find greener grass that does not exist. Just as it is impossible to find God "out there" somewhere, so it is with a soul mate. Both are found within and brought to life when lived.

The problem we have with living humanly is that we are not in a conscious relationship with God, or our life as a human being, or the universe. When my soul incarnated into my body, this established the only soul mate relationship I will ever have.

My body is mated to my soul, making me the human being I am now. God centered within my heart is another type of mating. God is centered within my mind I feel as my heart. Joy is feeling God is real within me inside my heart. Joy is a state of being. Joy becomes love relationally. God is joy and love as the physical and both are brought to life by the spirit. This establishes their identity, relationship, and independence. This is the soul mated to love as an ideal that is ongoing. Joy is mated to love, and these are mated to light, and these are mated to all that is.

My soul is mated to my mind, body, and spirit. The relationships my soul has with my mind are either pain or joy, with my body are either love or fear, and with my spirit are either light or dark. These are the relationships I have with God, planet, and universe. These determine one's purpose for being and path of service. As long as one feels something is missing from his or her life, he or she will feel neediness, discontentment, emptiness, lack, confusion, doubt, and uncertainty.

What fills our life is what we share with others and the life around us. My soul is in union with my body, making it the oneness of God and universe, establishing this as the relationship I have with my own life. When I am fully conscious of my life as the union and oneness of love and light, this is what ascends. Male and female are the inverse reversal of love and light into two differing states of being that share and evolve.

The differing types of relationships we have as our life are between God and the heart, the heart and the body, the body and the head, the head with the outer environment, and the entire self with the universe.

Appendix O
Oneness Versus Oneness

Oneness Versus Oneoness

Personal evolution is a curious process; it is not only personal, but it is also both relational and social. Evolution is the development of consciousness over time through space using catalysts, like pain, fear, darkness, and anything else we feel, think, and aspire to humanly. There are two ways oneness can be explained - as either an individualized understanding of something specific, or from an understanding that oneness is a collective state of existence. This appendix is the explanation of oneness versus oneness.

If an individual is focused solely upon him or herself, he or she will seek to find that state of oneness that is specific, like bliss, nirvana, or perfection. Specific states of being and knowing are only possible consciously when an individual considers him or herself an entity unto him or herself. This leads a person to seeking to discover an it or absolute of some kind, matching or mirroring his or her ideal about what oneness is from a perspective that is considered an entity unto itself. The aspirant seeks to find that state he or she considers an absolute. This requires exclusion, negation, and aversion to anything else. The statement made is, "I am it, therefore, there must be something that is also it." This perspective is only possible from belief that there is distance, isolation, differentiation, and other-than-me-ness. What a person states, to quote Chuang Tzu, is, "I am not you, and you are not me."

Individuality, treated in isolation, will only seek for an absolute of some kind considered it. The ancient Greeks, Hindus, and Buddhists sought for one state, giving rise to all states. Today physics use the same pursuit to discover the smallest particle, giving rise to the Big Bang and differing states of organization, like planets, stars, moons, and galaxies. What this tells us is, all of our knowledge is based upon individualized perspectives and interpretations about what exists as a collective. This version of oneness exists, due to individuality seeking to know from that perspective alone.

Contrasted against individuality and its interpretation of oneness is, collective consciousness knowing what oneness is as a single unified state of being that knows. This can be understood through mathematics. If an equation has several parts composing it, then the sum of the parts, its collective state, equals what it is as a single unified statement or equation.

Everything in existence is a collective of some kind. Everything has a composition to it. God has a companion to it giving it the ability to exist as a single state of reality or being. God is centered within the heart, surrounded by a state that is the exact opposite of what it is. Nothing within the universe exists independent of anything else. The universe is a binary vibrancy between what it is and what God is.

Built upon this state are several superimposed states existing, not only as us, but everything else in the universe. The universe is a single state. The parts composing it give God the experience it is varying forms of I am-ness. This means understanding oneness is actually only done through collective consciousness. This requires activating the entire brain to accomplish. The reason only 6% of the brain is active is, that is the part that pertains to and involves individuality. The other 94% pertains to and involves our collective state of being; this is no different than the universe existing as one state of being.

Oneness as an absolute, or oneness as a collective, are the only conflicts that exists within the universe. Each person decides whether he or she is an it of some kind, existing as an absolute, or as part of a larger collective involving opposite sex, society, the environment, and the universe.

Oneness versus oneness is often misconstrued as good versus evil. There are other versions of this conflict: as either/ or; perpetrator/victim; greater/lesser; right/wrong; and true/ false. This type of conflict can be thought about in the context of individuality versus all else. Individuality can be thought of as what is connected and integrated into a larger collective of some kind, beginning with the self existing as a collective state of being, extending and expanding into and through the opposite sex and society. The opportunity for wisdom about oneness lies within each of us. Some people choose to be an entity unto themselves. Others choose to be part of a collective.

Ascension also involves both individuals and collectives. Individual ascension is negative, while collective ascension is positive. Individuality is the active and negative aspect of the self. Collective states of being are positive by nature and design. Personal evolution is a person choosing to be and know him or herself, either as an entity unto him or herself, or as a collective state of being existing within larger collectives establishing and composing the entire universe.

Oneness versus oneness is the perspective one chooses to be and know and evolve as and through. For some, oneness is an absolute state of existence. For others, oneness is a collective state of consciousness. These two ideals evolve side by side. What one becomes conscious of as the self is the path. Collective consciousness is infinite, eternal, complete, and total, as-is as a state of oneness. Individuality considers itself to be the one and only - an absolute unto itself - and lives accordingly, while seeking for that state that confirms and validates its ideological point of reference and empowerment. Individuality requires adepts who blindly follow edits, rules, or laws needed to insure conformity and unwavering allegiance that the one followed is it.

There are several traditions built and based upon oneness according to an individual perspective. Any tradition where one person is the focus and source for knowledge is based upon this. Science, religion, politics, business, military, and education are the greatest culprits of oneness as a form of it. Collective states rely upon intuition and people, places, and things are not considered greater or lesser. Value is not given to inanimate things, like gold, jewels, money, or personal possessions. As long as people only think of themselves as their identity, and nothing else, oneness will only be a single state considered and the brain will only be 6% active.

Oneness as a collective is the true nature of existence with everything composing the universe. My mind, body, spirit, and soul are collective states. The only way I grasp whom I am collectively, is letting go of the idea I am an entity unto myself, and moving my awareness into what I am as a unified ideal of many differing states of being. This requires my letting go of the idea I am an entity unto myself existing only as and for that.

Appendix P
The Old Versus
the New Testament

The Old Versus the New Testament

Religion is as hotly contested today as it was hundreds of years ago. Christianity's first type of conflict existed between Catholics and Protestants. In addition, Christians believe several differing views concerning what personal devotion is and what faith is. People are just as intolerant today--about differing points of view--as they were 2,000 years ago. Jesus taught love, forgiveness, and doing unto others as unifying principles in the hope people would choose to accept one another and live in peace and harmony. The Bible is considered 'the document of faith' for practicing Christians. Some Christians feel only the King James Version of the Bible is legitimate. Christianity is divided against itself, and so is the Bible, with its conflicting points of view between the Old and the New Testaments. The Bible is a conflict of interest between the negativity of the Old Testament and the positivity of the New Testament. We, in our ignorance and arrogance, get to choose which Testament we place our faith in, aspire to follow, and live.

This statement poses a big problem for anyone who is a devout Christian. Many feel the Bible is "the infallible Word of God!" A man once stated that the Bible is "perfect" in every way. People believe the Bible is to be followed blindly through unquestioning faith. There are several places in the Bible where the Old Testament directly contradicts the New Testament.

In the Old Testament, there are the Ten Commandments, while in the New Testament there are the Be-attitudes. The Old Testament is fear-based, but the New Testament is love-based. People are instructed to fear God in the Old Testament, but they are advised to love God in the New Testament. The ways of the Old Testament are fear, judgment, and persecution, but the New Testament instructs us to love, forgive, and do unto others. The Old Testament advises, "An eye for an eye seventy times seven times," while, the New Testament advises, "To forgive seventy times seven times." Infractions incurred in the Old Testament were punishable by death. The New Testament warns, "Ye who are without sin cast the first stone." The Old Testament places big emphasis upon judgment, but the New Testament advises, "Judge not, lest ye be judged." The Old Testament has its version of Saul who refuses to change his negative ways, and meets his doom by the very forms of negativity he applied. In the New Testament, we are shown a different version of Saul, who changes his negative ways into living positively and conducively, thereby becoming a new man–renamed Paul–who finds personal salvation, or peace of mind, through his new way of living. The Old Testament focuses on personal struggle and social violence through taking possession of people, places, and things. The New Testament focuses upon personal healing by people living what is inherent and socially conducive through giving charitably to others. The Old Testament focuses upon taking, but the New Testament focuses upon giving.

We are taught in the Old Testament that opposites are in conflict through the belief of good versus evil. Contrasted against this is what we are taught in the New Testament, that inner peace and outer harmony are the ways of God's people. The Old Testament emphasizes guilt, while the New Testament demonstrates our true innocence through love and forgiveness. What is interesting, the Old Testament has "the Lord God Jehovah" who is an outer-based authority needing to be worshipped and appeased, while the New Testament has "Jesus the Christ" who is a living testimony demonstrating what it is to live according to how we were created. The Old Testament informs us of a covenant established between the Israelites and the Lord God Jehovah, making them his chosen people. The New Testament defines a new covenant, whereby individuals get to choose to have a relationship with God or not by choosing to live love as their personal ideal.

The Lord God of the Old Testament promises "the promised-land" to the faithful, who have to take possession of it through conquering, enslaving, and destroying others. The New Testament informs the faithful, "Seek ye first the Kingdom of God, and all things shall be added unto you." It also tells us, "The kingdom of the father is within," and that true faith in God establishes a relationship between God and the faithful that is real, and when fully realized, makes a person a way-shower, deliverer, and healer, like Jesus was. The reader of the Bible is always reminded in the Old Testament that Jehovah is God and great, while people are insignificant and inferior to Him. However, Jesus taught a simple truth: "If ye believe these things that I have done, ye shall do as I have done, even greater, for I go unto the father," thereby informing the reader of the equality between Jesus and those who are faithful.

The irony of choice is that people refuse to choose whom they will serve. People make the mistake of personifying both negative and positive emotions and thoughts. Choosing to personify the negative and the positive cancels both, creating impotency and ineffectiveness. The Bible states, "Ye cannot serve God and mammon." Negative faith leads to negative experiences, yet positive faith leads to positive experiences. Holding to both negative and positive ideas about anything creates discord within anyone who chooses to believe that conflict exists between components composing what exists. Conflict is impossible within anything that is infinite and eternal by nature and design. When people resolve their belief of opposites in conflict healing occurs and concern and confusion--leading to animosity, violence, and war--vanishes.

Choosing to live according to the doctrines of the New Testament (through the teachings of Jesus) ensures each aspirant will live according to love, not fear; innocence, not guilt; and kindness, not cruelty. The Old Testament glorifies the self, but the New Testament educates people into living what is socially conducive. Living to get or living to give is what the Bible teaches us. The only conflict that exists is people choosing to be both selfish and giving! Conflict is healed into peace when the opposites of the positive and the negative are lived as an equality and balance, establishing harmony between differing states and differing people. Resolving the conflict between the Old Testament and the New Testament requires choosing whether to follow the dictates of the Lord God Jehovah or the dictates of Jesus. People must choose between living fear, judgment, and persecution, or choosing to live love, forgiveness, and doing unto others.

Appendix Q
To Conquer or Not to Conquer

To Conquer or Not to Conquer

Understanding the distinctions between invading cultures and indigenous people is useful because invading cultures live according to the false doctrines of conquering, enslaving, and destroying others. Indigenous people live as they were created to exist as happy, peaceful, and harmonious. Invading cultures use a monetary system of exchange, while indigenous people barter. Invading cultures live according to doctrines needed to justify ill-advised social behaviors. Indigenous people live in harmony with each other and their environment according to what is consistent and conducive. Invading cultures seek to take possession of people, places, and things, whereas indigenous people share what they are already in possession of as an inherent truth or reality. The only conflict that exists socially is the ideological differences between invading cultures and indigenous people.

What exactly establishes a culture as invading? An invading culture is based upon very specific ideals through ideology accepted as cultural traditions. Every invading culture existing today lives according to the beliefs of: hierarchy, elitism, superiority, chosen-ness, and good versus evil, leading to the social behaviors of conquering, enslaving, and destroying others through war, greed, and slavery.

Contrasted against the invader culture mindset, is the way indigenous people live socially and environmentally. Their social intercourse is based upon equality, balance, relationship, purpose, and harmony, leading to the social behaviors of inspiration, kindness, and creativity through peacefulness, generosity, and respect.

Invading cultures live according to an either/or mindset, and that there is greater and lesser entitling those who are greater to take whatever they want from others under the guise it is 'divinely' sanctioned. Arbitrariness is why value is given to things, like people, gold, money, and land, and that these are what the invader must take possession of, making these his or her personal possessions defining who the person is, and giving him or her a sense of self-worth. The entire quest of an invading person is to take possession of as much as one can in one's lifetime. This is how one's life is measured.

Contrasted against this is what defines an indigenous person. He or she is defined by how well adapted he or she is within the culture as a whole. Indigenous people do not seek to 'better' themselves, as they accept who they are, as-is. The conflict between both cultures is one of self versus community, or individuality versus socialism. Does one live for self only? Or does one live for the culture, as a whole? Indigenous people live according to how they were created to live. Invader cultures live according to false doctrine. The contrast exists between living what is inherent, or what comes from an outer-based source of some kind. Invader cultures live according war, greed, and slavery. Indigenous people live according to peacefulness, generosity, and equality amongst its members.

Living as designed is not easy. Unabated, the conflict ensues between invading cultures and indigenous people. Returning to living in harmony with the land and people is an admirable quest everyone is wise to aspire to. Prior to this, people must embrace peacefulness, and demonstrate kindness toward each other. This is how humans were originally created to exist. Conflict is our responsibility to heal into peace and harmony. Choosing to live as designed, or according to those who enslave, defines each of us as either an invader or the image and likeness of God. Choose wisely.

Closing Remarks

Now that you have finished reading this book what do you do? I suggest you run screaming from the room yelling these ideas can't be true. Then burn the book after profaning it profusely.

It is difficult living this life as that ideal we embody. Further complicating life is no two people are the same, so our experiences differ from anyone else's. Any given person will have unique experiences that are strictly personal created through God's Will. People fail to grasp they are the 'victims' of their own mind.

I was told by a channeled source, that each of us humans decide the meaning and the purpose about the self, and it is this we live and portray for others who either agree, disagree, or ignore.

The path begins with God and ends with ascension. In between these is life, humanness, service polarity, oneness, healing, and wholeness, or the lack of these, as experiences. Our task is to be and know these on a personal level, and then a relational level, and then a social level, and then a planetary level, and finally a universal level. To do so, one must heal, by addressing those catalysts, making us the human being we personify. The catalysts I am speaking of are pain, fear, guilt, denial, arrogance, ignorance, indifference, and intolerance.

The path is grasping what God, life, and universe are as the self. Relying upon outer-based sources, no matter how evolved, only leads us astray. Reality and truth are within and only found within. It is here we seek and find what is real and true as our being-ness that knows and shares with others. Not with the intention others be just like us, but from knowing each of us as what we are, and that we can get along joyfully and lovingly if we desire to.

The importance we place on something is the key to how our life evolves and what we experience. Many are addicted and very attached to their identity and psychology. True they play the roles they do, but we are much more than just these. Beauty, fame, wealth, and talent are traps few resolve. People still cling to their individuality as if that is 'it.' Few people have a working knowledge of what gives rise to identity and the purpose this serves. Many people live their entire life as their psychology, career, gender, issues acting as catalysts, and talents.

Denial, irresponsibility, rejection, and projection are difficult to heal, as many outer based traditions demand we do so for our entire life. Fear and love denied have become the ideas we hold as Satan and God. Denial leads to idol worship and ritualized living.

Few people aspire to accept the self, life, and others and have an even-minded-ness about anything happening out there. People do not do a very good job of feeling something real, thinking something true, and then sharing these is ways kind and conducive to the enhancement of the entire creation.

Those who serve themselves are keeping us steeped in disease, disparity, conflict, slavery, greed, war, and death. So that health, equality, harmony, freedom, generosity, peace, and ascension do not exist personally or socially.

The earth is changing its polarity into what is positive based within its center. People are wise to do likewise if they hope to evolve beyond death and reincarnation within their planetary experience.

People are very lazy; refusing to do the work. People only experience their own creations. The end that comes is the healing of those fictions people choose to feel and think that do not exist outside or beyond the minds perpetrating negative ideals.

There is only being, that knows, that shares, and that ascends. What these are as the self is up to us to decide. What the self evolves into is determined by whom we serve and what we aspire to become.

The dying chooses heaven. The living chooses ascension. Knowing the self, serving others, and collectively ascending is what transpires humanly for all of us who seek to be and know our self as real and true. Those who serve themselves have been successful, over the eons of time, in preventing and stopping people from living and speaking out about injustices perpetrated by negatively polarized souls.

People are expected to deny their self and remain steeped in fear. The perpetrations of many are keeping us stuck in denial and remaining fearful. Almost every institution is teaching ideas that are negative and false based upon an ideology that denies who and what we are humanly. All for the sake of empowering those whose ideal is war, greed, and slavery. Almost every institution adheres to an ideology that is self-serving by nature. So called 'civilized man' has engaged in the practices of war, greed, and slavery for over 10,000 years.

Speaking the truth is against the law. Living what is real is against the law. Being and knowing what is real and true violates the mandates of those who serve themselves. The earth changes coming is the earth healing all of the negativity that has infected this planet. Those who are negatively polarized do not realize the end of their path is self-destruction. Death is this on a personal scale. Cessation of the body as the death experience shows everyone, that the person doing so was imbalanced and negative about his or her humanness. Negative collective experiences called natural disasters show us what happens to a group of people who subscribe to an ideology that is negative.

The end of the world is the end of negative polarity and all it encompasses. Anyone who has chosen involvement will face his or her demise according to how the earth heals these fictions. I am a living testimony to the truths I write about. Putting into words is and means making it real and personal. This is the true meaning of "In the beginning was the word," and "The word was made flesh." These mean God became manifested as the universe and as us.

I finally realize I have to be willing to stand up for myself and own what is God and universe as me. I have accepted the responsibility of being actively involved with my human being-ness, and my personal and social evolution.

What I am demonstrating is that anyone can become fully conscious of the self as God and universe, and any quality, like joy, love, peace and happiness, or talent desired. Truth and realness must be owned and shared regardless of the cost to one's life. Jesus did this, as did Martin Luther King, Jr. When people do this collectively, they will ascend, as the realness and truth of those qualities owned and shared.

This book is my attempt in assisting people choosing to be and know God and the universe as the self. The culmination of the completed work results in collective ascension for everyone who chooses to be and know likewise.

Author's Biography

Douglas Harold Melloy was born in Los Angeles, CA, and raised in San Francisco, CA. He graduated from George Washington High School and attended City College of San Francisco.

He is an accomplished writer and speaker. He is also a competent Toastmaster, and has done public speaking in a Unity Church in Bozeman, MT, and Rome, GA.

He studied Christianity, Hinduism, Buddhism, Sufism, and the works of Meher Baba. He is considered a scholar of various disciplines, having studied Western and Eastern Philosophy, Mysticism, and New Age.

He is the author of two previously published books, "**God-Planet-Universe**," (2002) and "**Love and Wisdom**," (2003). His poetry was published in, "*The Vineyard Quarterly.*" He wrote an article about Sun Yat-sen that was published in, "*The Tourch Of Victory.*"

He is a martial artist, and earned his Black Belt in Ed Parker's, Kenpo Karate in 1980. He taught this style for four years. He also studied Tai Chi, Tae Kwon Do, and Choi Li Fut Gung Fu.

He is an accomplished musician, and has performed with several bands, while living in Livingston, MT, and Rome, GA. He played Gospel music with Psalms 150 and the Gospel International Workshop Choir. He joined New Life of St. John Baptist Church and played as an in-house musician for two years.

He currently works for the State of Georgia with troubled adolescents and teens.

To contact Douglas H. Melloy, write to: 310 Mountain View RD SE, Rome , GA 30161, or contact him via email at: godisiam@bellsouth.net.

Reality is,

Self...

Defined!

References:

Jane Roberts, Seth, the Nature of Personal Reality, Prentice Hall, 1974

Elkins, Rueckert, McCarty, The RA Material, The Law of One Vols.
1-5, Whitford Press, 1984, 1982, 1998

Robert Monroe, Journeys out of the Body, Far Journeys, Ultimate Journey,
Doubleday, 1971, 1982, 1994

Neale Donald Walsch, Conversations With God Vol. 1, Putnam, 1995
Neale Donald Walsch, Conversations With God Vol.2, 3, Hampton Roads,
1997, 1998

Helen Schucman, A Course In Miracles,
Foundation For Inner Peace, 1975

Jay Z Knight, Ramtha, Jehovah tape, 1984

KJV Bible

Other books by Douglas H. Melloy:

├──────────□──────────┤

"**God-Planet-Universe**
is this life
I AM
now here being...
everything else is just a detail"
Franklin Press, Rome, GA 30165
June, 2002

"**Love and Wisdom**
are the art
of appropriateness"
Prince Media Group, Atlanta, GA 30142
May, 2003

├──────────□──────────┤

INNERCIRCLE PUBLISHING

Catalog of Original Titles

ISBN	Title
0-9720080-9-8	the sometimes girl by Lisa Zaran
0-9720080-5-5	A Metaphysical Interpretation of the Bible by Dr. Steven Hairfield
0-9720080-2-0	Return To Innocence by Dr. Steven Hairfield
0-9720080-3-9	Interview With An American Monk by Dr. Steven Hairfield
0-9720080-4-7	Interview II: Heath and Healing by Dr. Steven Hairfield
0-9723191-4-X	Poetry to Touch the Heart and Soul by Marla Wienandt
0-9755214-9-7	Touched by Spirit by Marla Wienandt
0-9723191-8-2	Stress Fractures by Andew Lewis
0-9723191-6-6	Life Rhymes by Rene Ferrell
0-9723191-7-4	One Hundred Keys to the Kingdom by Prince Camp, Jr.
0-9723191-0-7	the voice by Rick LaFerla
0-9755214-0-3	On the Edge of Deceny by Rick LaFerla
0-9723191-5-8	A Day in the Mind by Chad Lilly
0-9755214-6-2	uncommon sense by Chad Lilly
0-9755214-7-0	Peace Knights of the Soul by Dr. Jon Snodgrass
0-9755214-1-1	Petals of a Flower by Patricia McHenry
0-9755214-2-X	Poetry-Prose-Stories by J.L. Montgomery
0-9762924-0-8	The Weave that Binds Us by Martin Burke
0-9762924-2-4	Dare to Question by Jack Perrine
0-9762974-2-6	The Twelve Mastery Teachings of Christ by Lea Chapin
0-9762924-3-2	Alnombak by Ken Delnero
0-9762924-7-5	Life is a Song Worth Singing by Clarissa LeVonne Bolding
0-9762974-3-4	The Spirit Within by Susan Marie Ratcliffe
0-9720080-8-X	And the Angels Spoke by Rebecca J. Steiger
1-882918-00-2	From Ashes To Angel Light by Rebecca J. Steiger
0-9762974-6-9	The One Minute Miracle by Daniel Millstein
0-9762974-5-0	Unemployed: A Memoir by Reginald L.Goodwin
1-882918-03-7	Look and Remember by Marie taBonne
1-882918-02-9	Poetry of Comfort and Light by Marla Wienandt
1-882918-01-0	Life Happened Here by Marilyn Wendler

Are You Aware?
www.innercirclepublishing.com

Printed in the United States
77527LV00004B/4-51

9 780972 812726